T0352813

Politics and Cosmopolitanism in a Global Age

Ethics, Human Rights and Global Political Thought

Series Editors: Sebastiano Maffettone and Aakash Singh Rathore
Center for Ethics & Global Politics, Luiss University, Rome

Whereas the interrelation of ethics and political thought has been recognized since the dawn of political reflection, over the last sixty years — roughly since the United Nation's Universal Declaration of Human Rights — we have witnessed a particularly turbulent process of globalizing the coverage and application of that interrelation. At the very instant the decolonized globe consolidated the universality of the sovereign nation-state, that sovereignty — and the political thought that grounded it — was eroded and outstripped, not as in eras past, by imperial conquest and instruments of war, but rather by instruments of peace (charters, declarations, treaties, conventions), and instruments of commerce and communication (multinational enterprises, international media, global aviation and transport, internet technologies).

Has political theory kept apace with global political realities? Can ethical reflection illuminate the murky challenges of real global politics?

This Routledge book series *Ethics, Human Rights and Global Political Thought* addresses these crucial questions by bringing together outstanding monographs and anthologies that deal with the intersection of normative theorizing and political realities with a global focus. Treating diverse topics by means of interdisciplinary techniques — including philosophy, political theory, international relations and human rights theories, and global and postcolonial studies — the books in the Series present up-to-date research that is accessible, practical, yet scholarly.

Also in the Series

Wronging Rights? Philosophical Challenges for Human Rights
Editors: Aakash Singh Rathore and Alex Cistelecan
ISBN 978-0-415-61529-7

Conflict Society and Peacebuilding: Comparative Perspectives
Editors: Raffaele Marchetti and Nathalie Tocci
ISBN 978-0-415-68563-4

Global Justice: Critical Perspectives
Editors: Sebastiano Maffettone and Aakash Singh Rathore
ISBN 978-0-415-53505-2

Deprovincializing Habermas: Global Perspectives
Editor: Tom Bailey
ISBN 978-0-415-85933-2

Between Ethics and Politics: Gandhi Today
Editor: Eva Pföstl
ISBN 978-0-415-71064-0

Canned Heat: Ethics and Politics of Global Climate Change
Editors: Marcello Di Paola and Gianfranco Pellegrino
ISBN 978-1-138-02027-6

Secularism, Religion, and Politics: India and Europe
Editors: Peter Losonczi and Walter Van Herck
ISBN 978-1-138-79600-3

Politics and Cosmopolitanism in a Global Age

Editors

Sonika Gupta
Sudarsan Padmanabhan

Routledge
Taylor & Francis Group

LONDON AND NEW YORK

First published 2015 by Routledge

2 Park Square, Milton Park, Abingdon, Oxfordshire OX14 4RN
52 Vanderbilt Avenue, New York, NY 10017

Routledge is an imprint of the Taylor & Francis Group, an informa business

First issued in paperback 2019

Copyright © 2015 Sonika Gupta and Sudarsan Padmanabhan

All rights reserved. No part of this book may be reprinted or reproduced or utilised in any form or by any electronic, mechanical, or other means, now known or hereafter invented, including photocopying and recording, or in any information storage or retrieval system, without permission in writing from the publishers.

Notice:
Product or corporate names may be trademarks or registered trademarks, and are used only for identification and explanation without intent to infringe.

Typeset by
Solution Graphics
A-14, Indira Puri, Loni Road
Ghaziabad, Uttar Pradesh 201 102

British Library Cataloguing-in-Publication Data
A catalogue record of this book is available from the British Library

ISBN 978-1-138-82240-5 (hbk)
ISBN 978-0-367-17694-5 (pbk)

Contents

Abbreviations   vii
Glossary   ix
Acknowledgements   xi

Introduction   1
Sonika Gupta and *Sudarsan Padmanabhan*

Part I
Normative Cosmopolitanism: Statements

1. Cosmopolitan Democracy: Paths and Agents   17
   Daniele Archibugi and *David Held*

2. The Cosmopolitanization of International Law:
   Rethinking Global Constitutionalism   37
   Garrett Wallace Brown

3. Legitimacy in the Global Normative Order:
   Justificatory Practices in the Space of Reasons   59
   Eva Erman

Part II
Reconceptualizing Cosmopolitanism

4. Cosmopolitanism without Foundations   83
   Véronique Pin-Fat

5. Who are the People of the World?   103
   Sudhir Chella Rajan

6. Cosmopolitanism, Liberalism and Citizenship   121
   Arvind Sivaramakrishnan

7. Diasporas, Cosmopolitanism and Post-territorial
   Citizenship   137
   Francesco Ragazzi

8. The 'Domestic Abroad' and the Limits
   of Cosmopolitanism   166
   Latha Varadarajan

Part III
Towards a Postcolonial Critique

9. The Elusiveness of 'Non-Western Cosmopolitanism'   193
   Rahul Rao

10. Cosmopolitanism and Nationalism: A Re-examination   216
    Sonika Gupta

Epilogue
Imagining India: The Interplay of the Cosmopolitan
and the Vernacular   234
Sudarsan Padmanabhan

About the Editors   264
Notes on Contributors   265
Index   268

Abbreviations

AIEI	Association of Indian Engineering Industry
BSC	Biome Stewardship Council
CCEUS	Centre for Comparative European Union Studies
CPT	Comparative Political Thought
ECHR	European Court of Human Rights
EU	European Union
FACES	Filipino/American Coalition for Environmental Solidarity
FICCI	Federation of Indian Chambers of Commerce and Industry
GLOBE	Global Legislators for a Balanced Environment
ICC	International Criminal Court
ICISS	The International Commission on Intervention and State Sovereignty
ICJ	International Court of Justice
IITM	Indian Institute of Technology Madras
INC	Indian National Congress
IO	International Organization
KDP	Union of Democratic Filipinos
MNC	Multinational Corporation
NAFTA	North American Free Trade Association
NATO	North Atlantic Treaty Organization
NGO	Non-governmental Organization
NPT	Nuclear Non-Proliferation Treaty
NRI	Non-resident Indian
OSCE	Organization for Security and Cooperation in Europe
PIO	Person of Indian Origin
PPP	Public–Private Partnership
R2P	Responsibility to Protect

TRIPS	(Agreement on) Trade-Related Aspects of Intellectual Property Rights
UN	United Nations
UNSC	United Nations Security Council
WTO	World Trade Organization

Glossary

Anatta	Soul
Avidya	Ignorance
Bhakti	Devotion
Cit acit visishtam Brahman	The Ultimate Reality is qualified by the Conscious and the Unconscious
Demos	A group of individuals that share a name and a common territory and are aware of their identity as a community
Desa	Place
*Dharmasastra*s	Various codes of conduct in a fractured polity
Din-i-Ilahi	A new syncretized religion, centred on the ideal of one supreme reality
Dravida Nadu	Dravidian nation
*Gana sangha*s	Groups of various *sangha*s or social groups
Hindu Rashtra	Hindu nation
Hrvatsvo	Croatianness
Insan-i-Kamil	The perfect man
Italianità	Italianness
Kala	Time
*Kavya*s	Poetic works
Lakshana-lakshya	Categorization in the ancient Indian classical literary theory and musicology, cosmopolitan–vernacular socio-linguistic framework — formal–pragmatic
Laoi	Followers of a leader
Lokasamgraha	Welfare of the world at large
Marai	Veda
Mexicanidad	Mexicanness
Moksha	Liberation
Mujtahid	A scholar of Islamic jurisprudence
Neeti	Formal justice
Nermai	Honesty
Niskama karma	Non-attached action

Nyaya/Nyayam	Fairness
Paramarthika satta	Transcendent realm
Paramarthika, Vyavaharika	Distinction between the realm of Sanskrit cosmopolis and the vernacular
Plethos	Mass of disorderly people
Praja	A civic nation; people or subjects
Pravasi Bharatiya	Indians abroad
Rajabhasha	Official transactions; royal transactional language
Saranagati	Self-surrender
Sarva dharma sama bhava	Equal treatment of all religions
Sastra	Scientific/formal authoritative texts on religion, science and law
Shariat-tareeqat	Distinction in Islamic law and jurisprudence; canonical practice
Sulh kul	The concept of universal toleration
Sunyata	The concept of emptiness
Swaraj	Self-rule
Vaidika	Ritualistic practices pertaining to the Vedas
Varthamana	Contemporary context
Vedantic	Philosophical
Vishwa Bharati	Global India
Vyavaharika satta	Level of everyday reality
Watan	Nation

Acknowledgements

The editors would like to thank the generous support from the European Commission under which the Centre for Comparative European Union Studies (CCEUS) was set up at the Department of Humanities and Social Sciences, Indian Institute of Technology Madras (IITM), India. This volume is a dialogue among an international network of scholars established by the CCEUS that came together to discuss the different facets of the overarching theme of democracy, globalization and international relations. We acknowledge the participation and support of all the contributors and discussants at the international conference at which the papers included in this volume were presented.

This book has greatly benefited from the comments of the anonymous reviewers. The editors would like to thank all the individual chapter reviewers and the publisher's reviewer for their critical comments.

We also thank the Department of Humanities and Social Sciences and IITM for providing the academic and infrastructural space to conceive of, and execute, this project. A word of thanks is due to Professor V. R. Muraleedharan for his support and for putting together the initial team for the project.

Dr V. Rajesh and Bharathi Kannan, project associates, are owed a special word of thanks for their contribution in making this project and its related events a success.

Aditi Rao and G. Janani, project associates, IITM China Studies Centre, contributed to fine-tuning the manuscript in its final stages. We gratefully acknowledge their contribution.

The editors are grateful to the editorial team at Routledge who have steered the publication of this volume with great dedication and professionalism. Thanks are due to Aakash Singh Rathore, the Series Editor for *Ethics, Human Rights and Global Political Thought*, for his critical comments and editorial contribution towards the bringing together of this book.

Introduction

Sonika Gupta and *Sudarsan Padmanabhan*

Global politics today is grappling with moral and epistemological questions arising out of the skewed distribution of power in the world. In this context, examinations of justice and equality are attended to with urgency in the contemporary cosmopolitan discourse that recasts the relationship between state and citizen within the framework of humanity. Cosmopolitanism addresses the loss of agency for the individual in the face of overwhelming state power, in the process engaging with the crisis of moral authority that the state as an agent faces today. As a redressal, cosmopolitanism offers the idea of cosmopolitan democracy that bridges the gap between those who take decisions and those who bear the consequences of these decisions. In this, cosmopolitanism demands and creates the discursive space for reinterpreting political community beyond the nation state.

This volume critically examines cosmopolitanism as a normative discourse and is an attempt at political and intellectual decolonization of the cosmopolitan discourse. Existing literature on cosmopolitanism does a comprehensive job of laying out the philosophical foundations, categorizations and critiques of the cosmopolitan principle and hence this volume does not restate these (Brown and Held 2010; Delanty 2012a). The purpose of this collection of essays is to take the debate on the foundations and critiques of cosmopolitanism in newer directions. We argue that till now the critique of cosmopolitanism has operated within the boundaries of the post-modern critique of modernity. In doing this, while the cosmopolitan discourse vigorously challenges the tyranny of modernity, it yet reproduces the epistemological and even historical mapping of modernity. This volume attempts both an immanent as well as a transcendental critique of cosmopolitanism to re-examine its moral and epistemological underpinning. It examines the former by exploring the ontological and political foundations of cosmopolitanism and the latter by offering a postcolonial critique of cosmopolitanism. This volume examines the dehistoricizing imperative of the cosmopolitan project in the context of postcolonialism.

The cosmopolitan discourse and its ethical concerns are now firmly established as a legitimate field of inquiry in political philosophy, international political theory, law, and sociology and politics (Beitz 1975; Schlereth 1977; Nussbaum 1996; Brennan 1997; O'Neill 2000; Pollock et al. 2000; Pogge 2002; Singer 2002; Dower 2003; Vertovec and Cohen 2003; Beck 2004; Brock and Brighouse 2005). As encapsulated by Garrett Wallace Brown and David Held:

> In its most basic form, cosmopolitanism maintains that there are moral obligations owed to all human beings based solely on our humanity alone, without reference to race, gender, nationality, ethnicity, culture, religion, political affiliation and state citizenship or other communal particularities (2010: 1).

This overarching statement of cosmopolitanism is almost impossible to disagree with and allows even its critics to declare that 'we are all cosmopolitan today' (Miller 2010: 379). Or, in other words, it is difficult to deny the ethical basis of cosmopolitanism that looks at humanity as the organizing principle for providing a moral basis for equality. The cosmopolitan search for the aspirational political community is traced from Diogenes the Cynic, who declared himself to be a 'citizen of the world' to Immanuel Kant's *Perpetual Peace*. The common thread through this long philosophical unfolding of the cosmopolitan project is the focus on the individual as a referent of justice and equality. In more contemporary developments of the cosmopolitan project, the aspirational political community takes on a decidedly post-national tone (Held 1995; Archibugi et al. 2011). While not all cosmopolitan prescriptions move towards post-nationalism, liberal cosmopolitanism in its institutional form is essentially post-national. Daniele Archibugi and David Held's focus here is on progressing from 'building peace between democracies to a global democracy'.[1] Arising from this, the normative agenda of cosmopolitanism is being increasingly sought to be institutionalized through proposals for 'global' institutions and 'global' lawmaking. Liberal cosmopolitanism currently dominates the agenda for institutionalization of cosmopolitan norms into the institutions of global governance.

---

[1] Please see Archibugi and Held, Chapter 1, 'Cosmopolitan Democracy: Paths and Agents'.

The post-national cosmopolitan project is premised on three assumptions about transformative changes in the *nature* and *direction* of contemporary global politics. First, Cosmopolitanism posits that globalization has irreversibly transformed the nature of world politics in that certain issues like the environment, pandemics, financial flows, and migration are intrinsically global in nature and as such cannot be subject solely to territorially bound national decision-making (Held 2010: 304). Second, cosmopolitanism underlines the existence of layered and hybrid identities of individuals in the global village today (Cheah and Robbins 1998). Arising from fluid and transplanetary articulations of identity, the cosmopolitan discourse explores the social and political dynamics that decentring of the national brings to the table in evolving a cosmopolitan political community (Delanty 2009). Cosmopolitanism is also offered as an alternative to three approaches that viewed global social changes as follows: first, increasing homogenization culminating in world cultures; second, increased polarization hurtling towards clash of civilizations; and third, hybridization, which is a constant mixture of cultures that give rise to newer forms. In contrast, cosmopolitanism is considered a reflexive interrelation of cultures, a unity in diversity (Delanty 2012b: 44; Padmanabhan 2012: 463). Finally, cosmopolitanism engages with the evolution of the global institutions and processes that build solidarities across national boundaries in the context of the rights discourse. These include state-based institutions like the United Nations (UN), European Union (EU) and World Health Organization (WHO), as well as global social movements.

Based on the above understanding of the transformed nature and direction of global politics, cosmopolitanism makes an argument for redefining the basis for political community beyond the territorial state. However, even as cosmopolitanism opens up the space for challenging the hierarchies of modernity, it also assumes the universal relevance of the values of Enlightenment specifically in political practice. The cosmopolitan discourse assumes universality of its relevance based on the idea of a common humanity as it broadens categories of identity and citizenship beyond the territorial state. Identity and citizenship are linked directly to moral and political cosmopolitan concerns about redefining both the basis and the nature of political community respectively. As a moral discourse, cosmopolitanism provides a template for inclusion and equality of all human beings. It places the individual at the centre of political and moral concern. As a political discourse, cosmopolitanism relates citizenship not to political or cultural identity but to the membership of the human race. The role of the nation state in both cases is imagined as facilitator of its own increasing limitation in defining a cosmopolitan political community.

The call for institutionalization of cosmopolitan norms along liberal institutional lines is problematic as it assumes philosophical agreement on the fundamental constituents of a cosmopolitan society. While there is an engagement with the tyrannies of modernity, there is a broad agreement about the philosophical relevance of the Enlightenment values of liberalism and capitalism (See, for example, Archibugi and Held 1995). This forecloses the possibility of exploring any transformative changes in the structures of hierarchy that continue to provide the framework for much of the theory and practice of global politics. We argue that the transition from moral cosmopolitanism to political cosmopolitanism is essentially problematic as it contracts the universalism inherent in the former to a political consensus on norms thereby making cosmopolitanism an exclusionary discourse. Cosmopolitanism is a continuation of the liberal discourse of the period between the two World Wars with a reflexive turn and a strong normative prescription for creating conditions for global justice. The internal critique of modernity and its hierarchies is well reflected in the cosmopolitan discourse; however, a historical examination of the same is currently lacking. This volume attempts to examine the underlying epistemological assumptions of cosmopolitanism in the context of postcolonialism. One of the major arguments offered in here is that liberal cosmopolitanism is a dehistoricizing discourse. It needs to make space for historically antagonistic and mutually constitutive narratives of modernity and coloniality that continue to inform global hierarchies of power. In the lack of this space, the same hierarchies that cosmopolitanism seeks to challenge are reproduced as the philosophical foundations of liberalism continue to dominate the moral discourse of cosmopolitanism. Urging for a 'decolonizing' of the cosmopolitan's moral discourse, Walter Mignolo (2011) argues that liberal cosmopolitanism, by claiming that the Western liberal democratic nations have the moral resources to provide frameworks of global solidarity and justice, creates the same hierarchical relationships in global politics that it challenges. His critique establishes cosmopolitanism's reliance upon the moral-philosophical resources of the Enlightenment as privileged in the works of Immanuel Kant and Francisco de Vitoria as examples of the 'uni'-versal as opposed to the 'pluri'-versal foundations of cosmopolitanism (ibid.: 329). He quotes the silence of the 'cosmopolitanism localism' in cosmopolitan literature as evidence of this exclusion, giving the example of the indigenous concepts of cosmopolitanism of the South American peoples, namely the Incas and the Aztecs. Through this he demonstrates the dominance of the Eurocentric experience and epistemologies in the present cosmopolitan moral discourse (ibid.: 270–76). In his opinion, being 'critical' is not enough, urging instead for 'dewesternising' and 'decolonizing' the cosmopolitan project's epistemological mapping of the world in the context of the colonial difference, before it can engage in any meaningful manner with the idea of equal moral worth for all (ibid.: 258). This volume is an attempt toward the decolonization of the cosmopolitan discourse.

The context of cosmopolitan enquiry has produced a common concern with regard to excess of state power for creating an individual centred political community that can address the loss of agency. However, the creation of a political community solely on the basis of individualism is not representative of the diversity of political practice that exists both historically and philosophically. Vivienne Jabri contends,

> Just as liberal cosmopolitanism sees itself as a driver of the project of modernity, what it appears to deny, as post-colonial critics argue, is that this very project is experienced differently across the globe, a project that is at once both enabling and constraining (Jabri 2010: 723).

That is to say that the core values of cosmopolitanism, that is, individualism, egalitarianism and universalism as articulated by Thomas Pogge are sufficiently renegotiated at different cultural locations and cosmopolitanism must explicitly provide the discursive space for it (2010: 114).

Structure of This Volume

This volume offers statements, reconceptualizations and critiques of cosmopolitanism. Offering a statement of select key concepts in cosmopolitanism, Archibugi, Held, Brown, and Erman introduce urgent concerns that shape the cosmopolitan discourse in Part I. These chapters locate cosmopolitanism within its liberal assumptions about humanity and the good political community. This part of the book explores the specific institutional and philosophical challenges in constructing a cosmopolitan political community which provides the context for the subsequent critique of cosmopolitanism. The immanent critique address key concerns within the cosmopolitan debate relating to ontological foundations and political outcomes of assumptions of 'global' political community. Here there is an argument for unpacking categories of 'humanity' and 'good political community' in ways that bring to the fore the hierarchies of knowledge and practice that inhere in their production. There is also a critique of liberalism as a valid basis for reconceptualizing a global political community. This addresses the shortcoming of liberalism as a moral and political framework within which aspirational goals of global justice may be achieved. In Part II, the volume critically engages with the cosmopolitan assumptions about the nature and direction of global politics offering both immanent and external critiques of the cosmopolitan project. It offers a postcolonial critique of cosmopolitanism that explores the moral universalism and historical teleology inherent in cosmopolitan formulations. The postcolonial critique is not necessarily only an external critique, but also engages with ontological issues with the framing of cosmopolitanism as a moral discourse (Balibar 2012). However, there is a strong critical component inherent in the postcolonial critique aimed at the ahistorical universalizing tendency of the cosmopolitan discourse. Each of these themes is explored ahead in a chapter-wise discussion of this volume.

Archibugi and Held provide a statement of liberal cosmopolitanism and address the critique of their earlier work on cosmopolitan democracy by identifying specific agents and paths for the creation of a global cosmopolitan order. The authors examine existing institutions of global governance, such as the states, international organizations, global judicial and administrative courts, and the global framework of *lex mercatoria* (commercial law), to argue that these institutions with some specific reforms can provide the building blocks of a cosmopolitan democracy. They support the creation of a World Parliamentary Assembly (Falk and Strauss 2001) along the lines of the European Parliament for a broader citizens' participation in global governance. To make the above prescriptions work,

Archibugi and Held identify specific cosmopolitan groups or agents, as they call them, who will work towards creating the conditions for reform to a cosmopolitan order. These include transnational political communities; the dispossessed; migrants; cosmopolitan groups comprising famous public personalities such as sportsmen, artistes, intellectuals and writers; global stakeholders and global civil society; international political parties, trade unions and labour movements; and MNCs. This chapter provides a context for further discussion, which Sudhir Chella Rajan (in Chapter 5) and Brown (in Chapter 2) specifically respond to in this volume.

Brown, in Chapter 2, critically discusses the processes of constitutionalization of cosmopolitan norms by examining the premise that expansion of international regimes can have a positive impact on the behaviour of nation states and individuals. Brown identifies the different understandings of constitutionalization and brings them together to define constitutionalization as a process that can work simultaneously through 'traditional contractarian principles of consent, treaty and formal contract, or, generated by way of a more sociologically iterative process of mutual norm compliance'. He cautions that increased constitutionalization need not always reflect the cosmopolitan position, partly because the process of constitutionalization also creates a certain path-dependence which might be opposed to cosmopolitical changes that are being advocated by cosmopolitan scholars. He notes the subaltern critique of constitutionalization argues that it is yet another aspect of the Western civilizing mission. He argues for normative cosmopolitan theory to inform scholarship on constitutionalization as the latter has tended to work within dominantly positivist frameworks, largely focused on the institutional experience of the EU and has often conflated the processes of globalization with increased constitutionalization.

Eva Erman (Chapter 3) identifies the inefficacy of democracy in a globalized world order and the problems in global distributive justice, with increasing poverty and inequalities as two most daunting challenges faced by contemporary political philosophy and international relations. Erman argues that the obfuscation of the distinction between democratic theory and moral theories of legitimacy had led to the failure to understand the normative aspects of the challenge. For Erman, the normative dilemma of democracy or justice is a false dichotomy. Through a three-layered analysis of global normative order, Erman proposes 'multiple citizenship', where citizens are democratic agents and agents of democracy. From democracy as rule by people, Erman derives two conditions: first, political equality and the second, political bindingness. Erman utilizes Habermas' discourse theory of democracy in developing the 'equal influence principle' which emphasizes participatory and deliberative democracy.

Part II of this volume raises ontological and institutional questions with regard to conceptualizing and realizing cosmopolitanism. Véronique Pin-Fat steers the conversation back to the theoretical challenges in identifying the foundations of cosmopolitanism. In her grammatical examination of cosmopolitanism, Pin-Fat explores the relationship between language and ontological foundations, arguing for the ineffability of cosmopolitanism. Employing Wittgenstein's use of language games, she argues against seeking ontological foundations for the cosmopolitan concepts of universality, humanity and generality; identified by Thomas Pogge (1992: 48) as common to all cosmopolitan conceptions. Pin-Fat replaces language games with cosmopolitanism, arguing that scholars have created a dichotomous ontology, hard and soft ontologies based on a theory of linguistic representations. She calls cosmopolitanism a soft ontology since it defies precise characterization according to the tenets of analytic philosophy. Yet she mounts a defence of universality in the process of exploring how the meaning of universality is produced. Pin-Fat emphasizes the relational or co-constitutive nature of the cosmopolitan project that simultaneously challenges the universal as well as locates ways of identifying the universal. This endeavour is not in search of a successful or authoritative understanding of cosmopolitanism (or its practices), but to create conditions that 'make ethico-political contestation and engagement possible'. Using Lewis Carroll's *Hunting of the Snark* as a heuristic literary strategy, she makes an argument against drawing of exclusionary lines by investing language with an ability to represent multiple meanings, which it does not have. Without foundations, cosmopolitanism can only be understood as the domain of ethico-political contestations, asserts Pin-Fat, which gives it vitality, plurality and dynamism.

Rajan poses the following question: 'Who are the people of the world, of cosmopolitanism?' Even as cosmopolitanism seeks to transcend or displace the territorially bounded political community, it must contend with the enormity of locating the new 'global community'. Rajan's chapter argues that the most fruitful approach to building a cosmopolitan political community is to shift the focus from collectivities identified with a definite history and culture to social imaginaries at the transnational scales. In doing this, Rajan sets up a debate on the arguments advanced in this volume by Latha Varadarajan (Chapter 8), Sonika Gupta (Chapter 10) and Francesco Ragazzi (Chapter 7) in emphasizing the rootedness of identities and the reach of the territorial state into transnational spaces. He contends that existing post-national forms of politics, manifesting hybrid and overlapping identities, are in a position of engaging with 'global power' more effectively and in a reflexive process of change through iterative 'acts of power'. He uses the example of a global parliament and biome stewardship council to introduce the idea of a global political community that is internally consistent towards a cosmopolitan vision.

Providing a critique of the liberal foundations of cosmopolitanism, Arvind Sivaramakrishnan (Chapter 6) engages specifically with the idea of rights and citizenship, as framed in the liberal discourse as an untenable basis for achieving the cosmopolitan ideals. He problematizes rights-based liberalism, which assumes agency and autonomy of individuals, for failing to recognize the clashes of rights in some instances and holding rights as absolutes in some other. He argues that rights reflect societal, cultural and political agreements on the definitions of good in society. This agreement is contextual to shared ways of life, languages and cultures and therefore will inevitably clash with other definitions of the same. He contends that disagreements over rights and their definitions are as likely to be part of the cosmopolitan world as they are of others. Sivaramakrishnan also argues that rights-based liberalism neglects the role of the state, whereas neoliberalism's market economy has only deepened social, political and economic inequities. This chapter then raises questions with regard to the trajectory of institutionalization proposed by Archibugi and Held and constitutionalization as discussed by Brown, respectively, of cosmopolitan principles in global politics in this volume.

Ragazzi (Chapter 7) argues against automatically investing political spaces beyond the territorial state with normative cosmopolitan politics. He also challenges the conflation of the 'national' with a bounded territorial conception, arguing that the presence of transnational communities does not necessarily translate into a cosmopolitan post-national understanding of political community. He contends that it is faulty to presume that state power is purely territorial and that there are processes beyond the reach of the state and therefore ruled only by 'individual (ethical) or global (human rights) norms'. He offers the concept of post-territorial citizenship, as opposed to post-national citizenship, defined in terms of ethnocultural markers of identity rather than a territorial qualification of place of residence by tracing the 'territorialization' of the nation. Ragazzi historically examines the attempts at territorializing nations and problems associated with the conception of citizenship tied to territories with reference to 18th and 19th century imperial powers. In the globalized world, he argues, there is more of a redistribution of the features of citizenship rather than emergence of cosmopolitan norms of citizenship, as the state continues to securitize the citizens.

Varadarajan (Chapter 8) critiques the concept of a 'global citizen' based on the increasing irrelevance of territorial boundaries in the light of 'rapid and intensified movement of people, capital, ideas, and technology'. Employing the category of the 'domestic abroad', Varadarajan challenges the assumption that the existence of diaspora and their political engagement by the state of origin breaks down the inside-outside binary that is intrinsically linked to a territorial concept of state. Instead, the author argues that diasporas reinforce the nationalist imaginary and the authority of the state. She argues that diasporic cosmopolitanism does not in essence transform material conditions or the class cleavages. On the contrary, the author asserts, attempts in postcolonial literature to portray the diaspora as a liberated space and a challenge to the dominance of nation state, which is likened to imprisonment, have themselves been suborned by the domestic abroad phenomenon which is itself state driven. Varadarajan argues that current attempts of the Indian state to court the domestic abroad emanates out of neoliberal economic policies and that its 'transnationally informed policy-making' is not cosmopolitan by any stretch of the imagination, but fuelled by strong global capitalist forces. Varadarajan explains that there is a convergence of cosmopolitan, post-modern and postcolonial thought on diaspora, and in most cases the post-modern post-nationalism is conflated with cosmopolitanism.

Finally, this volume offers a postcolonial critique of cosmopolitanism questioning some methodological assumptions and exploring the relationship between nationalism and the cosmopolitan discourse. This section draws upon the Indian intellectual traditions as well as the Indian national movement for framing the critique of cosmopolitanism.

Rahul Rao (Chapter 9) critiques the hold of Western ontological and methodological frameworks on existing scholarship on cosmopolitanism. He also emphasizes the failure of political philosophy and theory to substantively engage with non-Western spaces. Rao is specifically critical of the social contractarian approaches led by John Rawls' prolific writings on justice as fairness, with emphasis on the veil of ignorance and original position. The question that Rao raises is whether cosmopolitanism is merely an extension of the Western intellectual and theoretical framework or can there be a genuine cosmopolitan perspective from the non-Western perspective? He argues that there is a possibility of alternative cosmopolitan perspectives not entirely incubated in the West, but which germinate in the 'peripheries' such as that of M. N. Roy, an avowed Indian communist who contested Lenin's advocacy of a tactical alliance between bourgeois nationalists and communists during the anti-colonial struggle. He also emphasizes the need to look for marginalized and border-crossing practices, and their link to cosmopolitan moral obligations.

Gupta (Chapter 10) argues that liberal cosmopolitanism negates nationalism's plural history in the search for building a cosmopolitan political community. Gupta asserts that liberal cosmopolitanism does not view nationalism as a legitimate location for the evolution of political community despite its historical role in creating self-aware and self-governing communities. She argues for a historically contextual evaluation of nationalism in contemporary global politics, especially with regard to postcolonial states. Gupta examines the liberating role of nationalism through a reading of Gandhi's seminal text *Hind Swaraj*. She argues that nationalism in the West and in the postcolony performs and fulfils different historical functions and the current cosmopolitan discourse must explicitly accommodate this rather than urge for a universal relevance of transcending to the post-national.

In the Epilogue, Sudarsan Padmanabhan argues that the polity, culture, society, religion, and language of the Indian subcontinent could be imagined only as contestation and negotiation between the cosmopolitan and the vernacular. Padmanabhan contends that from ancient times through the modern age and to the contemporary epoch, the dialectical relationship between the cosmopolitan and vernacular has manifested in manifold ways. He discusses the dialectical relationship between the Sanskrit cosmopolis and the vernacular linguistic traditions that created a unique way of imagining India — a unity in diversity — and how this imagining permeated religious, social, cultural, and political institutions, even challenging the caste system. He also focuses on the medieval period in Indian history, when many social, cultural and religious movements harnessed the dialectical nature of the cosmopolitan and vernacular debates with a renewed emphasis on humanism, illustrated by the Hindu Bhakti and Islamic Sufi movements led by saint-poets from all classes, castes and religions.[2] He maps how the creative tension between the cosmopolitan and the vernacular metamorphosed into a modern understanding of justice, secularism and the diversity of the Indian nation. He draws attention to how such an understanding was the bedrock of the Indian constitution, as envisaged by thinkers such as Gandhi, Ambedkar and Nehru, as it was sensitive to the postcolonial sociopolitical climate, stability of the fledgling nation state, accommodative of the linguistic-regional aspirations and, above all, ensuring justice to the hitherto subjugated voices.

Cosmopolitanism as a normative discourse raises fundamental questions of agency and location and production of power in the world. The value of this discourse lies in the challenge it presents to hegemonic understandings of the relationship between individual and state. This allows for exploring alternate structures of governance, citizenship and identity. However, beyond this, cosmopolitanism is also a reflexive movement in political philosophy that allows for a critical re-examination of its own fundamental assumptions. While offering this critical re-examination, the principle of humanity as an organizing principle is not weakened but strengthened. Strengthening the ethical statement of cosmopolitanism by contextualizing it within a historical context is what

---

[2] Rulers such as Akbar recognized and acknowledged the creative tension between the cosmopolitan and vernacular traditions of India.

this volume attempts. While there is much more to be said in this regard, the critique offered in this collection of essays is just the beginning of this conversation.

≈

References

Archibugi, Daniele (ed.). 2003. *Debating Cosmopolitics* (New Left Review Debates), Verso, London and New York.

Archibugi, Daniele and David Held. 1995. *Cosmopolitan Democracy: An Agenda for A New World Order*, Polity Press, Cambridge.

Archibugi, Daniele, Mathias Koenig-Archibugi and Raffaele Marchetti (eds). 2011. *Global Democracy: Normative and Empirical Perspectives*, Cambridge University Press, Cambridge.

Balibar, Etienne. 2012. 'Citizenship of the World Revisited', in Gerard Delanty (ed.), *Routledge Handbook of Cosmopolitanism Studies*, Routledge, London, 291–301.

Beck, Ulrich. 2004. 'Cosmopolitical Realism: On the Distinction Between Cosmopolitanism in Philosophy and Social Sciences', *Global Networks* 4(2): 131–46.

Beitz, Charles R. 1975. 'Justice and International Relations', *Philosophy and Public Affairs* 4(4): 360–89.

Brennan Timothy. 1997. *At Home in the World: Cosmopolitanism Now* (Convergences: Inventories of the Present), Harvard University Press, Cambridge, MA.

Brock, Gillian and Harry Brighouse (eds). 2005. *The Political Philosophy of Cosmopolitanism*, Cambridge University Press, Cambridge.

Brown, Garrett W. and D. Held (eds). 2010. *The Cosmopolitanism Reader*, Polity, Cambridge.

Cheah, P. and B. Robbins (eds). 1998. *Cosmopolitics: Thinking and Feeling Beyond the Nation*, Minnesota University Press, Minneapolis.

Delanty, Gerard. 1999. 'Self, Other and World: Discourses of Nationalism and Cosmopolitanism', *Cultural Values*, 3(3): 365–75.

———. 2009. *Community*, Routledge, London.

——— (ed.). 2012a. *Routledge Handbook of Cosmopolitanism Studies*, Routledge, London.

——— (ed.). 2012b. 'The Idea of Critical Cosmopolitanism', in Gerard Delanty (ed.), *Routledge Handbook of Cosmopolitanism Studies*, Routledge, London, 38–46.

Dower, Nigel. 2003. *An Introduction to Global Citizenship*, Edinburgh University Press, Edinburgh.

Falk, Richard and Andrew Strauss. 2001. 'Toward Global Parliament', *Foreign Affairs* 1(1): 212–20.

Held, David. 1995. *Democracy and the Global Order: From the Modern State to Cosmopolitan Governance*, Stanford University Press, Stanford.

———. 2010. *Cosmopolitanism: Ideals and Realities*, Polity Press, Cambridge.

Jabri, Vivienne. 2010. *War and the Transformation of Global Politics*, Palgrave Macmillan, Basingstoke.

Mignolo, Walter. 2011. *The Darker Side of Western Modernity: Global Futures, Decolonial Options*, Duke University Press, Durham.

Miller, David. 2010. 'Cosmopolitanism', in Garrett W. Brown and David Held (eds), *The Cosmopolitanism Reader*, Polity, Cambridge, 377–92.

Nussbaum, Martha C. 1996. *For Love of Country?* Edited by Joshua Cohen for *Boston Review*, Beacon Press, Boston, MA.

O'Neill, Onora. 2000. *Bounds of Justice*, Cambridge University Press, Cambridge.

Padmanabhan, Sudarsan. 2012. 'Unity in Diversity: The Indian Cosmopolitan Idea', in Gerard Delanty (ed.), *Routledge Handbook of Cosmopolitanism Studies*, Routledge, London, 463–76.

Pogge, Thomas W. 1992. 'Cosmopolitanism and Sovereignty', *Ethics* 103(1): 48–75.

———. 2002. *World Poverty and Human Rights: Cosmopolitan Responsibilities and Reforms*, Polity Press, Cambridge

———. 2010. 'Cosmopolitanism and Sovereignty', in Garrett W. Brown and David Held (eds), *The Cosmopolitanism Reader*, Polity Press, Cambridge, 114–33.

Pollock, Sheldon, Homi K. Bhabha, Carol A. Breckenridge, and Dipesh Chakrabarty. 2000. 'Cosmopolitanisms', *Public Culture* 12(3): 577–90.

Schlereth, Thomas J. 1977. *The Cosmopolitan Ideal in Enlightenment Thought: Its Form and Function in the Ideas of Franklin, Hume, and Voltaire, 1694–1790*, Notre Dame University Press, Notre Dame, Indiana.

Singer, Peter. 2002. *One World: The Ethics of Globalisation*, Text Publishing, Melbourne.

Vertovec, Steven and Robin Cohen. 2003. *Conceiving Cosmopolitanism: Theory, Context and Practice*, Oxford University Press, New York.

Part I
Normative Cosmopolitanism: Statements

1

Cosmopolitan Democracy: Paths and Agents*

Daniele Archibugi and *David Held*

Twenty Years After

When at the end of the Cold War and at the beginning of a new wave of democratization we suggested the idea of a cosmopolitan democracy (Archibugi and Held 1995; Held 1995), we were aware that we were pouring old wine into new bottles. The attempt to make world politics more transparent, more accountable, more participatory, and more respectful of the rule of law had pioneers spanning from Immanuel Kant to Richard Falk. Still, the idea that 'democracy' as a concept and a practice could and should be applied beyond nation states was somehow innovative.

If we read the international relations textbooks prior to 1989, we may be surprised to note that many of them do not even contain the word 'democracy'. When the word appears, it is generally in reference to the internal political system of states and certainly not in relation to the possibility of subjugating world politics to demo-cratic rules. Even international organizations were mostly seen as purely intergovernmental bodies and the prospect of making them more democratic was not contemplated. The European Union (EU), the first international organization composed exclusively by democratic regimes and with some germs of democratic norms in its modus operandi, was mostly discussed in relation to the limits it imposed on its member countries rather than in terms of its abil-ity to deal publicly with transnational issues. The state of the art was not very different in the realm of democratic theory. Most of the textbooks dedicated to democracy, including the first edition of the work of one of us (Held 1987), did not contain any reference to the problem of democracy beyond borders. Many of these text-books addressed in detail how decision-making within town halls,

---

* This essay is a revised version of 'Cosmopolitan Democracy: Paths and Agents', *Ethics & International Affairs* 25(4): 433–61. Reproduced with permission from Cambridge University Press.

counties and central governments could foster or hamper democracy. But democratic theory ended at state borders: it had nothing yet to say beyond this level of analysis. Today the state of the art is substantially different: international relations and democratic theory both take for granted that 'democracy beyond borders' is an issue to be discussed. Most of the recent international relations handbooks devote at least a chapter to the question of democracy within international organizations and of the impact of globalization on national democracies. The same applies to handbooks on democracy, which often devote the last chapter to the challenge of expanding democratic values to the international system.

Of course, not everybody is convinced that a cosmopolitan democracy is needed or desirable. Opponents are clearly more numerous than supporters. Robert Dahl, Ralf Dahrendorf, David Miller, Philippe Schmitter and many others have more or less politely declared that the idea of applying the concept of democracy beyond the state is premature or even naïve. However, other scholars, including Jürgen Habermas, Richard Falk, Ulrich Beck, Mary Kaldor, Tony McGrew, Jan Aart Scholte, and Saskia Sassen have contributed to the development of this vision from a variety of disciplinary backgrounds. Moreover, the hope of cosmopolitan democracy has reached the hearts and minds of many young scholars, which are increasingly providing fresh ideas and sophisticated analytical tools.

The aims of the cosmopolitan democracy project have never been limited to academic discourse. On the contrary, the ambition was mostly to provide the intellectual arguments to achieve elements of transformation in the real world. It should be recognized that, while the academic discourse has been unexpectedly successful, the hopes to obtain a democratic transformation of world politics have achieved so far very modest results. In fact, most of the proposals put on the table in the last two decades have not been implemented; a fact that is not entirely surprising, given how long it takes to change and reshape institutions. A change in the rhetoric, at least, is perceivable: since the beginning of the 1990s, statesmen are less likely to justify their actions on the ground of national interests, while international organizations are now keener to be accountable not only to diplomatic circles but also to public opinion at large. It is difficult to foresee now if this change will remain a simple cosmetic coverage or if it might lead to substantial transformations.

In this chapter we address an issue that has not yet been satisfactorily discussed in our previous work: who are the agents that might promote cosmopolitan democracy? While we have elsewhere illustrated the reasons that justify the need and the possibility of a cosmopolitan democracy (Held 1995, 2010; Archibugi 2008; Archibugi et al. 2011), and others have discussed its possibility (Koenig-Archibugi 2010), we have not yet discussed the social, economic and political processes that may lead some agents to support the political innovations suggested by the model. We are well aware that political transformations occur because of a combination of idealistic and materialistic motivations and that both top-down and bottom-up forces do contribute to the development or obstruction of change. In the next section we single out a few areas where changes in line with cosmopolitan democracy have been debated, while the subsequent sections are devoted to identifying the top-down and bottom-up agents that could promote cosmopolitan democracy.

Paths towards Cosmopolitan Democracy

If we ever manage to achieve a form of global governance that embeds some of the values and norms of democracy, it is very unlikely to happen as a result of a single grand plan. It is, on the contrary, more likely that various changes and reforms introduced at the local, national, regional and global levels will together contribute to a progressive transformation of world politics, and that each innovation provides inspiration and encouragement for further changes. The idea of a cosmopolitan democracy was never intended to provide a closed recipe, but as a unifying framework for a battery of proposals and campaigns that, in different ways, aim to develop global governance in a democratic direction.

Many ideas for reforming global governance have been debated by diplomats and activists, governmental authorities and nongovernmental organizations (NGOs), businessmen and scholars, at the United Nations (UN), the G8 and G20 summits, the World Economic Forum and the World Social Forum. Some suggest reforms to current international organizations and others argue for new ones. Some stress the role of social movements, others the need to give more space to selected groups of stakeholders. There are campaigns that insist on the crucial importance of legal institutions, while other groups suggest giving to the business sector a more prominent role in managing global issues (see Held 2004). We do not consider this variety of proposals competing against each other. On the contrary, we tend to look at most of them as complementary attempts to move towards a world order that progressively encompasses at least some forms of democracy. We sketch below some of the areas where transformations have been advocated.

States as Champions of Cosmopolitanism

States can be champions of cosmopolitanism within their own borders. Most states have to deal with a citizenry with diverse languages, religions, ethnicities, and ideologies. Each state has the opportunity to experiment with different forms of political participation, and with those minority rights that have been advocated by multiculturalists. Many states, especially Western states, are also facing an increasing challenge from migration. Aliens have fewer rights than natives in most states and, with transborder flows of people on the increase, this is making accommodation more problematic and it is generating mounting internal tensions. A state willing to become a champion of cosmopolitanism should make an effort, where possible, to reduce disparities between natives and strangers and offer to aliens the political rights enjoyed by its citizens. The expression 'cosmopolitan state' may at first appear an oxymoron, but cosmopolitanism is a set of values and practices that can be implemented by any political institution, including the state (Beardsworth 2011; Brown 2011). International institutions can also be a positive stimulus to induce states to introduce more progressive standards in this regard. The UN Human Rights Council, the Council of Europe and the EU all have monitoring programmes that critically assess respect for minority rights within their member countries.

For a Democratic Foreign Policy

One of the core demands of cosmopolitan democracy is to obtain a substantial change in national foreign policy priorities, especially those of the liberal and powerful Western states. A democratic state should use its foreign policy instruments to become a good member of the international community even at the expense of short-term disadvantages. For example, consolidated democracies should support foreign political parties and activists willing to foster democracy in despotically ruled countries rather than those who might be more congenial to their own national interests. For too long democratic countries have passively accepted or even actively supported dictatorial regimes when this was in their interest. A new foreign policy doctrine based on solidarity among democratic forces is now needed. This does not necessarily mean that democratic countries should create new institutions to exclude other despotic governments, as suggested by the proposal for a League of Democracies (see Carothers [2008] for an assessment). Such a proposal risks creating a further divide among countries and could have the paradoxical effect of creating international cohesion among despotic countries and the isolation of democratic movements within these countries.

The Reform of International Organizations

International Organizations (IOs) embed some elements of democracy as they are based on treaties and charters, their actions must not violate international law, their operations are transparent to a certain extent, and their activities and policies are accountable to their member states to a degree. But many of the core ideas of democracy, such as the principle of equality among citizens, are not applied. Most IOs started as clubs for national governments, but they progressively incorporated, often in a decorative role, larger numbers of stakeholders. As a result of the participation of the business sector and NGOs, IOs have managed to expand their authority and legitimacy. Yet, while plans to reform the UN and other IOs have emerged from policy debates and academic writings, they have not been implemented. The bulk of these proposals aim to increase the role and functions of IOs and to enlarge participation and accountability. Many of the reform proposals could substantially enhance the independent political role of IOs, making them something other than simple instruments of national governments. This would help make them one of the core institutions of a cosmopolitan democracy. Perhaps surprisingly, opponents of these proposals are not only found among autocratic states, but among democratic ones as well.

Global Judicial Authorities

The rule of law and its enforcement is an essential component of any democratic system. Cosmopolitan democracy supports the development of a more effective global rule of law, while remaining sceptical of the enhancement of coercive supranational powers in general. Several IOs, including the EU and the UN, already have complex legal norms and embryonic judicial power. These bodies have a weak authority in world politics since they lack enforcement capacity. Nevertheless, if international norms and jurisdictions become more sophisticated, it will be increasingly costly for governments to violate them. There are at least three aspects of the global judicial authority that should be taken into account: the emerging global criminal justice system, the need to reinforce legal solutions to interstate controversies and the need to provide adequate transnational administrative rules for both the public and the business sectors.

Criminal Justice

The creation of several ad hoc international courts and, above all, the International Criminal Court (ICC) have generated new hopes to hold egregious criminals, including politicians, accountable for their actions. Indeed, the ICC is the most significant institutional innovation introduced in the post-Cold War era. Much could still be done to make the ICC fully operative, and to induce all countries to accept its jurisdiction. But it is already possible to assess its first few years of activities (see Glasius 2009). To date, the ICC has mostly acted on suspected African culprits, and on insurgents fighting against, and denounced by, incumbent governments, the case opened against the Sudanese president, Omar al-Bashir, is a significant exception. All investigations undertaken are well documented, but the coverage is still highly selective. There is the danger that the ICC will be perceived as an instrument of incumbent governments against rebels and another burden of the white man over the black man. Those who hoped that the ICC could also be an instrument in defence of the weaker against the most powerful have so far been disappointed. There is the need to balance the action of the ICC to cover cases in which the crimes are committed by Western individuals. For these reasons, the operation of the ICC can be stimulated and reinforced by other bottom-up initiatives, such as Opinion Tribunals, which may be selective and politically motivated, but are less influenced by diplomatic negotiations and could call the attention of public opinion and of the official criminal courts to cases that have been overlooked.

Lawful Conflict Resolutions

Interest in the ICC has somewhat overshadowed an equally important problem, namely the need to address interstate controversies through legal instruments. The International Court of Justice (ICJ), the body within the UN system that should address these controversies, is highly underused mostly because it can be activated only when both parties in a dispute are willing to accept its jurisdiction. Unfortunately, this happens very rarely and too often is activated for relatively insignificant controversies. If we read the sentences and the opinions provided by the court, we will have a distorted view of the world history of the last sixty years. The Vietnam War, the invasions of Hungary and Czechoslovakia, the Iraq war, the legitimacy of nuclear weapons and many other key international controversies have not received any attention from the court for the very simple reason that states were not willing to submit cases of vital importance to their national interest to its judgement. A major expansion of the global rule of law would require empowering the ICJ with compulsory jurisdiction, making the court not just a sort of 'referee' among two states but a proper tribunal (Falk 1998). This does not necessarily imply that the ICJ would have the power to enforce its own judgements. But even in absence of enforcement, a judgement denouncing the behaviour of some states would have an important impact on international relations. And, again, this is a change that each state could implement individually; several states have already accepted the compulsory jurisdiction of the ICJ.

International Administrative Courts

One of the most relevant trends in international law is the development of judicial or semi-judicial authorities for administrative purposes and the business sector. Rather than using national courts, both public and private players prefer to activate elements of *lex mercatoria* (the global framework of commercial law) and to use special courts set up for the purpose of hearing such cases. This new network of judicial institutions is in fact replicating, at the global level, the functions of the state: namely arbitrating in cases of controversy. At the same time, these legal developments show that there are some possibilities to obtain conflict resolutions also in the absence of a coercive power of last resort.

Citizens' Participation in Global Politics

Cosmopolitan democracy advocates giving citizens political representation also at the global level. This cosmopolitan participation should not replace the political participation that citizens have in national democracies through elected assemblies. The aim of cosmopolitan democracy is to create assemblies representing world citizens (such as the Assemblies of the non-governmental organizations recognized by the UN), or even directly elected assemblies (on the model of the European Parliament), in parallel and independently from the already existing national political institutions. There is a wealth of proposals aimed at creating this, but the most straightforward way to achieve it would be to create a World Parliamentary Assembly, similar in composition to the European Parliament. Such an institution would be the natural and most effective way to help bring together the peoples of the earth, allowing them to deliberate on common issues (Falk and Strauss 2001). It is unlikely that such an organ would have effective powers (at least in the short and medium period), but even if it were simply a forum reflecting and deliberating upon global public opinion, it could play an important role in identifying and confronting policies on world issues. This assembly would not necessarily be involved in every aspect of global political life, but it could concentrate on the most relevant and pressing issues: for example, those with a high impact on global life (for example, the environment) or those with huge political significance (for example, major violations of human rights). On some occasions, the World Parliamentary Assembly could provide suggestions on what is the most appropriate constituency to address issues that cut across borders. Such a new institution would complement the UN General Assembly and could work in close connection with it. It could provide political representation in global affairs to individuals and collective groups that are so far deprived of it: ethnic or political minorities within states, stateless groups, immigrants, refugees and, more importantly, peoples who still live under authoritarian regimes. Its usefulness will not just be for groups at the margins of political representation: individuals living in consolidated democracies would also have the advantage of engaging with a new level of governance and representation.[1]

---

[1] The Campaign for the Establishment of a United Nations Parliamentary Assembly has even prospected the electoral systems and the number of

Political Communities without Boundaries

Deliberative communities are not necessarily based on a territorially contiguous space. Increasingly, there are more areas in which political problems are non-territorial or involve stakeholders in very different capacities (Gould 2004). Professional associations, ethnic communities, groups of citizens linked by common diseases or by strong economic interactions may be willing to address their problems through democratic procedures. The capacity to address these challenges is strongly limited by the current representation of interests in world politics, whereby most foreign affairs issues are addressed by national governments. While many of these specific groups have neither the interest nor the capacity to become a state and claim sovereignty over a given territory, they may nevertheless find it necessary to have a political space to address their problems and that it is recognized by states and IOs (Dryzek 2006; Macdonald 2008). The number of transnational actors that are in charge of specific domains is increasing, as is the number of administrative bodies involving both public and business members. Transnational movements for social justice have already experimented with many ways to link players across borders.

Recognizing the importance of non-territorially bounded political communities composed of individuals with common interests raises a crucial question for political theory: who are the legitimate stakeholders? For better or worse, the organization of political communities based on states provides a straightforward answer: it is the state that decides who the citizens are and how to represent their interests on the international scene. In cases of other forms of political representation, it will be much more difficult to assess who the stakeholders are. Who are the stakeholders of the oil industrial complex? We can name the shareholders of the oil companies, the employees of the industry, the consumers of the industrial society, and the citizens of oil-producing countries, among many others. All of them are legitimate stakeholders, but this still leaves open the relative weight that each of these categories should have in the political process. In some cases stakeholders themselves will find the system of representation congenial to their interests, but

---

deputies of such a World Parliament (see http://en.unpacampaign.org/news/374.php [accessed 17 July 2014]).

in more controversial cases it is likely that they will need to rely on an external assignment of competences and electoral weights. A World Parliamentary Assembly may be the instrument that could minimize political exclusion by providing political representation to dedicated functional areas where the relative importance of stakeholders is not properly acknowledged. In controversial cases, the World Parliamentary Assembly could also provide opinions on who should be competent for what. There are, in fact, several cases of conflicting competencies: Who should be in charge of refugees — the neighbouring states or the whole international community? Who is entitled to vote in referendums concerning self-determination? These are the cases in which a World Parliamentary Assembly may help to minimize conflicts by providing independent assessments.

Top-down and Bottom-up Agents of Cosmopolitan Democracy

We have briefly discussed a number of areas and institutions that could make world politics more democratic. It is now important to ask: which political and social agents might have an interest in supporting these reforms? Political change occurs when there are interests at stake and agents willing to mobilize. The question just posed can in part be answered by reflecting on those social groups that are today excluded from political participation, that find the traditional channels to access world politics insufficient or that feel strongly motivated to act in selected domains. These are the players that should have an interest in generating more democratic global political institutions.

The 'Dispossessed'

The first group of agents that could have an interest in minimizing exclusion in world politics and that have access to decision-making are the dispossessed, those that Frantz Fanon (1963) labelled the 'wretched of the earth'. These are people concentrated in under-developed countries, with very low living standards, and that are more vulnerable to environmental, economic and political crises. A significant part of this grouping has also experienced major political instability associated with failed states. This group has also been called 'the bottom billion' (Collier 2007) but perhaps its number is even higher. It is a group of people that rely heavily on the support provided by international agencies and donors. The structural weakness of this group does not allow its voice to be heard directly in world politics, to reach world markets, and often even to participate actively in the domestic politics of their own country. If its voice is heard at all in global fora, it is because of extreme actions, humanitarian catastrophes or because other players report its needs and its opinions. International relief agencies and NGOs call attention to the conditions of these people as they are not sufficiently powerful and organized to obtain it themselves. The dispossessed have even had to rely on Western celebrities as their spokespersons.[2] In principle, this is the group of people that could benefit most from a cosmopolitan democracy: within states the dispossessed obtained substantial advantages when they achieved the franchise, and empowering them with political rights in world institutions could be an important step in improving their bargaining power.

Migrants

Migration flows motivated by economic reasons are generating major changes in affluent countries. Most of these migrants move to countries that are not only wealthier but also have democratic regimes. Authorized immigrants are seldom guaranteed the same economic, social and, above all, political rights as the natives, while unauthorized immigrants can have no rights at all. This is creating an increasing discrepancy between the rights and the duties of these citizens. Immigrants are engaging in forms of civil disobedience such as the Great American Boycott on 1 May 2006 in the United States[3] or the 'Sans-Papiers' movement in France and other European countries.[4] Immigrants are not isolated and they have often been supported by civil society groups, trade unions and other organizations, creating a social and political coalition supporting their rights (see Cabrera 2010). The immediate target of these

---

[2] Paradigmatic cases are George Clooney as campaigner for Darfur and Angelina Jolie as Goodwill Ambassador for the United Nations High Commissioner for Refugees.

[3] On 1 May 2006, immigrants in the United States boycotted businesses, shops and schools to show how important their presence was to the American economy and society.

[4] The Sans-Papiers ('without documents') movement started in France in April 2007, when a group of undocumented immigrants occupied the Church Saint Paul in Massy claiming their right to be regularized.

protesters is the government of the host country and the principal aim is to get their status recognized. But these protests go far
beyond national boundaries: there is a more general claim towards
freedom of movement — that it does not correspond to the state
only (see Benhabib 2004). Most democratic states are also associated to IOs that monitor their human rights regime, including
the treatment of aliens. Individual EU member states, for example,
have often been reproached by the EU and the Council of Europe
for unfair treatment of immigrants.

Cosmopolitan Groups

There are already some collective groups that are already sociologically 'cosmopolitan'. Some rock stars, football players and actors
have not only become global icons but they already live in conditions that make national boundaries irrelevant to them. While
these icons are the most visible cosmopolitans, they are certainly
not alone: cosmopolitans also include many intellectuals, businessmen, public officers, and social activists. This group has periodically
attracted the hostility of nationalistic and totalitarian leaderships
and have often been called, derogatorily, 'rootless cosmopolitans'
(Kofman 2007). It is not easy to identify the size of this cosmopolitan group, and even less so to what extent they simply belong to
the group of privileged elites. It is, however, possible to distinguish
between two relevant analytical factors: that is, between having a
personal cosmopolitan lifestyle and holding cosmopolitan values.
The cosmopolitan democracy project needs more support from the
latter than from the former.

The available empirical evidence shows that as many as 15 per
cent of the world's inhabitants perceive their principal identity as
post-national (either regional or cosmopolitan), compared with
38 per cent who privilege their national identity and 47 per cent
their local identity (Norris 2000). Moreover, identification with
a global identity increases among young people and among those
with a higher educational level, suggesting that, in the near future,
cosmopolitan identity might become considerably more important.
It might be argued that it is the privileged elites who hold these
cosmopolitan values, but this assumption is disproved by other
empirical evidence which, on the contrary, indicates that the share
of cosmopolitan values is spread evenly between the elites and the
population at large (Furia 2005). The existence of cosmopolitan

values does not, of course, necessarily translate into political mobilization, but if and when it does, it could resonate with a considerable proportion of the world population.

Global Stakeholders and Global Civil Society

Political mobilization in favour of a more progressive world politics rests on two important and often overlapping groups: global stakeholders and the global civil society. Global stakeholders include sectors of governance, networks and social movements, as well as other groups with sectoral interests. In all cases, these groupings do not necessarily overlap with established political communities nor receive a mandate from states. These stakeholders are very active and have considerable mobilizing and lobbying capacities which they can direct at both national authorities and international institutions. Often these global stakeholders are better informed, technically more competent and certainly more motivated to pursue their agenda than their national or international counterparts (Macdonald 2011). As might be expected, in many areas stakeholders have managed to secure key positions in decision-making and can even act as suppliers of global governance without an explicit delegation. In other areas, stakeholders are dispersed and less organized and their political contributions unheard or heard only in international fora when national governments are willing to support them.

Mary Kaldor (2003) and her collaborators have also described and mapped another important player: global civil society.[5] Global civil society is often the most vocal supporter of progressive changes in world politics, including the democratization of global governance and reform in IOs. NGOs and other players have become increasingly important in drafting the agenda of global politics and often also in delivering public goods in areas of crisis. Global civil society is, according to Kaldor and her colleagues, also transforming the canons of international politics, providing often more effective solutions to local problems than national governments or even IOs and acting as a powerful counterweight to traditional power politics (Kaldor et al. 2003). This 'politics from below' carried out by the global civil society is often pushing for a different organization

---

[5] See the *Global Civil Society Yearbook* produced by LSE Global Governance since the year 2000, which has produced a wide range of analyses on the significance and activities of global civil society.

of interest at the various levels of policy actions — local, national and also global.

International Political Parties

Several political parties also have a transnational affiliation. As is widely known, the loyalty to this affiliation is low and the political priorities of parties are largely dictated by national interests rather than by the parties' international ideologies. Within the EU, parties have greater international coordination and this is associated with the powers and functions of the EU as well as with the existence of the only directly elected international assembly: the European Parliament. In fact, in the European Parliament national parties are organized within European groups. This is far from reflecting a genuine Westminster-style majority and opposition (see Hix 2008), but it still provides a sense that, certainly at the European level, there are different options. The European example indicates that institutions do shape the ways in which interests are organized. It is therefore possible that international political parties could act as promoters of democratic reforms in the UN and other IOs. The Socialist International (2005), for example, has already published a far-reaching document on UN Reform which urged member parties in government to actively support the proposals made.

Trade Unions and Labour Movements

The labour movement is seriously challenged by economic globalization. The labour movement built its political power at the national level, when, in alliance with left-wing political parties, it managed to guarantee labour rights, labour standards and the welfare protection of the lower and middle classes. Ideologically, however, the labour movement always had an internationalist standpoint, as shown by its mobilization against many wars and colonialism. One of the most important challenges of the labour movement in the 21st century is to guarantee to the working classes adequate standards of living and economic and social rights in a global economy dominated by multinational corporations (MNCs) and high mobility of capital (see Munck and Waterman 1999). The labour movement's mandate to defend wages and jobs at the national level is now in tension with notions of the transnational solidarity of the working class. This tension is reflected in the ambivalent attitude of labour movements towards trade liberalization and migration. Most trade unions have been actively involved in defending the labour rights of immigrants, but some of them have been hostile to uncontrolled trade liberalization and inflows of labour when these risk reducing employment and wage levels.

How could the labour movement face a much better equipped transnational business sector? The differences in labour costs and labour rights at the world level are still so high that it is difficult to create an effective alliance linking labour interests in countries as different as Sweden and China, the United States and India. This issue has been addressed in the attempt to standardize and upgrade labour standards through the International Labour Organization (ILO) and to prevent unfair trade practices through the World Trade Organization (WTO). Expanding from labour rights to other social and economic rights, and ultimately to political rights, might allow the labour movement to become a powerful agent in democratizing global governance.

Multinational Corporations

Multinational corporations are formidable players and drivers of the global economy. A few hundred MNCs account for a very large share of world income, employment and technology generation and are also very efficient in lobbying to protect their interests. To secure materials, to organize their production and to reach markets, MNCs need to overcome institutional barriers, including barriers to trade, capital movements and migrations. MNCs have also shown the capacity to shape global governance in line with their interests, as they have done with national governments.

Some scholars believe that MNCs will always act against the democratization of global governance since they can satisfy their agenda by lobbying or functional networking, rather than through transparent and accountable policymaking. This is certainly part of the story, but not all MNCs' interests are convergent and often their agenda also needs effective and accountable global governance. In some core areas, such as telecommunications, transport, technical standards, crime prevention and law enforcement, MNCs require more effective and transparent global governance. In the area of business law and property rights, the lack of appropriate transnational jurisdiction often makes transactions less certain and more risky. In such cases, MNCs push for transnational legislation and law enforcement (see Crane et al. 2008). They are also increasingly using international arbitration and public or semi-public judicial powers.

Effective Combination of Top-down and Bottom-up Politics

The two sections above have presented two lists, neither of which pretends to be comprehensive. The first is a list of actions that can be taken to advance cosmopolitan democracy. The second is a list of the political and social players that may be either interested or ideologically motivated to introduce greater transparency, accountability and participation in global governance. Of course, the various players do not necessarily have an ultimate and coherent agenda for pursuing the democratization of global governance; their agency is often dominated by mixed motives. Table 1.1 displays the list, mapping the uneven and combined agency which might pursue cosmopolitan democracy. It indicates that the vision of a more transparent, accountable and participatory global governance has roots in current economic, social and political processes, and that the cosmopolitan project has social and political anchors.

To what extent can the actions and the players mentioned in Table 1.1 be labelled 'top-down' or 'bottom-up'? The very idea of democracy rests on a glorious bottom-up struggle to make political power accountable. But this bottom-up process is not necessarily fostered only by bottom-up pressures. We know that the English, American, French, and Russian revolutions, all fought in the hope of empowering the bourgeois, the citizen and the proletariat, were led by the elites. But, as Mary Kaldor has shown, political change also occurs through less imperative levers and that light ties among individuals, associations and unofficial political movements may generate snowball effects of unpredictable consequences. The end of the Cold War and the re-unification of Europe provide a powerful example of this (see Kaldor 1991).

The cosmopolitan democracy project is shaped by this hope: it aims to analyse the current transformations, to identify the areas where institutional innovations are needed and are possible, to foster linkages and to understand what the main political players require. It does not have a fixed final goal since we are convinced that history will continue to surprise even the most optimistic thinker. And it adjusts routinely to the evolution of politics. It is perhaps

Table 1.1: Paths and Agents of Cosmopolitan Democracy

Agenda for Cosmopolitan Democracy	Agents of Cosmopolitan Democracy						
	Dispossessed	Immigrants	Cosmopolitan Groups	Global Stakeholders and Global Civil Society	International Political Parties	Trade Unions and Labour Movements	Multinational Corporations (MNCs)
Cosmopolitan States	–	Request for social, economic and political rights for immigrants	Contribute to a public sphere to obtain from states respect for cosmopolitan standards	Social and political actions to guarantee cosmopolitan standards within states	Instruments to secure citizenship within and beyond states	Request social and economic rights for immigrants	Pursuit of integrated markets
Democratic Foreign Policy	Request donor states to contribute to development aid and policies	Actions to remove the causes of migration	Request to apply consistent principles at home and abroad and also support democratization	Ensure that foreign policy is transparent and accountable	Press national parties to respect democratic standards and to support democratic forces in authoritarian countries	–	Tension between business interests and business ethics
Reform of International Organizations (IOs)	Direct participation in relief and other on-field activities of IOs	Guarantee the human rights of immigrants and also freedom of movement	Pressure for citizens' participation in IOs	Active participation in IOs also to augment transparency and accountability	Urge members of parties in government to support reform in IOs	Enlarge IOs' stakeholders when labour interests are at stake	Interest in getting effective global governance through IOs
Global Criminal Justice	Protection against major human rights violations in deprived areas	–	Ensuring impartiality of official international criminal courts, also through the promotion of Opinion Tribunals	Reinforce global criminal justice through opinion tribunals	Pressure to obtain adhesion and participation in the ICC of member parties in government		

Table 1.1: (*Continued*)

Table 1.1: (Continued)

Agenda for Cosmopolitan Democracy	Agents of Cosmopolitan Democracy						
	Dispossessed	Immigrants	Cosmopolitan Groups	Global Stakeholders and Global Civil Society	International Political Parties	Trade Unions and Labour Movements	Multinational Corporations (MNCs)
Lawful Interstate Conflict Resolution	Minimize international conflicts and aim for peaceful conflict resolution	–	Public opinion pressure for a global rule of law	Opposition to wars and to other forms of international coercion	Press member parties in governments to accept compulsory jurisdiction of the ICJ	–	–
International Administrative Courts	–	–	–	Enhance timely and effective arbitration	–	Promote effective transnational administrative networks	Promote effective and timely contract adjudication
Citizens' Participation in Global Politics	Steps to be taken towards political representation at the global level	Activate channels for transnational political participation	Campaigns to develop political rights and electoral franchise at the regional and global levels as well	Generate transnational democratic networks in specific areas	Enlarge participation in world politics	–	–
Non-territorial Political Communities	Request direct participation in relief programmes and development aid	Possibility to connect politically to their home country	Organization of transnational public opinion	Develop and self-organize ad hoc democratic communities	–	Promote active transnational links between employees	Participate in transborder economic and political activities

Source: Prepared by the authors.

this suppleness that is the very essence of democratic thought and practice. Today this needs to confront a globalizing society.

✍

References

Archibugi, Daniele. 2008. *The Global Commonwealth of Citizens Toward Cosmopolitan Democracy*, Princeton University Press, Princeton.

Archibugi, Daniele and David Held (eds). 1995. *Cosmopolitan Democracy: An Agenda for a New World Order*, Polity Press, Cambridge.

Archibugi, Daniele, Mathias Koenig-Archibugi and Raffaele Marchetti (eds). 2011. *Global Democracy: Normative and Empirical Perspectives*, Cambridge University Press, Cambridge.

Beardsworth, Richard. 2011. *Cosmopolitanism and International Relations*, Polity Press, Cambridge.

Benhabib, Seyla. 2004. *The Rights of Others: Aliens, Residents and Citizens*, Cambridge University Press, Cambridge.

Brown, Garrett W. 2011. 'Bringing the State Back into Cosmopolitanism: The Idea of Responsible Cosmopolitan States', *Political Studies Review* 9(1): 53–66.

Cabrera, Luis. 2010. *The Practice of Global Citizenship*, Cambridge University Press, Cambridge.

Carothers, Thomas. 2008. *Is a League of Democracies a Good Idea?* Carnegie Endowment for International Peace, Washington.

Collier, Paul. 2007. *The Bottom Billion. Why the Poorest Countries are Failing and What Can Be Done about It*, Oxford University Press, Oxford.

Crane, Andrew, Dirk Matten and Jeremy Moon. 2008. *Corporations and Citizenship*, Cambridge University Press, Cambridge.

Dryzek, John. 2006. *Deliberative Global Politics*, Polity Press, Cambridge.

Falk, Richard. 1998. *Law in an Emerging Global Village: A Post-Westphalian Perspective*, Transnational Publishers, Ardsley.

Falk, Richard and Andrew Strauss. 2001. 'Toward Global Parliament', *Foreign Affairs* 1(1): 212–20.

Fanon, Frantz. 1963. *The Wretched of the Earth*, Grove Weidenfeld, New York.

Furia, Peter. 2005. 'Global Citizenship, Anyone? Cosmopolitanism, Privilege and Public Opinion', *Global Society* 19(4): 331–59.

Glasius, Marlies. 2009. 'What is Global Justice and Who Decides? Civil Society and Victim Responses to the International Criminal Court's First Investigations', *Human Rights Quarterly* 31: 496–520.

Gould, Carol. 2004. *Democratizing Globalization and Human Rights*, Cambridge University Press, Cambridge.

Held, David. 1987. *Models of Democracy*, 1st edition, Polity Press, Cambridge.

———. 1995. *Democracy and the Global Order: From the Modern State to Cosmopolitan Governance*, Polity Press, Cambridge.

———. 2004. *Global Covenant. The Social Democratic Alternative to the Washington Consensus*, Polity Press, Cambridge.

———. 2010. *Cosmopolitanism. Ideals and Realities*, Polity Press, Cambridge.

Hix, Simon. 2008. *What's Wrong with the European Union and How to Fix it*, Polity Press, Cambridge.

Kaldor, Mary, (ed).1991. *Europe from Below: An East-West Dialogue*, Verso, London.

———. 2003. *Global Civil Society: An Answer to War*, Polity Press, Cambridge.

Kaldor, Mary, Helmut Anheier and Marlies Glasius. 2003. 'Global Civil Society in an Era of Regressive Globalisation', in Mary Kaldor, Helmut Anheier and Marlies Glasius (eds), *Global Civil Society 2003*, Oxford University Press, Oxford, 3–34.

Koenig-Archibugi, Mathias. 2010. 'Is Global Democracy Possible?', *European Journal of International Relations* 16(4): 1–24.

Kofman, Eleonore. 2007. 'Figures of the Cosmopolitan. Privileged Nationals and National Outsiders', in Chris Rumford (ed.), *Cosmopolitanism and Europe*, Liverpool University Press, Liverpool, 239–56.

Macdonald, Kate. 2011. 'Global Democracy for a Partially Joined-up World. Toward a Multi-level System of Public Power and Democratic Governance?', in Daniele Archibugi, Mathias Koenig-Archibugi and Raffaele Marchetti (eds), *Global Democracy: Normative and Empirical Perspectives*, Cambridge University Press, Cambridge, 793–812.

Macdonald, Terry. 2008. *Global Stakeholder Democracy*, Oxford University Press, Oxford.

Munck, Ronaldo and Peter Waterman (eds). 1999. *Labour Worldwide in the Era of Globalization: Alternative Union Models in the New World Order*, St. Martin's Press, New York.

Norris, Pippa. 2000. 'Global Governance and Cosmopolitan Citizenship', in Joseph Nye and J. Donahue (eds), *Governance in a Globalizing World*, Brooking Institution Press, Washington, 155–77.

Socialist International. 2005. 'Reforming the United Nations for a New Global Agenda', SI Position Paper 2005.01.24, New York.

2

The Cosmopolitanization of International Law: Rethinking Global Constitutionalism

Garrett Wallace Brown

There is a growing literature regarding the constitutionalization of international law and international institutions. Appeals to constitutionalization are often made in response to increased interconnectedness at the global level and are often presented as a normative response to the negative effects of globalization. As issues of 'global crisis', global warming, increased nuclear proliferation, the H1N1 pandemic, and global economic meltdown capture our headlines, many scholars have suggested that these problems result from a failure to appropriately regulate these concerns at the global level and that they are indicative of a lack of unified authority and institutional accountability (Beck 1999; Archibugi 2008; Held 2010b). As a response, many argue that what is needed is the increased constitutionalization of international law and international institutions, which can reign in states (Kumm 2004), create compliance pull (Teubner 2004), and generate a more appropriate response to collective concerns of global cohabitation (Rosenau 2002). Furthermore, many constitutionalization scholars suggest that we are in some sense already moving positively in this direction, where the slow accumulation of international law and international institutions have started to display aspects of a more robust constitutional order (Habermas 2006; Waldron 2006). As Jan Klabbers suggests, 'constitutionalism carries the promise that there is some system in all the madness, some way in which the whole system hangs together and is not merely the aggregate of isolated and often contradictory movements' (Klabbers 2004: 49). In this sense, many scholars have used the language of constitutionalization as a method to both legitimate the expansion of international regimes at the global level and as a way of pursuing a more cosmopolitan normative agenda.

Nevertheless, there remain many unresolved questions and ambiguities with these appeals to constitutionalization and it is unclear whether these processes of global constitutionalism are actually ushering in a more cosmopolitan order. In particular, there are considerable ambiguities regarding what conditions are being grounded within the processes of constitutionalization and whether this legal and institutional order is actually creating the type of legal cosmopolitanism that is often assumed. In response to these ambiguities, and as a means to help clarify the debate, this chapter attempts to outline what current appeals to constitutionalization mean as well as to suggest some key theoretical alterations that will be necessary in order to bring constitutionalization under the guiding normative principles of a potentially expanding cosmopolitanization.

Constitutionalization and the Idea of Global Constitutionalism

As suggested above, the concept of constitutionalization 'is drawn from international legal theory as a means of defending the legitimacy of international law despite its expanded scope and increasing distance from the consent of states' (Fine 2007: 69). As is often argued, international legal regimes can have a positive impact on the lives of ordinary people despite their state citizenship and there is compelling evidence to suggest that international regimes can command compliance to international covenants. Because of this expansion of international legal regimes and the meaningful authoritative impact it can have on the behaviour of states as well as individuals, many scholars have sought to hail this condition as illustrating an ongoing process of constitutionalization and as a movement towards something resembling a global constitution. Nevertheless, it is not always exactly clear what is meant when scholars invoke the term constitutionalization or how this constitutionalization process works, for it seemingly has multifarious applications with broadly different descriptive and normative dimensions (Wiener et al. 2012). It is because contemporary uses of the term constitutionalization have manifold meanings, which are not always specified or consistently applied, that it is necessary to examine what is being invoked when claims of constitutionalization are made and when more globally minded scholars make normative appeals for robust forms of global constitutionalism. By doing so, it can provide a more salient location for what an appeal to constitutionalization is meant to suggest as well as to allow further examination of why these current appeals for constitutionalization may remain underdeveloped and normatively impoverished. So what is meant by constitutionalization? In terms of definition, the word constitutionalization seemingly refers to explanatory notions of legal process, subjectification and objectification, and makes reference to at least three corresponding features. First, the most common understanding and use of constitutionalization is in relation to describing the formal legal and political processes involved in constituting a global legal order of some kind. The objectification of this legal order can be expressed through a singular hierarchical structure or it can be expressed through a network of interconnecting and iterative legal regimes that act as a procedural structure for some form of authoritative legal order. In this regard, to 'constitutionalize' something is to establish formal legal processes where legal rights and duties are codified and where the authoritative mechanisms for legal adjudication are clearly delineated (Ackermann 1997; Werner 2007). Second, the term constitutionalization also refers to the act of making an entity subject to the legal jurisdiction of an established constitutional order. In relation to the first definitional property, legal regimes or entities that were once independent of this constitutional process (or in an unclear legal relationship) are explicitly brought under the jurisdiction of this formal legal system, which in effect supercedes prior legal relationships and which ultimately secures a sense of mutual legal obligation (Schorkopf and Walter 2003). Third, the term constitutionalization can additionally refer to informal and extra-legal processes of norm solidification and normative convergence. This is where common norms emerge from various processes of legal and political interaction that act as extra-legal iterations toward a more procedurally authoritative and constitutionalized legal order. Although similar to the first definition, the difference is that under this understanding of constitutionalization, what matters is the continued building of norms and extralegal commitments, which over time provide the juridical material necessary for the establishment of a more objectified constitutive order (de Wet 2006; Habermas 2006; Milewicz 2009).

We can see these meanings played out within many constitutionalization arguments and it is common to see repetition of these three descriptive elements within most debates about the constitutionalization of international law and international institutions. For example, in relation to the first element outlined above, many scholars have suggested that constitutionalization represents the extent to which the international legal system has constitutional features comparable to the legal frameworks found in national structures (Klabbers et al. 2009). In this case, constitutionalization at the international level refers to formal and objectified legal arrangements and their corresponding authority mechanisms, which in comparison to the legal orders found within nation states, are seen to generate compliance pull, a rule of law and formal legal obligation. This form of constitutionalization has found particular salience within the study of European integration and in debates about European Union (EU) laws (Weiler and Wind 2003). As is often noted, there are interesting analogies between domestic constitutional orders and the emerging legal order at the European level and it is often believed that the EU offers heuristic insights in relation to broader processes of international constitutionalization (Eriksen et al. 2004).

In other cases, global constitutionalization is defined as a phenomenon occupying the legal spaces that result from various transformations associated with globalization and the subsequent 'de-constitutionalization' of domestic legal structures in an increasingly interdependent world (Peters 2006). According to this argument, states remain key actors within the international system, but because of global interconnection, the ability for states to remain as a self-contained constitutional entity is no longer practically feasible or legally tenable. As a result, many constitutionalization scholars argue that domestic state constitutions can no longer act as a 'total constitution' in the strictest sense, since state constitutional mechanisms are unable to regulate the entirety of governance structures that affect them in a thoroughgoing and comprehensive fashion (Gerstenberg 2001). In other words, this conceptualization holds that globalization is challenging the saliency of domestic constitutions and as a result obliges states to increasingly operate in legal systems outside of traditionally prescribed domestic constitutional spheres. In scholastic debate, these arguments have also found particular relevance in discussions explaining the expanding lawmaking capacities of the EU (Rittberger and Schimmelfennig 2006), the supra-constitutionalism involved with the European Court of

Human Rights (Lacroix 2002; Stone-Sweet 2012), and within debates about the limits to which states should willingly abdicate autonomy to external authorities (Collins and White 2011).

Yet for others, international constitutionalization represents 'a vertically integrated legal regime conferring judicially enforceable rights and obligations on all legal persons and entities, public and private, within the sphere [of a mutually applied rule of law]' (Haltern 2003: 14). Similar to the first definition above, this conception of constitutionalization refers to a hierarchical system of law that establishes legal authority while clearly delineating and codifying the legal rights and obligations that are to exist between all constitutional parties. Again, like the aforementioned use of constitutionalization, these discussions about the codification and specification of rights and duties into international law have been seen to have significance in relation to the EU. For it is often argued that Article 49 of the EU Maastricht Treaty provides a mechanism for EU integration and constitutionalization, which clearly sets out legal rights and obligations while also bringing all member states under the umbrella of EU law (von Bogdandy 2003). Furthermore, as is commonly argued, the 1963 Rome Treaty in essence created a 'constitutional instrument' to promote greater legal obligation between member states and sought to create direct legal relationships via a formal constitutional process (Shaw 2000).

Alternatively, some have attempted to broaden the idea of constitutionalization to include a more customary dimension of legal and extralegal coordination at the global level. This is exemplified in its most expansive form by the work of Jürgen Habermas, who argues that through continued reiterative processes the expanding body of international law and institutional regimes come to resemble a form of global constitutionalism. As Habermas suggests, it is from these processes that a more robust form of cosmopolitan order can be established from current legal regimes. According to Habermas, these legal processes create 'a rule of law that can normatively shape existing power relations, regardless of their democratic origins, and direct the exercise of political power into legal channels' (Habermas 2008: 316). Thus, in this way, international law creates legal and extralegal norms that become increasingly 'self-referential', 'constructive' and 'part of a circular learning process' (ibid.: 321). It is through this learning process that states become increasingly 'constitutionalized' towards a more legally constituted order by way of 'stages and degrees of constitutionalization' (Habermas 2008: 318). As Habermas claims, this process of constitutionalization is not dependent on a single authoritative body of positive law, like those found in the constitutional structures of nation states, but is reliant on something like an Schachterian notion of an already established 'proto-constitution' of international law and international legitimacy. It is from these proto-constitutional legal tenets that duties and obligations to the international legal community become reiterative principles for further supranational organization, which in turn generate new procedural principles of world community (Habermas 2006: 141). In this sense, constitutionalization represents a socializing 'process' where present norms shape and influence the creation of new norms and legal relationships, from which more formal constitutional properties can begin to emerge and to eventually be objectified into international covenants.

In an attempt to collect these formulations together, I propose the following general definition. When used as a descriptive device, constitutionalization is meant to denote the processes of legal codification towards the establishment and incorporation of entities into a coherent and legally objectified body of law, where legal parties, legal rights, legal obligations, and legitimate centres of adjudicating power are specified. This process of legal codification and objectification can take place through two interrelated processes of constitutionalization. It can take place via traditional contractarian principles of consent, treaty and formal contract, or it can be generated by way of a more sociologically iterative process of mutual norm compliance that, with time, starts to resemble legal and extralegal conditions that are similar to more robust constitutional orders. In addition, constitutionalization refers explicitly to processes of compliance and/or vertical legal authority (with varying levels of authority), whether to international institutions or to international law. In this regard, whatever constitutionalization is as a phenomenon, it relates to structural processes and to how these processes generate legal, institutional and normative authority at the international level. However, as alluded to above, it is not always clear what exactly these processes are and in what ways these constitutional processes create a universally valid and legitimate 'rule of law'. Furthermore, it would seem that current discussions regarding increased constitutionalization are based on unsettled empirical and normative assumptions about the socializing forces of international law and its corresponding ability to generate state compliance. This raises questions about the normative claims often made by advocates of constitutionalization and gives merit to those who advance more critical reflection. For as it will be explored below, it is not immediately clear whether more constitutionalization is always reflective of a cosmopolitan position and that it would be misguided to always assume a progressive trajectory within the processes of constitutionalization.

Constitutionalization or Cosmopolitanization?

Within the constitutionalization literature it is sometimes possible to find a prevailing logic. This logic posits that more international law and more international institutions represent a more robust form of constitutionalization. In addition, it is also possible to find an almost teleological presupposition that more constitutionalization is better cosmopolitanism and an idea that the more states are brought under the normative influence of customary law and international institutional practice the better this will be for the international environment in general (Habermas 2006). However, there are many interrelated theoretical and empirical challenges that should temper an immediate enthusiasm about this calculation.

By calculating constitutionalization in this fashion, it seemingly ignores alternative interpretations that suggest that more law and the creation of more international institutions can actually disperse legal authority horizontally in ways that can contradict a 'vertical' constitutionalization or cosmopolitan process (Armingeon and Milewicz 2008). Specifically, the creation of more institutions and international law can often create blurred institutional and legal jurisdictions, which create multiple channels for non-compliance and which create alternative avenues for unilateral expressions of political power (Goldsmith and Posner 2005). As many scholars of global governance and international political economy rightfully suggest, powerful states often create new international institutions (Brown 2010), or switch allegiance to an alternative institutional or legal body (Krisch 2005; Sarooshi 2005), in order to sidestep existing legal and institutional regimes that no longer serve their interests (Johnson 2005). In addition, it is also not uncommon for certain powerful states to explicitly pursue this strategy as a tool of foreign policy and do so as a direct rejection of international constitutionalization (Bolton 2000; Shiro 2000). Because of the political, economic and legal complexities involved with what constitutes constitutionalization, it would be fallacious to assume that more international law and the creation of more international institutions *automatically* represent a condition of robust constitutionalization or emerging cosmopolitics.

In relation, calculating constitutionalization in this way also seemingly ignores a pathway-dependent dark side associated with constitutionalism. As defined in the first section, constitutionalization refers to the establishment of formal legal processes where legal rights and duties are codified and where the authoritative mechanisms for legal adjudication are clearly delineated. In this regard, not only does a constitutionalization process bring subjects into a legal relationship, but it also locks them into this relationship (Elster 2000). This is because constitutional arrangements are notoriously conservative in the sense that once this legal relationship has been codified and objectified, then any alteration of this constitutional arrangement must be performed within the 'pathways' of this legal order (Krisch 2005: 377). In other words, constitutional arrangements are by definition conservative and restrictive. As a result, a potential negative feature of this 'locking-in' is that there is no reason to assume that an already existing constitutional arrangement at the global level is not antithetically predisposed to the kind of positive cosmopolitical change many constitutionalization scholars seem to want.

In relation, and as a thought experiment, let us assume that the world is currently operating under conditions of ongoing constitutionalization and that this order represents a constitutional order in some fairly meaningful sense, as many constitutionalization scholars suggest. If this is so, then it is arguable that this same order propagates and 'locks-in' the very institutional arrangements that have led to the collective action problems of global crisis that currently dominate our headlines. This is because, historically speaking, it is this same constitutional regime that has been ineffective in tackling climate change, unable to prevent genocide, unable to secure people from poverty, to stop preventable diseases, and, of current importance, has been unable to defend states or peoples from the present economic meltdown. In fact, and to stay on the topic of the economic crisis, it could be argued that the entire reason the economic meltdown occurred is because the current 'global economic constitution' upholds the legal and institutional mechanisms that allow the opportunities for economic bubbles to take place (Gamble 2009). For it is not unreasonable to suggest that this constitutionalized system is not only ineffective in regulating such a crisis (despite our knowledge of past ones), but that the neoliberal economic policies embedded within current constitutionalization processes actively 'channel' the kind of accelerated economic regulatory conditions where meltdowns can happen (Cohen 2004). Again, this raises theoretical and empirical questions about whether more constitutionalization creates a more progressive cosmopolitanism, or whether more constitutionalization simply equates to just more of the same.

Interestingly, and related to the former points, calculating constitutionalization descriptively as 'more is better' says little about the substance or quality of the constitutionalization process or about what it is we are in fact constitutionalizing. For example, the Agreement on Trade-Related Aspects of Intellectual Property Rights (TRIPS Agreement) clearly creates a body of international law and institutional structure that regulate intellectual copyrights, protects corporate patents, and creates a series of legal norms that demand international compliance through enforcement by the World Trade Organization (WTO) (Muzaka 2011). However, as it is often noted, this body of law arguably favours the protection of the interests of certain economically powerful states and it has not been to the mutual benefit of a majority of human interests (Deere 2009). This raises important questions in regard to the processes of constitutionalization and in relation to what norms are being objectified. Specifically, this raises the question as to whether all international law and institutional regulation act as part of the constitutionalization process, and if so, can the normative claim that more is better hold? In response to this, it is my suspicion that most cosmopolitan scholars would intuitively reject TRIPS as forming an integrally normative part of an expanding constitutionalization process and that many global constitutionalists would critique TRIPS in relation to the demands of global justice. Nonetheless, this still begs the question as to whether constitutionalization as a descriptive tool should refer to all laws and institutions or whether it should refer to only those instruments that capture a certain normative component (Peters 2009a). However, making a further distinction in this way will require a better discussion about what is actually being constitutionalized, how it is being constitutionalized, and whether this process actually resembles any sense of cosmopolitan justice or mutual benefit. In other words, what is seemingly missing from many discussions about constitutionalization are the crucial questions about whether we are constitutionalizing the right legal tenets, if we are creating the right international institutions, and whether these regimes actually reflect any sense of cosmopolitan justice or legal reciprocity. For without this better distinction, as Stephen Gill aptly notes, the constitutionalization process will represent 'binding constraints' on various forms of human conduct and these constraints will remain largely favourable to some while remaining systematically repressive to most others (Gill 1995).

Lastly, and in immediate relation to the last point, there is a concern about the role of power within the socializing processes of constitutionalization. As many postcolonialists, Marxists, and post-structuralists argue (as found in this volume), it is not wholly unreasonable to view the current process of constitutionalization as simply entrenching Western political and economic power (Gill 2002; Krisch 2005; Thomson 2005). Furthermore, as some have argued, constitutionalization could represent nothing more than a form of neo-imperialism and the legal and institutional dominance of the most powerful states (Hobson 2011). Or that constitutionalization represents a possible form of civilizing mission that potentially threatens a plurality of cultural traditions through its universalizing and pro-Western orientation (Harlow 2006). These opinions are not limited to those who usually critique all things neoliberal, for even more liberally minded scholars suggest that by conceptualizing constitutionalization as being universally oriented, it runs a risks of also 'dressing up strategic power-plays' as having a progressive form and that this can obscure a more insidious hidden agenda (Cohen 2004: 10). As Deborah Cass has suggested, it is important to be aware that 'social legitimacy is being artificially constructed through the use of constitutional language' and that this may be painting a highly unrealistic portrait in regards to the legitimacy of global governance and international law (Cass 2005: 208). Once again, this raises questions about what is actually being constitutionalized, who is it constitutionalized for, and what normative and moral implications this has on the long-term socialization of global order.

Disciplinary Confusion and the Need for Cosmopolitan Normative Theory

An explanation for why these questions have been seemingly neglected within the mainstream constitutionalization literature is threefold. First, most scholarship on constitutionalization has taken place between international lawyers and scholars of international relations who employ a positivist methodology that often looks specifically at the formation of legal regulation, international law and with how these legal tenets have been complied with or rejected by states. Traditionally, this maintains a rather narrow focus that looks specifically at positive interpretations of law, the mechanisms for legal enforcement and the empirical existence of legal compliance (Krisch 2005: 372). In this regard, international relations and legal scholarship has often avoided many normative considerations and the moral implications involved within constitutionalization, preferring to operate within the strict disciplinary boundaries of legal realism and legal positivism (Buchanan 2004). Furthermore, it has only been within the last twenty years that a more substantial shift towards the importance of customary law has been made. Nevertheless, even here, the focus has tended to be limited to issues of law formation and compliance in the absence of an overarching world authority and there is still considerable debate between international lawyers and international relations theorists regarding the significance and empirical robustness of customary law (Çali 2010).

Second, a significant amount of the scholarship on constitutionalization seems to have been primarily focused on the EU and on the legal and institutional processes involved with European integration. This research has certainly provided useful and interesting debates about constitutionalization and about the development of a constitutional Europe. Nevertheless, it could be argued that studying the constitutional processes of European integration relies on a different set of cultural, legal, economic, historical, and sociological foundations (Howse and Nicolaidis 2003: 75). In this regard, as it has been argued, it is not immediately clear that transplanting these analytical tools to the global order provides the best way to examine the processes of global constitutionalization

(Goldsmith and Posner 2005). For it may very well be the case that the empirical background conditions involved with the constitutionalization of Europe far exceed those available at the global level and that transplanting this set of constitutionalization criteria to the global level is methodologically inappropriate and normatively deceptive.

Third, many theorists in international relations, international law and political theory have seemingly conflated increased globalization with a process of increased constitutionalization (Peters 2007). This is because there has traditionally been an assumption that increased interconnectedness equates to an increased constitutionalization of global norms (Greider 1997; Wolf 2004). However, by making this move, it is possible to downplay the fact that globalization and constitutionalization are both dialectical, in the sense that their processes are positive and negative, and/ or that they may actually be in opposition to one another. In this regard, although the processes of globalization and constitutionalization are certainly connected, and both have promoted more interconnectedness, economic markets, democracies, and peaceful legal relations between global powers, these same forces have also produced greater economic inequality, increased cultural tension, legitimated corporate exploitation, and have resulted in a general failure to secure human development. In other words, globalization and the resulting iterations of constitutionalization have made the opportunities for a more robust constitutional process possible and in many ways visible, but this does not necessarily represent a progressive constitutionalization trajectory with inherent cosmopolitan consequences. In addition, there is also considerable evidence to support the argument that an opposite trajectory is true (Gill 2002; Lane 2006). In particular, and as mentioned before, it is not hard to find research which suggests that what is actually being constitutionalized at the global level is nothing more than the hegemonic norms and interests of Western power and that globalization (and it's growth of legal and institutional components) represents only a form of neoliberal triadization and does not translate into a meaningful sense of unifying globalization (Hirst and Thomson 1996).

Consequently, there are many unanswered questions involving the substantive issues of constitutionalization and that its current conceptualization remains underdeveloped in relation to the nature of its processes and in regard to its positive or negative socializing effects. Because of this, it is not entirely unreasonable for critics of constitutionalization to argue that it remains an under-evaluated concept and that it currently rests on questionable empirical and sociological foundations (Hirsh 2006). This unfortunately helps to render constitutionalization as a rather unpersuasive normative concept, for it is not always clear what processes we should be adopting and how those processes can effectively produce a legitimate source of constitutionalization. In order to rectify this, constitutionalization scholarship will need to better clarify the relationship between globalization and constitutionalization and to untangle the various processes that are often assumed to interconnect and similarly motivate the two. In addition, there needs to be a more effective normative delineation between having more constitutionalization and having better cosmopolitanization and that this will need to be clarified before the concept can have a high level of persuasiveness.

Nevertheless, to do so this understanding will ultimately have to start from an ontological position that understands that the processes of constitutionalization can be as constitutionally reinforcing of domination and power as they might be progressively cosmopolitan. Thus, an effective response to these challenges will require a greater sensitivity about the legitimacy of global legal and institutional norms as well as a better understanding regarding the colonizing forces of power and wealth that exist within current forms of constitutionalization (Walker 2007). Furthermore, it will require greater normative clarity regarding what 'good' constitutionalization should represent as well as what moral conditions must be satisfied before claims of cosmopolitan justice can also be exerted. The last section below explores some potential ways forward.

From Constitutionalization to Cosmopolitanization: Taking the Agenda Forward

Throughout this chapter it has been argued that an assumption often takes place within the constitutionalization literature that seemingly conflates more constitutionalization with better cosmopolitanization. This is problematic because it is questionable whether more constitutionalization necessarily produces a constitutionalized legal order in line with cosmopolitan principles. As was suggested, calculating constitutionalization in this fashion assumes that it has a progressive trajectory and it was suggested that cosmopolitans should be weary of conceptualizing constitutionalization in such a simplistic fashion.

As was argued earlier, this begs the following conceptual question: should constitutionalization refer to all laws and institutions or should it refer to only those instruments that can capture a certain normative component? In my opinion, making a distinction of this type is crucial if the concept of constitutionalization is to have the kind of normative strength many globally minded scholars suggest it has. This is because constitutionalization as it is currently conceptualized lacks a coherent and consistent moral compass that can help differentiate between the various negative and positive aspects involved within its processes.

Consequently, what is required is a better fusion between cosmopolitan theory and the more legally focused work of constitutionalization scholars. This is because cosmopolitanism as a political theory is potentially well equipped to provide the additional moral and normative criteria needed to underpin a reinvigorated research agenda that can begin to address many of the theoretical concerns outlined above. For cosmopolitanism, as a global political theory with its focus on issues of global justice, has the philosophical material available to provide the necessary moral criteria from which the gaps between theory and practice should be measured. Nonetheless, making this move will first require a better conceptualization of what is actually being constitutionalized, how it is being constitutionalized, and whether this process actually resembles any sense of global justice and mutual benefit. For what is currently lacking from many constitutionalization arguments is a thorough response to key questions about whether we are constitutionalizing the right legal tenets, if we are creating the right international institutions and, most importantly, whether these regimes actually reflect any sense of cosmopolitan justice. These shortcomings are important to be mindful of, especially if we are to understand constitutionalization as providing a foundation for an effective cosmopolitan response to increasing issues of global cohabitation.

In an attempt to respond to this lacuna, there have been some recent efforts to reflect upon the heuristic, hermeneutic and critical qualities of the idea of constitutionalization. In these more critical and reflective approaches, which have increasing salience with *moral cosmopolitanism*, the first step is to re-examine constitutionalization in light of certain normative principles, in order to draw our attention to various shortcomings and injustices associated with contemporary international law. By exposing these shortcomings, the goal is to tie key normative principles to the valuation of what a 'global constitution' ought or ought not to capture. In general, but certainly not representationally exhaustive, it is possible to locate three critical/reflective themes that offer potential movement towards making a distinction away from normatively devoid notions of constitutionalization and which could potentially provide movement towards a more globally just understanding of cosmopolitanization.

First, scholars like Marrti Koskenniemi have suggested that the 'virtue of constitutionalism in the international world' is to expose fundamental global injustices so as to then exercise critical judgement upon these existing features of global order. In other words, by thinking in terms of constitutionalization and a global constitution, it can help to generate a 'universalizing focus' within legal debates, from which critical reflections and global reforms could be generated (Koskenniemi 2007: 35). This 'universal focus' nicely mirrors past cosmopolitan efforts to use morally grounded cosmopolitan principles to expose and then make normative recommendations for institutional reform. In particular, this first critical component seeks to evaluate current practice in relation to universally valid duties of global justice, the protection of human rights and the reformation of unjust international systems, so that they are in line with cosmopolitan principles. This critical dimension maps onto many debates of institutional cosmopolitanism, which focus primarily on examining what institutional designs (or reforms) might best implement the normative demands of its moral counterpart. As a result, the normative considerations of moral cosmopolitanism can act as a litmus test or normative compass from which more universally valid constitutional processes can be delineated. This is especially the case in terms of applying conditions of global justice, which can set conditions that purposely oppose current legal orders that represent colonization through unjust or unsubstantiated power. In summary, by examining international law in terms of constitutionalization and the extent to which these processes meet the demands of cosmopolitanism, we can better come to judgements about where legitimacy gaps between cosmopolitan theory and legal practice exist. Although this will not give us an exact roadmap on how to institutionally bridge the gap between theory and practice (Brown 2008), it can provide a much-needed normative blueprint from which current institutional models can be critiqued and measured. From this it becomes possible to make specific normative recommendations as to how the current structure fails to capture concerns of global justice and can generate further recommendations on how to reform existing legal relationships towards a cosmopolitanization of international law.

Second, in an attempt to further peg the study of constitutionalization to some overarching normative evaluative measure, some scholars have started to suggest that the idea of constitutionalization should be made synonymous with corresponding elements of democratization and democratic legitimacy. For scholars like Anne Peters, an appeal to 'global constitutionalism requires duel democratic mechanisms ... these should relate both to government within nation states and to governance "above" states, thus to multiple levels of governance' (Peters 2009b: 264). Without pegging the process of constitutionalization to the legitimization of law via democratic inclusion (Held 2010a), participatory lawmaking (de Burca 2008) or to a form of republican virtue ethics (Klabbers 2007), it opens the potential to 'fraudulently create the illusion of legitimate global governance' and universalizable principles of international law, despite remaining inequalities and structural abuses of power. In relation to cosmopolitanism, associating the legitimacy of constitutionalization with principles of democratic inclusion comes remarkably close to recent arguments for cosmopolitan democracy and its demand that legitimacy is best generated from procedurally driven public reason formation, and not legitimated solely through legal positivist notions of authority and the ability to coerce compliance (Held 2010b).

Third, in questioning the reasonable scope of a global constitution, some scholars have agreed that the language of constitutionalism has the potential to incorporate a 'responsibilizing' agenda into the legal discourse, but have remained less enthusiastic about the prospects for a truly 'progressive' global constitutional authority. As an alternative, these scholars suggest that the lessons to be taken from critically examining the processes of constitutionalization is to favour conceptualization in terms of plural constitutionalism

or metaconstitutionalism, which conceives constitutional authority as distributed horizontally between a plurality of constitutional
structures, which are only tied loosely to a metaconstitutional
mechanism that can act like an instrument for intersubjective
deliberative adjudication (Walker 2002). Similar to debates found
within theories of cosmopolitan democracy, between world state
cosmopolitans (Marchetti 2008) and those advocating more pluralistic multilevel schemes of global governance (Held 1995), the
question here pertains to what institutional mechanisms can best
promote a globally just and publically reasoned structure of global
governance and constitutionalization. In comparison, the question
for cosmopolitans is not whether the processes of constitutionalization should be measured against some understanding of cosmopolitan global justice and universal public reason (this is already
held as a valid theoretical foundation), but about the best way
to ground this cosmopolitan condition of justice institutionally
(whether vertically or horizontally), so as not to threaten the core
emancipatory foundations themselves (Brown 2008).

If we unpack the normative elements involved with these
attempts to provide a more morally substantiated vision of constitutionalization, it becomes possible to discern three primary principles that connect these visions of constitutionalization to what
I have been terming cosmopolitanization. First, both cosmopolitanism and more normatively conscientious global constitutionalists
maintain the normative position that individuals should have reasonable opportunities to affect their lives and that the legitimacy of
international constitutional structures should be measured against
how well this normative aim is fulfilled in practice. Second, both
cosmopolitans and normatively astute global constitutionalists suggest that the legal order should be founded on egalitarian application
of the 'rule of law' so that individuals, governmental representatives
and peoples can engage in meaningful debates and adjudication(s)
regarding the substance and practice of international law. This is
seen as crucial because it not only fosters meaningful deliberations
of public reason and collective decision-making, but also promises
eventual resolution of collective action problems and the further-
ance of a legitimate legal order that is able to generate sociological
identifications associated with *constitutional patriotism* (Habermas
2001). Third, both cosmopolitans and more normatively cognizant

global constitutionalists share a foundational sense of global justice as the overriding litmus test involved with the evaluation of constitutionalization (Wiener et al. 2012). In its basic form, there is seemingly a key normative principle promoted within these arguments, which suggests that constitutionalization, in order to be globally just, must be seen by participants as being the result of a legitimate process of public reason, in that the process of law formation, and the actions taken thereafter, can be seen as acceptable by all stakeholders involved.

In conclusion, there is presently a theoretical deficit in our current thinking about constitutionalization and the formation of a global constitution. As has been argued, filling this lacuna requires a more sensitive treatment and evaluation of the processes of constitutionalization and what normative principles can help us distinguish constitutionalization as simply representing more of the same, from a global constitution that is more closely representative of the cosmopolitan project. Without these further conceptual distinctions, constitutionalization will continue to lack normative purchase, for it is only by grounding the processes of constitutionalization in a cosmopolitan fashion that it will then be possible to more accurately suggest that there are positive movements towards the cosmopolitanization of international law.

～

Acknowledgements

I would like to thank Luis Cabrera, Raffaele Marchetti, Richard Beardsworth, Antje Wiener, and the members of the 'Global Crisis and Constitutionalization' workshop at the University of Birmingham as well as the conference attendees at the Indian Institute of Technology Madras (IITM) for their helpful comments and suggestions. In addition, part of this work has drawn upon material from Brown, Garrett Wallace. 2012. 'The Constitutionalization of What?', *Global Constitutionalism* 1(2): 201–28. Reproduced with permission.

References

Ackermann, Bruce. 1997. 'The Rise of World Constitutionalism', *Virginia Law Review* 83: 771–97.

Archibugi, Daniele. 2008. *The Global Commonwealth of Citizens*, Polity Press, Cambridge.

Armingeon, Klaus and Karolina Milewicz. 2008. 'Compensatory Constitutionalism: A Comparative Perspective', *Global Society* 22: 179–96.

Beck, Ulrich. 1999. *World Risk Society*, Polity Press, Cambridge.

Bolton, John. 2000. 'Should we Take Global Governance Seriously?' *Chicago Journal of International Law* 1: 205–22.

Brown, Garrett Wallace. 2008. 'Moving from Cosmopolitan Legal Theory to Cosmopolitan Legal Practice: Models of Cosmopolitan Law', *Legal Studies* 28(3): 430–51.

———. 2010. 'Safeguarding Deliberative Global Governance: The Case of the Global Fund to Fight AIDS, Tuberculosis and Malaria', *Review of International Studies* 36(2): 511–30.

Buchanan, Allen. 2004. *Justice, Legitimacy and Self-Determination: Moral Foundations for International Law*, Oxford University Press, Oxford.

von Bogdandy, Armin (ed.). 2003. *Europaisches Verfassungsrecht*, Springer, Heidelberg.

de Burca, Grainne. 2008. 'Developing Democracy Beyond the State', *Colombia Journal of Transnational Law* 46: 102–58.

Çali, Başak. 2010. *International Law for International Relations*, Oxford University Press, Oxford.

Cass, Deborah. 2005. *Constitutionalization of the WTO*, Oxford University Press, Oxford.

Cohen, Jean. 2004. 'Whose Sovereignty? Empire versus International Law', *Ethics and International Affairs* 18(3): 1–23.

Collins, Richard and Nigel White (eds). 2011. *International Organizations and the Idea of Autonomy: Institutional Independence in the International Legal Order*, Routledge, London.

de Wet, Erika. 2006. 'The Emergence of International and Regional Value Systems as a Manifestation of the Emerging International Constitutional Order', *Leiden Journal of International Law* 19(2): 579–610.

Deere, Carolyn. 2009. *The Implementation Game: The TRIPS Agreement and the Global Politics of International Property Reform in Developing Countries*, Oxford University Press, Oxford.

Elster, Jon. 2000. *Ulysses Unbound*, Cambridge University Press, Cambridge.

Eriksen, E., J. Fossum and A. Menendez (eds). 2004. *Developing a Constitution for Europe*, Routledge, London.

Fine, Robert. 2007. *Cosmopolitanism*, Routledge, Abingdon.

Gamble, Andrew. 2009. *The Spectre at the Feast: Capitalist Crisis and the Politics of Recession*, Palgrave, Basingstoke.

Gerstenberg, Oliver. 2001. 'Denationalization and the Very Idea of Democratic Constitutionalism: The Case for the European Community', *Ratio Juris* 14(3): 298–325.

Gill, Stephen. 1995. 'Globalization, Market Civilization, and Disciplinary Neoliberalism', *Millennium: Journal of International Studies* 24(3): 399–423.

Gill, Stephen. 2002. 'Constitutionalizing Inequality and the Clash of Globalizations', *International Studies Review* 4(2): 47–65.

Goldsmith, Jack and Eric Posner. 2005. *The Limits of International Law*, Oxford University Press, Oxford.

Greider, William. 1997. *One World, Ready or Not: The Magic Logic of Global Capitalism*, Penguin, London.

Habermas, Jürgen. 2001. *The Postnational Constellation*, Polity Press, Cambridge.

———. 2006. *The Divided West*, Polity Press, Cambridge.

———. 2008. *Between Naturalism and Religion*, Polity Press, Cambridge.

Haltern, Ulrich. 2003. 'Pathos and Patina: The Failure and Promise of Constitutionalization in the European Imagination', *European Law Journal* 9(1): 14–44.

Harlow, Carol. 2006. 'Global Administrative Law: The Quest for Principles and Values', *The European Journal of International Law* 17(1): 187–214.

Held, David. 1995. *Democracy and the Global Order: From the Modern State to Cosmopolitan Governance*, Polity Press, Cambridge.

———. 2010a. 'Reframing Global Governance: Apocalypse Soon or Reform!', in Garrett Wallace Brown and David Held (eds), *The Cosmopolitanism Reader*, Polity Press, Cambridge, 293–311.

———. 2010b. *Cosmopolitanism: Ideals and Realities*, Polity Press, Cambridge.

Hirsh, David. 2006. 'Cosmopolitan Law: Agency and Narrative', in Michael Freeman (ed.), *Law and Sociology*, Oxford University Press, Oxford, 377–98.

Hirst, Paul and Graham Thomson. 1996. *Globalization in Question*, Polity Press, Cambridge.

Hobson, John. 2011. *Defending the Western Interest*, Cambridge University Press, Cambridge.

Howse, Robert and Kalypso Nicolaidis. 2003. 'Enhancing WTO Legitimacy: Constitutionalism of Global Subsidiary?', *Governance: An International Journal of Policy, Administration, and Institutions* 16(1): 73–94.

Johnson, Douglas. 2005. 'World Constitutionalism in the Theory of International Law', in Ronald MacDonald and Douglas Johnson (eds), *Toward World Constitutionalism: Issues in the Legal Ordering of the World Community*, Martinus Nijhoff, Leiden, 1–24.

Klabbers, Jan. 2004. 'Constitutionalism Lite', *International Organizations Law Review* 1(1): 31–58.

———. 2007. 'Possible Islands of Predictability: The Legal Thoughts of Hannah Arendt', *Leiden Journal of International Law* 20: 1–23.

Klabbers, Jan, Anne Peters and Geir Ulfstein. 2009. *The Constitutionalization of International Law*, Oxford University Press, Oxford.

Koskenniemi, Marrti. 2007. 'Constitutionalism as a Mindset: Reflections on Kantian Themes about International Law and Globalization', *Theoretical Inquiries in Law* 8(1): 1–27.

Krisch, Nico. 2005. 'International Law in Times of Hegemony: Unequal Power and the Shaping of the International Legal Order', *European Journal of International Law* 16(3): 369–408.

Kumm, Mattias. 2004. 'The Legitimacy of International Law: A Constitutionalist Framework for Analysis', *European Journal of International Law* 15(5): 907–31.

Lacroix, Justine. 2002. 'For a European Constitutional Patriotism', *Political Studies* 50(5): 944–58.

Lane, Jan-Erik. 2006. *Globalization and Politics: Promises and Dangers*, Ashgate, Aldershot.

Marchetti, Raffaele. 2008. *Global Democracy: For and Against*, Routledge, London.

Milewicz, K. 2009. 'Emerging Patterns of Global Constitutionalization: Toward a Conceptual Framework', *Indiana Journal of Global Legal Studies* 16(2): 413–36.

Muzaka, Valbona. 2011. *The Politics of Intellectual Property Rights and Access to Medicines*, Palgrave, London.

Peters, Anne. 2006. 'Compensatory Constitutionalism: The Function and Potential of Fundamental International Norms and Structures', *Leiden Journal of International Law* 19(3): 579–610.

———. 2007. 'The Globalization of State Constitutions', in Janne Elisabeth Nijman and Andre Nollkaeper (eds), *New Perspectives on the Divide Between National and International Law*, Oxford University Press, Oxford, 251–308.

———. 2009a. 'Membership in the Global Constitutional Community', in J. Klabbers, A. Peters and G. Ulfstein (eds), *The Constitutionalization of International Law*, Oxford University Press, Oxford, 126–50.

———. 2009b. 'Duel Democracy', in J. Klabbers, A. Peters and G. Ulfstein (eds), *The Constitutionalization of International Law*, Oxford University Press, Oxford, 263–341.

Rittberger, Berthold and Frank Schimmelfennig. 2006. 'Explaining the Constitutionalization on the European Union', *Journal of European Public Policy* 13(8): 1148–67.

Rosenau, James. 2002. 'Governance in a New Global Order', in David Held and Anthony McGrew (eds), *Governing Globalization*, Polity Press, Cambridge, 70–86.

Sarooshi, Dan. 2005. *International Organizations and their Exercise of Sovereign Powers*, Oxford University Press, Oxford.

Schorkopf, F. and C. Walter. 2003. 'Elements of Constitutionalism: Multilevel Structures of Human Rights Protection in General International and WTO-Law', *German Law Journal* 12(4): 1359–70.

Shaw, Jo. 2000. *The Law of the European Union*, Palgrave, Basingstoke.

Shiro, Peter. 2000. 'The New Sovereigntists', *Foreign Affairs* 79(6): 1–5.

Stone-Sweet, Alec. 2012. 'A Cosmopolitan Legal Order: Constitutional Pluralism and Rights Adjudication in Europe', *Global Constitutionalism* 1(1): 53–90.

Teubner, Gunther. 2004. 'Societal Constitutionalism: Alternatives to State Centered Constitutional Theory', in Christian Joerges, Inger-Johanne Sand and Gunther Teubner (eds), *Transnational Governance and Constitutionalism*, Hart Publishing, Porltand, 3–28.

Thomson, Graham. 2005. 'The Limits of Globalization', in D. Held (ed.), *Debating Globalization*, Polity Press, Cambridge, 52–58.

Waldron, Jeremy. 2006. 'Cosmopolitan Norms', in Robert Post (ed.), *Another Cosmopolitanism*, Oxford University Press, Oxford, 83–101.

Walker, Neil. 2002. 'The Idea of Constitutional Pluralism', *Modern Law Review* 65(3): 317–59.

———. 2007. 'Making a World of Difference?: Habermas, Cosmopolitanism and the Constitutionalization of International Law', in O. Shabani (ed.), *Multiculturalism and Law: A Critical Debate*, University of Wales Press, Cardiff, 219–34.

Weiler, J. H. H. and Marlene Wind (eds). 2003. *European Constitutionalism beyond the State*, Cambridge University Press, Cambridge.

Wiener, Antje, Anthony Lang, James Tully, Miguel Poiares, and Mattias Kumm. 2012. 'Global Constitutionalism: Human Rights, Democracy and the Rule of Law', *Global Constitutionalism* 1(1): 1–15.

Werner, W. 2007. 'The Never-ending Closure: Constitutionalism and International Law', in Nicholas Tsagourias (ed.), *Transnational Constitutionalism: International and European Perspective*, Cambridge University Press, Cambridge, 329–67.

Wolf, Martin. 2004. *Why Globalization Works*, Yale University Press, New Haven.

3

Legitimacy in the Global Normative Order: Justificatory Practices in the Space of Reasons

Eva Erman

Asymmetries between rule-makers and rule-takers, inequalities among states and between poor and rich, and disparities between global political problems and the capabilities of existing state institutions have stimulated massive growth in governance measures beyond traditional state structures in the last decades. One major concern is the democratic deficit of global governance structures and how to best rethink democracy to find solutions adapted to these 'new' circumstances of politics (Held 1995; Archibugi 2004, 2008; Cabrera 2010; Archibugi et al. 2010). While the institutional suggestions have been numerous and often mutually incompatible, the varied justifications offered on their behalf underscore that conceptual unclarity still reigns concerning the normative ideal of democracy as collective decision-making or self-determination, that is, 'rule by the people'. How is such an ideal to be brought to bear on a global context where states remain important but not sole actors? Another concern is the growing inequalities, severe poverty and the question of global distributive justice (Beitz 2004; Tan 2004; Caney 2005; Pogge 2002, 2007). In order to meet these two challenges, contemporary political philosophy and international relations theory offer different ways of approaching the question of the legitimacy of the global normative 'order'.

The aim of this chapter is twofold. First, it discusses the smudging of the distinction between democratic theory and moral theories of legitimacy in the literature addressing the former of these two concerns, prohibiting a deeper understanding of the normative aspects of these challenges. It is argued that this has lead to questionable ways of conceptualizing democracy and democratic legitimacy in a transnational and global context. Second, against a backdrop of this critical analysis, this chapter elaborates a discourse-theoretical view of the global normative order (understood in discursive terms as the 'global space of reasons') as consisting of three justificatory practices in three different contexts of justification, namely contexts of moral justification, contexts of political justification and equal stakes contexts. An advantage of working with different criteria of rightness or normative principles in different contexts is that we are able to elaborate several normative ideals simultaneously, thereby avoiding to reduce the problem of the legitimacy of global governance structures to being a problem of democracy or of justice.

It is indeed the case that short-term projects of devising workable institutional frameworks for transnational and global democracy in light of the prevailing circumstances of world politics, are much needed, such as formulating strategies for developing practical proposals of realizing democratic ideals under non-ideal circumstances. However, long-term normative-theoretical proposals (on the ideal-theoretical level) that elaborate these very ideals by analysing their underlying principles and necessary conditions are important as well. For only against such idealized evaluative and critical yardsticks could specific short-term institutional proposals be assessed and compared (Macdonald and Marchetti 2010: 13–18). While both kinds of projects are crucial if we are to take steps towards more legitimate and democratic global governance, this chapter constitutes a proposal of the latter kind.

Working from an agency-based standpoint, a discourse-theoretical view presupposes that not only moral but also democratic agency is an intersubjective human practice, without which there could be no democratic self-determination. At the same time, unlike moral theories in general, democracy is not always an applicable normative ideal. Rather, against those who argue in favour of the ideal of democracy in all political circumstances — for example, cosmopolitan democrats drawing on some version of the so-called 'all affected principle' — I argue that democracy is only desirable under certain political circumstances. However, this does not mean that democracy could not be instrumentally justified to the extent that it, for example, delivers other desirable goods, from the point of view of other normative ideals such as justice. The three contexts of justification are to be understood in descriptive terms, and are neither mutually exclusive nor mutually constitutive. Rather, they are best seen as three 'layers' of the space of reasons, such that political contexts are one kind of moral context, whilst equal stakes contexts are one kind of political context.

This chapter is structured as follows. The first section starts out by elaborating two basic conditions of democracy that in my view are hard to dismiss, namely political equality and political bindingness. Together they will constitute a normative yardstick for analysing contemporary proposals for globalized democracy. Thereafter, it illustrates how the distinction between democratic theory and moral theories of legitimacy and justice is sometimes conflated in the present debate on global democracy, and how this has led to misconceptualizations of democracy and democratic legitimacy in a transnational and global context. In light of these examples, a discussion of political equality highlights the relevance of distinguishing between moral and political equality, while a discussion of political bindingness highlights the difference between individual rights and individual (democratic agency) and collective (democratic legitimacy) political practices (Section I).

In a second step, against the backdrop of a discursive view of agency that is briefly presented, I develop my three-layered approach to the global normative order, consisting of three different contexts of justification, drawing on the work of Rainer Forst and Jürgen Habermas. While it is argued that the basic building blocks of Forst's discourse theory fit well with this discursive view of agency by emphasizing the right to justification as the proper criterion of rightness in moral and political contexts of justification, I demonstrate why this criterion is not immediately translatable to a criterion of democratic legitimacy in equal stakes contexts. Instead, what I call 'the equal influence principle' more appropriately offers such a criterion. Moreover, on the proposed view, each context of justification corresponds with a particular duty, relating to a specific normative ideal (Section II).

Finally, in this three-layered view the global normative order lays out the conceptual and normative ground for theorizing legitimacy in transnational and global governance in terms of two kinds of legitimacy, namely political legitimacy and democratic legitimacy, elaborated through what is speculatively called 'multiple citizenship'. The concept of multiple citizenship here is to be understood in explorative terms, opening the door for and illustrating the manifold roles that citizens could and ought to play in such governance, not only as 'democratic agents', that is, as members of a democratic community, but also as 'agents of democracy' or 'agents of justice', in relation to different normative ideals such as justice and democracy (Section III).

The Essence of Democracy and Why It Gets Lost in Translation

This chapter shares the concern that transnational and global governance structures suffer from a democratic deficit. However, while it might under certain circumstances be urgent to transfer democracy from the state to the transnational level, we need to explore the essence of democracy, that is, its basic conditions (conceptual as well as empirical), in order to know what exactly we transfer. In fact, this seems to be increasingly important as the concept of democracy is used by all kinds of political and economic actors today for numerous different purposes, and the looser the term becomes, the easier it can be hijacked for purposes that are harmful. So while democracy is highly contested, similar to most (if not all) normative concepts, defining indispensable conditions for democracy is not just an academic philosophical exercise, since if clear criteria are not specified, then the term democracy may be misused in all kinds of contexts to justify oppression, exclusion and injustices. On the one hand, we know for a fact that there is not one way to do democracy, and specific practices of democracy have been highly diverse across the world and over time. Similarly, in the academic debate, competing conceptions of democracy are proposed as being the most appropriate for the 'new' circumstances of world politics. Indeed, perhaps it is not even desirable to try to reach consensus on the best way to organize a political organization democratically. On the other hand, if we cannot agree on some minimal common requirements for the concept of democracy, we cannot disagree about what transnational or global democracy ought to look like either, since also such a disagreement must presuppose some common characteristics, without which we wouldn't speak about the same thing.[1] It is argued that any theory or conception of democracy that wishes to hold on to democracy as a normative ideal of

---

[1] Indeed, even to the extent that we would agree on the basic conditions of democracy, democratic theorists would certainly disagree on what needs to be done in order to fulfil them. However, we should distinguish the question of what democracy is from what it requires. The latter question is not of immediate interest in this section.

democratic self-determination ('the rule by the people') — from the local to the global level — must take up this challenge.

So, what conditions are required for an arrangement to qualify as democratic? In broad strokes, what seems indisputable is that democracy, 'the rule by the people', is a form of political arrangement in which the people collectively rules itself as political equals. If we unpack this idea, two conditions come to the fore as fundamentally important and seem to be hard to dismiss for any modern account of democracy. The first condition is political equality. What distinguishes democracy from other forms of government, such as dictatorship, monarchy or aristocracy, is that it has components that express and secure some form of political equality, according to which anyone who is relevantly affected by a political decision (or law) has an equal opportunity, secured through an equal right, to participate (directly or indirectly) in the decision-making about it (Christiano 2006).

But apart from this 'deontological' dimension of being, given an equal opportunity to participate in the decision-making procedure through equal rights, the rule by the people also involves a 'teleological' dimension, in that people rule over themselves and shape their institutions if they, at least a sufficient number of them, act politically by 'exercising' their political equality.[2] In other words, democracy requires some sort of democratic practice (through informal and/or formal processes, depending on which conception of democracy is favoured). I call this condition political bindingness. More specifically, in order for people to rule over themselves through a political authority, thereby making themselves authors of the laws, they have to bind themselves as equals to this authority, which requires certain forms of political action. Under modern conditions this authorization is usually made by taking part (directly or indirectly) in the decision-making or at a minimum accepting the constitutionalized procedures as valid, without which the right to participate would not have any binding force. We will return to this.

---

[2] On this point, compare Rawls' theory of justice as fairness, which insists on the 'equal worth of political rights' (Rawls 2001). Of course, what is considered a 'sufficient number' will vary between different conceptions or models of democracy.

Several attempts to theorize democracy beyond the state have difficulty accommodating one or both of these conditions. Let me illustrate with two examples. One approach in the contemporary debate sets its hopes on the civil society. The present circumstances of world politics, in which the political space is less and less mapped as territorial places, have fuelled a trend among democratic theorists to investigate the role of transnational non-state actors — ranging from social movements to non-governmental organizations (NGOs) and corporations — to achieve more transnational or global democracy. Instead of stressing legal aspects, as is often done by cosmopolitan theorists, it is argued that civil society offers a rich soil to reformulate democracy globally. Civil society is said to be inhabited by a growing range of social actors that create new political spaces, not delimited by territorial nation-state borders and therefore more suitable for confronting the globalized political problems that we face today. More specifically, non-state actors could play crucial roles in global democracy because they give voice to marginalized groups and local stakeholders that cross-cut global power relations and hierarchies (Dryzek 2006; Macdonald 2008; Scholte 2005; Steffek and Nanz 2008).

For example, Jan Aart Scholte (2005) notes that under traditional international law, non-state actors did not have any particular legal status and their participation in international organizations was at best informal. This is slowly changing. In recent years, partly as a response to the criticism of the democratic deficits in global governance, there has been a strong tendency towards increased participation of non-state actors in global governance. Many international organizations have opened up formal and informal avenues for political participation. In Scholte's view, civil society activism offers significant possibilities to come to terms with the major democratic deficit of international organizations in an era when the conventional state formula of democratic legitimacy is not sufficient for expanding global governance arrangements. This is already happening, according to Scholte. Most notably, civil society actors have increased and continue to increase the democratic accountability of international organizations by promoting transparency of global governance operations; by monitoring global policies and policymaking; and by pushing for the creation of formal accountability mechanisms to monitor and control the agencies concerned (ibid.: 93–98).

In a similar vein, Terry Macdonald outlines a multi-stakeholder model that in her view has the potential of being applied within a global polity without the need for either formal electoral mechanisms or the establishment of state-like structures of global public power (Dryzek 2006; Macdonald 2008: 192). According to this deliberative model, the decision-making procedure is underpinned by a 'dualist' conception of equality. In the first instance, stakeholders should be accorded equal opportunities to identify the interests that are supposed to be represented in a deliberative decision process. Second, since these stakeholder interests are not aggregated to reach a decision, as is the case in traditional nation-state models, but are advanced by stakeholder representatives, they must be accorded equal consideration by these representatives in the deliberative process (Macdonald 2008: 143).

While it seems plausible to presume that we need to theorize the role of a globalized civil society to the extent that we wish to globalize the ideal of democracy, the normative role of civil society actors in this approach is not spelled out properly. On closer examination, it seems as if these proposals blur the distinction between democratic theory and the moral theories of legitimacy and justice. The question is this: what sort of institutions can reliably secure such non-electoral representation of NGOs, and what makes these arrangements recognizably democratic? Consider the claim that NGOs would increase democracy in international organizations by promoting more transparency or monitoring the policymaking. While Scholte is right that this supposedly would increase the accountability of those organizations, it seems premature to conclude that democratic accountability is thereby increased too. In order to translate any moralized conception of accountability into democratic accountability, political equality and some form of political bindingness must be fulfilled. Indeed, the same difficulty faces Macdonald's dualist conception of equality, which seems equally unable to accommodate these two conditions, thereby securing equal political power or influence (Erman 2012).

Another common route to theorizing the democratic legitimacy of transnational and global governance is not primarily via civil society activity, but via human rights. While democracy and human rights as two normative standards often stand in a troubled relationship, even domestically, human rights are ascribed a central role in most accounts of democracy beyond the state, in part of course because one central set of human rights are rights to political participation (Erman 2005, 2011). It is generally (and reasonably) agreed that to the extent that we wish to apply democracy globally, we must apply some basic political rights globally too.[3] At the same time, the conceptualization of human rights in these proposals is often unclear. A wide range of scholars tend to reconceptualize global democracy in terms of human rights.

For example, while Michael Goodhart reformulates global democracy through a set of human rights securing the basic principles of freedom and equality, which in his view as a minimum require constraints on the exercise of power and political agency (Goodhart 2008: 406). Such a set constitutes 'ethical standards for legitimate governance at all levels and binding on all actors' (ibid.: 403). Similarly, but from a republican rather than liberal perspective, James Bohman lays out the conceptual foundations of transnational democracy by way of a theory of republican federalism, the normative core of which is freedom as nondomination. This is done through the so-called democratic minimum, which is sufficient to accommodate 'not only the constitutive features of democratic citizenship, but also the necessary conditions for nondomination' (Bohman 2007: 43). More specifically, this minimum alludes to the 'minimum set of powers and conditions that would make it possible for citizens to not be dominated and thus be free to make claims to justice' (ibid.: 35) viz. for citizens to be able to form and change the terms of their life (ibid.: 46).

Again, it is argued that this route is a deadlock because it does not sufficiently acknowledge the normative implications of the distinction between democratic theory and moral theory. It leaves two gaps unfulfilled: between individual rights and collective decision-making, and between (moral and legal) rights and agency. First, we can have perfectly enforced individual human rights without any collective decision-making whatsoever at any level (Erman 2008). Democratic decision-making is a joint endeavour. Second, even if

---

[3] The idea that we need to globalize basic political rights in order to globalize democracy is separate from the question of whether there ought to be a human right to democracy. Even if philosophers that argue in favour of a human right to democracy of course globalize basic political rights too, the opposite is not necessarily the case (see Cohen 2004; Benhabib 2007a, 2007b; Forst 2010).

we fulfilled the condition of political equality by universalizing the political right to participation in the democratic decision-making, rights do not say anything about *practices* such as democratic agency and political influence. Indeed, we might be bearers of numerous rights but never use them. By the same token, democracy is premised on political participation (Erman 2011, 2012, 2013).[4]

Three Layers of the Global Normative Order

So far I have illustrated the kinds of problems that we face when taking on the difficult task of transporting the essence of democracy, that is, the form of political arrangement in which the people collectively rule itself through political equality and political bindingness, to the transnational and global spheres. In different ways, normative ideals seem to get conflated, so that whatever normative improvements we see or theorize immediately get the label 'increased democracy'. This section attempts to resist this tendency by elaborating a three-layered view of the global normative order, which aims at specifying under what circumstances democracy is a desirable ideal, and where justice is the more appropriate ideal to apply. This is done by theorizing the different normative requirements that are placed on discursive agents and their institutions in three contexts of justification: contexts of moral justification, contexts of political justification and equal stakes contexts.

Let me begin by saying a few words about the particular discursive view of agency that underlies the proposed discourse-theoretical approach. On a discourse-theoretical outlook, moral, political and democratic agency have a similar underlying normative structure and originate from the same normative source, which understands agency in intersubjective terms. Of course, agency could be understood in many possible ways, appealing in other philosophical contexts. The only point made here is that a discursive

---

[4] Now, of course, different democratic models incorporate different ideas about how to best secure such agency, for example, through participation in direct and indirect egalitarian decision-making procedures, and through formal decision-procedures and informal civil society processes; they also incorporate different thresholds for how much of each of these political practices that are required for a system to be democratic. The point made here is merely that no matter how we define this, rights cannot alone transform a political community into a democratic community.

view is useful for dealing with some of the problems facing present proposals for theorizing democracy and legitimacy under globalized conditions.

Most moral philosophers agree that there is only one shared moral community, inhabited by moral agents. However, in contrast to much of the liberal philosophical literature on autonomy, the basic Brandomian idea behind the discursive view of agency is that autonomy must be understood as an exercise of autonomous agency. The status as autonomous (for example, moral or democratic) agent is not something to be distributed or ascribed (for example, through some moral principle), but is something that must be achieved. Agency is a concrete social achievement, as it were (Brandom 1994: 8; Erman 2007, 2010: 40). Further, from Brandom's normative pragmatic standpoint, a social status is understood as a normative status, without which there could be no agents. To recognize always means to attribute specific normative responsibilities in terms of entitlements and commitments. In this sense, recognition has to be mutual (Brandom 1994: 161–63).[5] Consequently, being autonomous, or being an agent at all, requires recognitive structures (Brandom 1999: 168–69; Darwall 2006; Erman 2007, 2010: 41).

In line with philosophers who assume there is only one moral community, the Brandomian view throws doubt upon communitarian or liberal-nationalist assumptions that there exist several such communities on discursive grounds. For example, on a communitarian outlook, the national and cultural community is the source of a moral language and of moral practice, and as such a precondition for moral agency and in relevant cases for democratic agency (Walzer 1977, 1984, 2004; MacIntyre 1984). By contrast, from the normative pragmatic vocabulary applied here, this suggests that there are multiple separate discursive communities, which sounds unintelligible as it would presume that there are bounded clusters

---

[5] Habermas expresses similar thoughts about commitments and responsibilities in terms of the raising of validity claims in discourse. Speech acts have an illocutionary force that has the capacity to motivate the hearer to respond. When we use communicative action, we explicitly or implicitly raise validity claims and expect that these be met, that is, that the targets of those speech acts accept them as valid (Habermas 1996: 107–8, 1998).

of mutually recognizing agents who share a world, such that recognitive relations are not possible across its boundaries.

Now, moving to the three layers of the global normative order and the exercise of moral, political and democratic agency in it. Here the term 'global normative order' is to be understood in broadly Brandomian terms, alluding to the space of reasons, which naturally consists of uncountable orders (and disorders for that matter) within a linguistic structure formed by human practices of giving and asking for reasons, constituting a community of justification. To begin with, with regard to contexts of moral justification, to the extent that we find the basic Brandomian framework persuasive, I argue that we have good reasons to subscribe to the cosmopolitan presumption that we as discursive agents ought to be equally respected as such in our justificatory practices. In Forst's view, the common source of all claims of validity in normative space is the principle of equal respect for autonomous agency, from which a basic moral right to justification is derived. This principle requires that we regard others as autonomous sources of normative claims within a justificatory practice such that each person is an 'authority' in the space of reasons, as it were (Brandom 1994, 1999). Justification on this view is understood as a discursive process whose primary addressees are those affected in relevant ways (Forst 2011: Ch. 1).[6] Thus, insofar as we get our normative statuses in practices of giving and asking for reasons, Forst argues we should have a moral right to justification in those very practices, that is, a right to be recognized as an agent who can demand acceptable reasons for any institution or structure which claims to be binding upon her or any action that claims to be morally justified (Forst 2010: 719).[7]

---

[6] As such, the principle of equal respect for autonomous agency is a 'dialogical' version of the all affected principle.

[7] This right accommodates two criteria, *reciprocity* and *generality*. In moral contexts, the criterion of generality takes the form of *universality* or 'generality in a strict sense' (Forst 2001: 363, 2010: 734), similar to Habermas' universalization principle (Habermas 1990, 1993, 1998; Erman 2007). However, in contrast to pure consent theories of moral justification, the criteria of reciprocity and generality allow for the justifiability of claims even in cases of dissent, because normative claims are justified to the extent that they are not 'reasonably rejectable', viz. as long as no reciprocal and

Moving to contexts of political justification, I agree with Forst that the right to justification ought to constitute the criterion of rightness here too, the difference being that moral contexts are concerned with interpersonal moral conduct, whereas political contexts are concerned with legal, political and institutional structures.[8] Indeed, on the discourse-theoretical view taken here, as soon as we are dealing with human rights, we have already moved from the moral to the political domain, since human rights have an inherently legal dimension. In other words, the difference between moral rights, such as the right to justification and human rights, is that the latter require a legal-political community (Habermas 1996; Besson 2011). For institutions to protect the equal respect for autonomous agency in contexts of political justification, the right to justification requires the fulfilment of two conditions in order for institutions to be politically legitimate. First, it requires the substantive condition that subjects' fundamental interests be secured through a set of basic rights, including political rights.[9] Second, it requires the procedural condition that channels and procedures are established on the basis of and through this set of basic rights, which secure the opportunity for discursive agents subjected to the decisions and laws of a political arrangement to demand acceptable reasons from it. Importantly, however, what is considered acceptable reasons will depend on the circumstances of the political community at hand.

However, apart from moral and political contexts, Forst claims that the right to justification also constitutes a criterion of democratic legitimacy. This way the ideal of justice and that of democracy

---

general reasons can be legitimately raised against them. Of course, within this dialogical framework, universalizing a maxim of action is not about an agent asking herself whether her action can be willed generally without contradiction in a monological fashion. Instead, justification is understood as a discursive process whose primary addressees are those affected in relevant ways. And disputes about 'relevantly affected' could only be addressed by way of a process of reciprocal and general justification (Forst 2011: Ch. 1).

[8] Forst does not separate the moral from the political in this way.

[9] However, these political rights would not include those rights commonly labelled 'democratic rights', such as the right to participate in the decision-making, which are only demanded from the point of view of democratic legitimacy in equal stakes contexts.

are knit together through the moral right to justification. For Forst, political contexts of justification are at the same time contexts of democratic legitimacy. His discursive conception of justice as non-domination (Forst 2007a: 260, 2007b: 299–300) is seen as inseparable from his conception of democracy since the moral point of human rights, that is, to have an active status as a justificatory equal, is not only about the protection of our agency, but also about expressing our agency and autonomy in practice as 'norm-givers'. Forst argues that human rights are best seen as rights that put an end to political oppression and relations of domination that deprive people of their access to a social status necessary to being persons of equal standing. This is articulated as a human right to democracy in terms of a basic right to democratic participation, viz. a right to full membership in a democratic community, which realizes for agents the right to justification in the political realm, and thus recognizes their equal right to effective political justification (Forst 2010: 724–35, 730, 2001: 362–70). Thus, rather than limiting the right to democracy by appealing to the principle of collective self-determination, which is a 'recursive' principle according to Forst, the border of the democratic community is to be decided and justified with reference to the right to democracy, viz. the right to democratic participation (Forst 2010: 730).

The problem with applying the ideal of democracy to all political contexts through the right to justification is that political equality, while being a necessary condition for democracy, does not suffice even on a minimal account. As was argued in the previous section, the idea that each political member is to be treated equally through an equal right to participation cannot constitute a criterion of democratic legitimacy standing by itself, since it doesn't say anything about collective decision-making, which is dependent on a condition of political bindingness, at a minimum requiring the acceptance of the constitutionalized procedures as valid. To repeat the argument against the human rights approach to global democracy: universal rights alone (legal or moral) cannot substantiate a normative theory of democracy because no matter how fully implemented, universal rights of any kind are individual rights, which could be enforced without any collective exercise of egalitarian decision-making whatsoever, on any level (Erman 2008, 2011). There are two points of importance here. First, in contrast to basic civil rights, such as freedom of speech, and basic socio-economic rights, such as the right to health care, a condition of political rights, at least of those labelled 'democratic' rights, is that they depend on them being exercised jointly with others. Thus, while I may have a right to vote, I cannot exercise this right any-time I want, but only in an election together with others. Second, if we all had a right to vote in an election but nobody ever did, we would not fulfil the condition of political bindingness since there would be no authorization involved. This would not be the case if we all had a right to health care but never got sick and had to exercise it. In other words, what is peculiar to democracy is that individual and collective autonomy are simultaneously at work when democratic legitimacy is generated.

In fact, drawing its normative force from the idea of 'affected-ness', the right to justification applied to 'democratic contexts' faces the same problem as the standard all affected (interests) principle stressed by cosmopolitan democrats, which roughly states that all whose significant interests are affected by a decision should have a say in deciding upon it (see, for example, Held 1995; Archibugi 1998; Benhabib 2004; Gould 2004). In order to show why such all affected principles are problematic from the point of view of democracy, let me introduce a third context of justification, namely equal stakes contexts.

It is not clear to me how any moral all-affected principle is able to take us from counting all interests equally (cosmopolitan democracy) or showing equal respect for autonomous agency (Forst), to political equality. Political equality is not only premised on the idea that members of a constituency are morally equal and as such have a right to participate in decision-making to the extent that they are affected, but also that they have a right to have an equal influence in the decision-making. The idea of 'one person, one vote' reflects precisely this conception of equality (that is, elec-toral mechanisms are one way to achieve political equality). The difference is crucial: the all affected principle allows for a propor-tional view of affectedness, according to which those who are more affected by a decision should have more influence than those who are less affected (see Gould 2004; Macdonald 2008). Indeed, sup-porting proportional influence seems sensible since it is affected-ness that motivates a right to participate in the decision-making in the first place. It is one of the features that make the principle so attractive from a normative point of view. Consider the alternative, according to which those who are affected should have the same degree of influence. This would draw an indefensible dividing line between those that are not at all affected and those that are very little affected. It would also undermine majority voting as a justified procedure from the standpoint of democracy, since voting on an issue would generate clear winners and losers in light of the fact that it will never be the case that people are equally affected. In a democracy, members are supposed to rule over themselves through a political arrangement that takes numerous decisions on a wide range of social, political, legal, and economic issues. To the extent that such arrangements have 'proportional influence' due to 'proportional affectedness', it is at set levels (for example, local municipality) within a legal-institutional framework that secures equal influence on each level.

This problem calls attention to a difference between moral and political contexts of justification, on the one hand, and equal stakes contexts, on the other. What distinguishes political equality, applicable in the latter, from moral equality is that to have an equal right to equal influence in the decision-making is premised on the members having *roughly equal stakes* — not in each and every decision but in the complete set of decisions in the democratic arrangement taken as a whole (Christiano 2006: 85–86). However, more needs to be said about this empirical condition since people can have roughly equal stakes for reasons that are irrelevant for democracy. More specifically, equal stakes contexts are contexts in which peoples' interests are interdependent, that is, they are a set of circumstances among a group of people in which the realization of nearly all of the fundamental interests of each person is connected with the realization of nearly all fundamental interests of every other (ibid.). While the call for collective decision-making and common institutions may emerge in other contexts too, it is argued below that democracy is a desirable normative ideal only in equal stakes contexts, in which the two empirical conditions of interdependent interests and roughly equal stakes are fulfilled.

Instead of following Forst's path to democracy, as an alternative discourse-theoretical strategy, I start instead in Habermas' discourse theory of democracy and defend what is here called the 'equal influence principle', which I argue offers a more plausible and convincing criterion of democratic legitimacy. In contrast to contexts of moral and political justification, in which the right to justification constitutes the criterion of rightness, it is argued that democracy is intrinsically justified only in equal stakes contexts, thus constituting a *partial* rather than comprehensive ideal (Robeyns 2008: 344). The equal influence principle borrows from Habermas the idea that democratically legitimate laws and political decisions must not win assent by those affected by them, but only by those subjected to them, that is, those whose actions are governed by them (Dahl 1989; Habermas 1996; Lopez-Guerra 2005). It is formulated as follows: 'Those that are systematically and over time subjected to an authority's laws, political decisions and rules, in the sense of being governed by them, should systematically and over time have an equal influence over its decision-making and in the shaping of the common institutions.' Influence here is to be understood in terms of political action and not merely the possibility of such action, which means that an arrangement in which there is formal political equality but no one ever exercised their political rights would not qualify as democratic. More specifically, influence at a minimum requires an ongoing democratic practice in terms of robust participation in both formal decision procedures (for example, through electoral vote) and informal processes (for example, in civil society and the public sphere), in which a large part of the members take part. Further, 'systematically and over time' suggests an institutional approach to democracy stating that this participation does not concern each and every decision but the complete set of decisions over time (Erman and Follesdal 2012).[10]

What follows from this discourse-theoretical approach is thus that discursive agents as members of the global space of reasons exercise their moral, political and democratic agency differently depending on context. For example, as members of a democratic community, they would not only be part of the one and only moral community, but also of a common political community through

---

[10] In contrast to those who see rights as a protection 'against' democratic rule-makers and democratic authority, my institutional approach, in line with Habermas, sees a set of rights protecting fundamental interests as an essential part of any reasonable conception of democracy applied to modern political societies, not only for the protection of members, but also in large part for non-members such as short-term residents, visitors and people seeking asylum.

human rights, international law, and transnational and global governance structures. As we have seen, the defended view holds that the space of reasons consists of three contexts of justification, constituting three layers of the global normative order. It is argued that each of these contexts corresponds with a particular duty, relating to a specific normative ideal. In moral and political contexts, the right to justification constitutes the criterion of rightness, generating two kinds of duties of justice. In contexts of moral justification, it foremost demands as a duty of individuals to respect each other as autonomous agents who have the right not to be subjected to actions or norms that cannot be properly justified to them. In contexts of political justification, every discursive agent can demand acceptable reasons for any political institution or arrangement that claims to be binding upon her or any action that claims to be morally justified (Forst 2010: 719). While it is primarily the duty of institutions to protect the right to justification by fulfilling the substantive and procedural conditions discussed earlier, it is the duty of those relevantly affected by such institutions to support them.

In equal stakes contexts, finally, the right to justification takes the form of the equal influence principle, which constitutes a criterion of democratic legitimacy. This principle entails a duty of institutions to include as political equals with equal influence in the decision-making those who are systematically and over time subject to their laws, decisions and rules. As an institutional duty of democracy, it is foremost a duty of the institutions in question to secure the inclusion required by the equal influence principle as well as a duty of its members to support such institutions. Further, it is secondarily a duty of institutions and discursive agents on the outside of this institutional structure to support in both these undertakings.[11]

Democracy, Justice and Multiple Citizenship

This three-layered view of the global normative order, distinguishing between different practices of justification, lays out the

---

[11] Of course, that the equal influence principle ought to be applied in equal stakes contexts rather than in 'all normative contexts' does not imply that it is acceptable to violate it outside of them. It is quite the reverse in fact. However, such a violation would, in political and moral contexts, primarily demand the right to justification and as such foremost be a matter of injustice rather than of undemocratic rule-making.

conceptual and normative ground for theorizing legitimacy in transnational and global governance in terms of two kinds of legitimacy, namely political legitimacy and democratic legitimacy, fruitfully illustrated through what I call multiple citizenship, which is meant to exemplify the multiple roles that citizens could and ought to play in such governance. This approach has several advantages.

To begin with, rather than starting out from a specific normative ideal, say, of democracy or justice, it opens the possibility of theorizing several normative ideals at the same time by analysing citizens in terms of 'democratic agents', 'agents of democracy' and 'agents of justice' simultaneously, at different governance levels and for different normative reasons. It thus contributes to the meagre dialogue between theorists of cosmopolitan democracy and the theorists of global justice by conceiving democratic institutions as devices for fulfilling several tasks in tandem, such as providing democratic self-determination through equal distribution of political influence over decision-making (intrinsic justification), and promoting and securing distributive justice by being more likely to remain responsive to the best interests of all citizens compared to alternative decision-making institutions (instrumental justification). Such a flexible division of normative labour between democracy and justice within territorial multilevel settings opens to a broader set of institutional arrangements, since citizens would have different obligations depending on context of justification, for example, as democratic agents in equal stakes contexts and as cosmopolitan 'citizens' of the world in political contexts, with different legal statuses (Erman and Follesdal 2012).

Second, the approach provides normative and conceptual tools for analysing the role of non-state actors in multilevel governance, not primarily as democratic agents, as is done by the civil society approach discussed above, but, at best, as agents of democracy or agents of justice. As agents of democracy they might push global governance institutions towards increased transparency or accountability or some other democratic quality and as such improve the prerequisites for democracy beyond the nation state. But democracy is not their main or only normatively desirable objective. They may also contribute to other important tasks of detecting and revealing human rights violations, pressuring states to ratify human rights treaties, and so on.

Third, it accommodates a pluralist view of human rights which acknowledges but does not reify several distinctions, such as that between passive and active human rights, or between those that secure basic needs more directly versus those that facilitate influence over institutions. As was evident in the human rights approach, political theorists who see human rights as one unitary package often overlook this. Thus some rights secure basic needs or the status of citizenship primarily in the form of protections (including civil and socio-economic rights), while others are better justified as essential for democratic agency, for example, for the equal possibility to participate in democratic decision-making. On this view, and in contrast to some theories of cosmopolitan democracy, not all human rights must be enforced at all levels of governance (Erman and Follesdal 2012).

I will conclude by specifying in more detail what kind of legitimacy the proposed three-layered approach would lend the global normative order. It suggests that there are two conceptions of legitimacy at work here, which are often conflated in the debate (Erman and Higgott 2010). In contexts of political justification, institutions in domestic, regional or international settings generate what we might call 'political legitimacy' insofar as they fulfil the right to justification by securing the substantive and procedural conditions. Political legitimacy is a weaker form of legitimacy from the standpoint of democratic theory. However, insofar as political arrangements in equal stakes contexts secure the equal influence principle, they generate *democratic legitimacy*. Working together, they make the global normative order as a whole more legitimate.

⁀

References

Archibugi, Daniele. 1998. 'Principles of Cosmopolitan Democracy', in Daniele Archibugi, David Held and Martin Köhler (eds), *Re-imagining Political Community: Studies in Cosmopolitan Democracy*, Polity Press, London, 198–229.

———. 2004. 'Cosmopolitan Democracy and Its Critics: A Review', *European Journal of International Relations* 10(3): 437–73.

———. 2008. *The Global Commonwealth of Citizens: Toward Cosmopolitan Democracy*, Princeton University Press, Princeton.

Archibugi, Daniele, Mathias Koenig-Archibugi and Raffaele Marchetti (eds). 2010. *Global Democracy: Normative and Empirical Perspectives*, Cambridge University Press, Cambridge.

Beitz, Charles. 2004. 'Human Rights and the Law of Peoples', in D. Chatterjee (ed.), *The Ethics of Assistance*, Cambridge University Press, New York, 193–215.

Benhabib, Seyla. 2004. *The Rights of Others: Aliens, Residents and Citizens*, Cambridge University Press, Cambridge.

———. 2007a. 'Twilight of Sovereignty or the Emergence of Cosmopolitan Norms? Rethinking Citizenship in Volatile Times', *Citizenship Studies*, 11(1): 19–36.

———. 2007b. 'Democratic Exclusions and Democratic Iterations', *European Journal of Political Theory* 6(4): 445–62.

Besson, Samantha. 2011. 'Human Rights and Democracy in a Global Context: Decoupling and Recoupling', *Ethics & Global Politics* 4(1): 19–50.

Bohman, James. 2007. *Democracy across Borders: From Dêmos to Dêmoi*, MIT Press, Cambridge, MA.

Brandom, Robert. 1994. *Making it Explicit*, Harvard University Press, Cambridge, MA.

———. 1999. 'Some Pragmatist Themes in Hegel's Idealism', *European Journal of Philosophy* 7(2): 164–89.

Cabrera, Luis. 2010. *The Practice of Global Citizenship*, Cambridge University Press, Cambridge.

Caney, Simon. 2005. *Justice Beyond Borders: A Global Political Theory*, Oxford University Press, Oxford.

Christiano, Thomas. 2006. 'A Democratic Theory of Territory and Some Puzzles about Global Democracy', *Journal of Social Philosophy* 37(1): 81–107.

Cohen, Joshua. 2004. 'Minimalism about Human Rights: The Most We Can Hope For?', *The Journal of Political Philosophy* 21(2): 190–213.

Dahl, Robert. 1989. *Democracy and Its Critics*, Yale University Press, New Haven.

Darwall, Stephen. 2006. *The Second-Person Standpoint*, Harvard University Press, Cambridge, MA.

Dryzek, John. 2006. *Deliberative Global Politics: Discourse and Democracy in a Divided World*, Polity Press, Cambridge.

Erman, Eva. 2005. *Human Rights and Democracy: Discourse Theory and Human Rights Institutions*, Ashgate Publishing, Aldershot.

———. 2007. 'Conflict and Universal Moral Theory: From Reasonableness to Reason-Giving', *Political Theory* 35(5) : 598–623.

———. 2008. 'On Goodhart's Global Democracy: A Critique', *Ethics & International Affairs* 22(4): 1–10.

Erman, Eva. 2010. 'Freedom as Non-Domination or How to Throw the Agent Out of the Space of Reasons', *Journal of Power* 3(1): 33–51.

———. 2011. 'Human Rights do not Make Global Democracy', *Contemporary Political Theory* 10(4): 463–81.

———. 2012. '"The Right to have Rights" to the Rescue: From Human Rights to Global Democracy', in Mark Goodale (ed.), *Human Rights at the Crossroads*, Oxford University Press, Oxford, 72–83.

———. 2013. 'In Search for Democratic Agency in Deliberative Governance', *European Journal of International Relations* 19(4): 847–68.

Erman, Eva, and R. Higgott. 2010. 'Deliberative Global Governance and the Question of Legitimacy: What can we Learn from the WTO?' *Review of International Studies* 36(2): 449–70.

Erman, Eva and A. Follesdal. 2012. 'Multiple Citizenship: Normative Ideals and Institutional Challenges', *Critical Review of International Social and Political Philosophy* 15(3): 279–302.

Forst, Rainer. 2001. 'The Rule of Reasons: Three Models of Deliberative Democracy', *Ratio Juris* 14(4): 345–78.

———. 2007a. 'Radical Justice: On Iris Marion Young's Critique of the 'Distributive Paradigm'', *Constellations* 14(2): 260–65.

———. 2007b. 'First Things First: Redistribution, Recognition and Justification', *European Journal of Political Theory* 6(3): 291–304.

———. 2010. 'The Justification of Human Rights and the Basic Right to Justification: A Reflexive Approach', *Ethics* 120(4): 711–40.

———. 2011. *The Right to Justification: Elements of a Constructivist Theory of Justice*, trans. J. Flynn, Columbia University Press, New York.

Goodhart, Michael. 2008. 'Human Rights and Global Democracy', *Ethics & International Affairs* 22(4): 395–420.

Gould, Carol. 2004. *Globalizing Democracy and Human Rights*, Cambridge University Press, Cambridge.

Habermas, Jürgen. 1990. *Moral Consciousness and Communicative Action*, trans. C. Lenhardt and S. Nicholsen, MIT Press, Cambridge, MA.

———. 1993. *Justification and Application: Remarks on Discourse Ethics*, trans. C. Cronin, MIT Press, Cambridge, MA.

———. 1996. *Between Facts and Norms: Contributions to a Discourse Theory of Law and Democracy*, trans. W. Rehg, MIT Press, Cambridge, MA.

———. 1998. *The Inclusion of the Other*, edited by C. Cronin and P. De Greiff, MIT Press, Cambridge, MA.

Held, David. 1995. *Democracy and the Global Order: From the Modern State to Cosmopolitan Governance*, Polity Press, Cambridge.

Lopez-Guerra, Claudio. 2005. 'Should Expatriates Vote?' *The Journal of Political Philosophy* 13(2): 216–34.

Macdonald, Terry. 2008. *Global Stakeholder Democracy*, Oxford University Press, Oxford.

MacDonald, Terry and Raffaele Marchetti. 2010. 'Symposium on Global Democracy: Introduction', *Ethics and International Affairs* 24(1): 13–18.

MacIntyre, Alasdair. 1984. 'Is Patriotism a Virtue?' *The Lindley Lecture at the University of Kansas*, University Press of Kansas, Lawrence.

Pogge, Thomas. 2002. *World Poverty and Human Rights*, Polity Press, Cambridge.

———. 2007. 'Severe Poverty as a Human Rights Violation', in Thomas Pogge (ed.), *Freedom from Poverty as a Human Right: Who Owes What to the Very Poor?* Oxford University Press, Oxford, 11–54.

Rawls, John. 2001. *Justice as Fairness. A Restatement*, Harvard University Press, Cambridge, MA.

Robeyns, Ingrid. 2008. 'Ideal Theory in Theory and Practice', *Social Theory and Practice* 34(3): 341–62.

Scholte, Jan Aart. 2005. 'Civil Society and Democratically Accountable Global Governance', in David Held and Mathias Koenig-Archibugi (eds), *Global Governance and Public Accountability*, Blackwell Publishing, Oxford, 87–109.

Steffek, Jens and P. Nanz. 2008. 'Emergent Patterns of Civil Society Participation in Global and European Governance', *Civil Society Participation in European and Global Governance*, Palgrave Macmillan, New York.

Tan, Kok-Chor. 2004. *Justice Without Borders: Cosmopolitanism, Nationalism, and Patriotism*, Cambridge University Press, Cambridge.

Walzer, Michael. 1977. *Just and Unjust Wars*, Basic Books, New York.

———. 1984. *Spheres of Justice*, Basic Books, New York.

———. 2004. *Arguing About War*, Yale University Press, New Haven.

Part II
Reconceptualizing Cosmopolitanism

4

Cosmopolitanism without Foundations

Véronique Pin-Fat

This chapter argues that cosmopolitanism has no foundations. Rather than using so-called 'anti-foundationalist' insights to critique cosmopolitanism, I use them to defend its ethico-political value. I suggest that it is the very lack of foundations that makes cosmopolitan commitments to universality so desirable.

What is Cosmopolitanism?

There appears to be a more or less standard formula for writing anything on cosmopolitanism. It usually begins by clarifying what might be meant by the term. In that sense, this chapter has not strayed from the formula. However, what I want to do here is to refuse to answer the question with a definition but to engage with it nonetheless. I hope to show how seductive such a definitional starting point can be and how it so quickly leads us to a search for the foundations of cosmopolitanism; that which is 'common to all'. More importantly, I engage with the question because I want to suggest that having a singular answer to the question may not be needed for cosmopolitanism to be both meaningful and ethico-politically defensible.

But, what is cosmopolitanism? Although I may not be interested in answering this question plenty of people are and have done so. There is no universal agreement on the meaning of cosmopolitanism. The array of definitions of cosmopolitanism and what they produce is so profuse that it has lead Holton, somewhat in exasperation, to declare: 'The study of cosmopolitanism threatens to become over-burdened with so many disparate elements and implications that it will become incoherent chaos' (Holton 2009: 3). But what is this near chaos and why be concerned?

Roughly speaking, scholars tend to group definitions around four categories: moral, legal, political, and, more recently, 'new' or 'actually existing' cosmopolitanism.[1] Moral cosmopolitanism's central concerns are commonly traced back to Kant (Wonicki 2009) and include the notion that 'every human being has global stature as an ultimate unit of moral concern' and that our moral concern should be universal in scope (Pogge 1992: 49).[2] It is a position wherein 'moral universalism takes precedence over moral particularism' (Holton 2009: 4). At stake here is the view that moral obligations extend to the whole of humanity and to each member of humanity equally. Consequently, the boundaries that divide humanity, such as race, gender, sexuality, and especially nationality, are considered morally arbitrary and, in the final analysis, morally irrelevant. Moral cosmopolitanism need not imply a commitment to any other form of cosmopolitanism but often does.

Legal cosmopolitanism 'concerns itself with developing laws and institutions that serve cosmopolitan ends' (Çali 2006: 1150).[3] It typically 'recognises individuals and groups in civil society, as well as states, as legal personalities. It is concerned with the rights and responsibilities of world citizens and the key problem it addresses is that the worst violators of human rights are often states' (Fine 2003: 452). The key point is that cosmopolitan law crosses the boundary that divides the inside (domestic) and outside of states. Often cited examples of cosmopolitan law include the Nuremberg Charter (1945), the Genocide Convention (1947), the Universal Declaration of Human Rights (1948) and, more recently, the Responsibility to Protect (2001) and the International Criminal Court (2002).

According to Fossum, political cosmopolitanism should provide a 'coherent approach to transformative politics beyond the prevailing Westphalian system of nation-states, a political project of politically reframing the world to sit better with cosmopolitan democracy and justice' (2011: 236). The key feature here is the idea of building global political institutions in order to create a cosmopolis or cosmopolitan world order. It may or may not include a commitment to the previous forms of cosmopolitanism but, typically,

---

[1] These are, of course, problematic. They can, and do, overlap.

[2] Examples would include universal human rights and global principles of justice.

[3] This may or may not involve a commitment to moral cosmopolitanism and/or political cosmopolitanism.

often does (Archibugi and Held 1995; Archibugi 2008) Indeed, the term 'cosmopolitics' has been coined in order to capture 'the connection of cosmopolitanism with visions of the good society (of which world government is one), with policies designed to enlarge and enhance citizenship (such as global human rights) and ways of generating increased social participation and social cohesion (such as global civil society)' (Holton 2009: 8).

Last but not least, according to new or actually existing cosmopolitanism we are all, presently, living in empirically new conditions; a 'cosmopolitan moment' of modernity that is not to be confused with globalization.[4] We are told that 'cosmopolitanization' has already arrived as

> the proliferation of multiple cultures (as with cuisines from around the world), the growth of many transnational forms of life, the emergence of various non-state political actors (from Amnesty International to the World Trade Organization), the paradoxical emergence of global protest movements, the hesitant formation of multi-national states (like the European Union) etc. There is simply no turning the clock back to a world of sovereign nation-states and national societies (Beck and Sznaider 2006: 10).

Unsurprisingly, different academic disciplines may be particularly attracted to one category over another. Philosophers, political theorists and international political theorists tend to be drawn towards moral cosmopolitanism; lawyers towards legal cosmopolitanism; scholars of international politics and political 'scientists' towards political cosmopolitanism, and social theorists, anthropologists and sociologists towards new cosmopolitanism. This is, of course, the very crudest of summaries, but we begin to see why Holton is worried about chaos — not only do we have different forms of cosmopolitanism but it seems each academic discipline that attempts to study it simply adds to its multiplicity and plurality.[5] How to tidy up this mess?

---

[4] According to Beck and Sznaider: 'Globalization is something that is taking place "out there", cosmopolitanization happens "from within"' (2006: 9).

[5] The crudeness of the summary doesn't capture the ways in which many scholars combine at least two forms of cosmopolitanism whilst still tending towards making one primary (either epistemologically or ontologically

A typical way would be to find what is common to all instances of cosmopolitanism such that our definition would refer to it and thereby provide us with an answer to the question 'what is cosmopolitanism?' The idea behind this approach is to identify the few essential elements of the reality of cosmopolitanism and its essence. Not only does this simplify things epistemologically and methodologically but it also makes the features of reality that cosmopolitanism addresses all the fewer (ontology). Simply, it is a search for and identification of foundations. Foundations are the very 'thing' that makes cosmopolitanism 'cosmopolitanism'. Without foundations the concern is that we couldn't distinguish cosmopolitanism from a 'deformed' cosmopolitanism or from communitarianism, realpolitik or anything else. If a form of cosmopolitanism is built on the correct foundations, then it is authentic, real or even, according to Ulrich Beck, 'non-deformed' (2006: 21). In sum, foundations are the 'real thing'. They are the essential ontology of cosmopolitanism and, apparently, they prevent us from getting horribly lost in the chaos that a multiplicity of meanings creates.

Frequently, the foundational ontology of cosmopolitanism — what is common to all instances of it — is taken to include both universality and humanity. Thomas Pogge's seminal articulation of common features is instructive. He says that individualism, universality and generality are the 'elements shared by all cosmopolitan positions' (1992: 48). Cosmopolitanism therefore refers to any position in which human beings are the 'ultimate unit of moral concern' (individualism), are so equally (universality) and where their moral status extends beyond arbitrary factors such as national boundaries (generality). Başak Çali similarly summarizes the plurality of cosmopolitanisms this way, 'what makes them all cosmopolitan is their explicit or implicit commitment to the equal worth of all human beings, regardless of social and political arrangements and affiliations of place' (2006: 1153).

What I intend to show in this chapter is that neither universality nor humanity can be, nor need be, foundational. This need not imply that cosmopolitanism is dead. On the contrary, I intend to

---

prior). Neither does it capture the plethora of distinctions that can be made within each category. For example, Pogge (1992) distinguishes between institutional moral cosmopolitanism and interactive moral cosmopolitanism.

show that the lack of foundations accounts for the vitality of cosmopolitanism and is desirable. However, to do this we must first examine the relationship between language and reality.

The Limits of Language: 'Hard' vs 'Soft' Ontologies

What universality is and what humanity might 'properly' mean for cosmopolitanism is a seemingly deep and profound question. Were we to locate the 'reality' of these things beneath the (misleading?) phenomenological surface of multiple definitions we would know what cosmopolitanism really is. And with that, much like the arrow on information maps in huge shopping malls that reassuringly tell us 'You Are Here', we could find our way out of confusion and be better placed to move towards a cosmopolitan future without going astray again. Using the philosophy of Ludwig Wittgenstein and my interpretations of him for this topic I seek to show: (*a*) that the idea of foundations which are 'common to all' instances of cosmopolitanism assume that language represents reality through naming; (*b*) that a representational understanding of language postulates a hard ontology; (*c*) that hard ontologies rest on a misunderstanding of our forms of language; (*d*) that instead 'the meaning of a word is in its use' and reality is linguistically constituted and that therefore; (*e*) 'foundations' (such as humanity, universality) cannot fulfil the formal requirement of logic that they exist outside and independently of language; and (*f*) nor need they in order to be meaningful. All this simply adds up to arguing that the ontology of reality and therefore cosmopolitanism can be read as soft.

Wittgenstein's notion of language games presents an insurmountable problem for any form of explanation that rests on the 'discovery' of a property that is common to all instances of phenomena under investigation. Wittgenstein uses 'games' to illustrate his point, which is worth quoting at length:

> Consider for example the proceedings we call 'games'. I mean board-games, card-games, ball-games, Olympic games and so on. What is common to them all? — Don't say: 'There *must* be something common, or they would not be called "games"' — but look and see whether there is anything common to all. — For if you look at them you will not see something that is common to all, but similarities, relationships, and a whole series of them at that. To repeat: don't think, but look! ... And the result of this examination is: we see a complicated network of

similarities overlapping and criss-crossing: sometimes overall similarities, sometimes similarities of detail (1958: 66).

Instead of considering 'games' we could consider the words 'cosmopolitanism' and, indeed, 'universality' and 'humanity' that are its purported essence. As the first section of this chapter amply shows, there are several 'games' of cosmopolitanism: moral, political, legal, and 'new'. Cosmopolitanism as a term is not captured or explained by 'discovering' an element which is common to all purported instances of it. The seductiveness of searching for an element common to all instances of phenomena is (almost) irresistible in the case of cosmopolitanism because the fundamental and dominant idea is that cosmopolitanism must have a universal foundation so that it applies to all human beings equally.[6] Paraphrasing Wittgenstein, the metaphysical urge is to say: 'There must be something common or it could not be called 'cosmopolitanism'.

But why do we become seduced by the promise of finding foundations; that which is common to all? For Wittgenstein, when we say things like 'individualism, universality and generality are the elements shared by all cosmopolitan positions', we think we are outlining a thing's nature and are captivated by it because of the view that language and thought represent reality (Pogge 1992: 48). In other words, that the role of language and thought is representational or a 'mirror of nature' (Rorty 1980).

Such a view holds that

> the individual words in language name objects — sentences are combinations of such names. In this picture of language we find the roots of the following idea: Every word has a meaning. This meaning is correlated with the word. It is the object for which the word stands (Wittgenstein 1958: 1).

In this view, the relationship between language and reality comes through naming. Language can represent reality because names name objects and configurations of names depict possible configurations of objects in the world. In this way, language can represent possible states of affairs because it shares the same structure.

---

[6] For a full discussion of this, and reading grammatically, applied to human rights, see Pin-Fat (2000).

Thus, the truth or falsity of a proposition depends on whether it agrees or disagrees with reality (Wittgenstein 1922: 2.223, 4.05). What this means, of course, is that language names objects outside itself. These objects are foundational and are aspects of reality. Consequently, this picture of language generates the idea that there must be a super-order between super-concepts — a 'hard' connection between the order of possibilities common to both thought and world (Wittgenstein 1958: 97); a hard ontology. More simply, this view pictures our words as anchored to hard objects (foundations) deep beneath the surface of language. It is these foundations that give the word meaning.

But, isn't this picture of how language functions and its relationship to reality 'common sense'? Wittgenstein suggests that one of the reasons why such a picture is so seductive is precisely because it does seem obvious. As he says: 'The aspects of things which are most important for us are hidden because of their simplicity and familiarity' (ibid.: 129). The suggestion here is that the role of naming in language is so familiar that we no longer notice it. What happens if we actually do pay attention to naming? Wittgenstein suggests that naming, as an act of conferring meaning, does not get its efficacy from the existence of or its reference to an object. Rather, meaning comes from context — 'the rest of our proceedings'.

Wittgenstein does not only use the language game metaphor to question the need for foundations, but uses it to emphasize both the role of practice (use) and rules in conferring meaning. Of this, he says:

> When one shows someone the king in chess and says: 'This is the king', this does not tell him the use of this piece — unless he already knows the rules of the game up to this last point: the shape of the king (ibid.: 31).

Wittgenstein's analogy that naming the king does not tell us how to move the king in chess is constructed to bring to light the idea that one's ability to name an object is not sufficient for one to be able to claim that one has understood or grasped the meaning of a word. Rather, what is required for understanding is that one be able to use a word and, even more importantly, be able to use it correctly.

Meaning can come from the way in which a word is used in particular contexts and not naming. Hence the famous quotation:

'For a large class of cases — though not for all — in which we employ the word 'meaning' it can be defined thus: the meaning of a word is its use in the language' (Wittgenstein 1958: 43). But, equally, understanding the meaning of a word involves the ability to be able to use the word in the appropriate contexts correctly. For Wittgenstein, then, understanding is associated with the capacity to do something, which is why naming cannot be a move in chess since the ability to name chess pieces does not, in itself, include the capacity to be able to play the game (that is, use the pieces). To say that naming means being versed in the practices that surround it (the context) challenges the very idea that the source of meaning lies outside language and must be singular; in other words, that a word like cosmopolitanism must have foundations outside language. Moreover, it implies that ontology is soft. The meaning of words is not hardwired in the structure of reality but rather, is written by us, by our practices and uses of them. This makes understanding the meaning of words like universality, humanity and cosmopolitanism a superficial exercise; an exercise that 'stays on the surface of language' or, less poetically, that keeps us engaged in understanding the multifarious human practices of 'humanity' for example. Such practices may well include some of the cosmopolitans referred to in the first section and their academic practices of explanation, but it also can include anyone else who uses the word humanity or evokes it. For example, the claim 'I'm human too' spoken from the bloodied and broken jaw of someone being tortured for being a 'terrorist' isn't best understood as an act of naming I suggest.[7] Rather, it is an act that emphasizes that the torturer's practice of humanity is violent and clearly excludes *them* and, moreover, that the people who are doing the torturing are responsible for creating this violent, exclusionary version of humanity.

In sum, the metaphysical urge to dig to find a 'below-the-world foundation' is where we run up against the limits of language. There is no below the surface of language that language represents and, therefore, there are no foundations for cosmopolitanism, universality and humanity. If this is so, then our attempts to

---

[7] It seems to me that the person is not saying, 'You have made a category mistake. I am a human, too.' On the contrary, he is calling into question the very configuration of the category itself.

understand them 'may in no way interfere with the actual use of language; it can in the end only describe it. For it cannot give it any foundation either. It leaves everything as it is' (Wittgenstein 1958: 124). In that sense I, along with Wittgenstein, am proposing that inquiring about cosmopolitanism, universality and humanity is flat/superficial. In this very specific sense, 'nothing is hidden' because everything lies on the surface of language (ibid.: 126). There is, as I hope this section has shown, no need to defend cosmopolitan commitments to universality or humanity with further commitments to essentialism and foundationalism. Universality, humanity and cosmopolitanism are plenty meaningful enough without foundations. I suggest instead that the ontological basis upon which a defence to cosmopolitan commitments to universality and humanity can be mounted are superficial and soft. It is to this that I turn next.

(Im)possible Universality

I want to defend universality, no matter what its form, simply because it serves as a reminder for particular purposes which I, personally, hold to be ethico-politically desirable. I want to defend universalism because it must always fail at representation. I absolutely will not defend it because it can succeed now or possibly in the future. For me, the ethics of universality lies in it never being fully possible — its grammatical (im)possibility.

Before I go any further, let me explicitly say that I am not offering a new, different kind of universalism. My greatest hope is that I'm offering no 'thing', and adding nothing whatsoever. I hope that the universality that I am defending 'leaves everything as it is' (ibid.: 124).

Universality is a fantastic word because, with no need to get metaphysical at all, in everyday usage its meaning always evokes implications of all cases and/or everyone. It's an all or nothing kind of word. It makes no sense to say, in ordinary language, 'That's about 38 per cent universal' or 'That's a lot universal' for example. Were one to say such things, we could reply, 'You seem to have misunderstood the word universal.' Leaving metaphysics aside then, I would like to defend universality and our uses (practices) of it, whether in language games of cosmopolitanism, international relations theory, language games of universal human rights, or everyday language, for example, because it always evokes senses of all and/or everyone. That it makes such an all embracing universal claim leaves open, always, the possibility of questioning, whether it does include everyone and/or all cases of something. All it takes to throw universality into a crisis of meaning where it is no longer universal is to find one example of exclusion; one person who is left out; one case that isn't covered and so on. After all, the meaning of universality seems to have gone awry if someone claims, 'Well, never mind that my understanding of universal humanity doesn't include humans who are suspected terrorists in the "war on terror", it's still universal.'

The first reason why I want to defend universality, then, is a very superficial one. The use of the word is always an invitation that asks whether there are any exceptions — asks if we have drawn lines (distinctions), where and how hard — and I want to defend the ethics of such an invitation. Personally, I want to accept the invitation as an ethico-political opportunity to challenge the practices of hardness that universality can render conspicuous. We may find that staying on the surface of language is an ethico-political practice of challenging the drawing, legitimization, policing, and authority of lines as though they were ontologically hard. As this chapter works towards its end, I will keep revisiting the significance of such an opportunity with the grammatical remarks that follow.

The second reason why I want to defend universality is also superficial and, again, is related to line drawing. Accepting now that we are no longer seduced by the notion that universality names 'the real thing', like a bottle of Coca-Cola™, we are in the business of trying to understand how the meaning of universality is produced. Were we to examine the universal commitments of the cosmopolitans mentioned in the first section of this chapter, we could see that it is a grammar of (im)possibility that produces universality. I openly admit that calling such a grammar (im)possible is nothing deeper than heuristic — shorthand for assembling reminders for the purpose of challenging hardness, in this case.

Each cosmopolitan above, but in very different ways, seeks to identify what constitute the conditions of possibility for cosmopolitanism, including universality. In doing so they are also articulating the conditions of its impossibility. Of course, as the first section of this chapter emphasized amply, the details of what they name differs, but it is not this that matters here. Rather, what I wish to emphasize is that, grammatically speaking,[8] these binary opposites are entirely dependent upon each other and mutually serve a role in producing the meaning of universality; what universality can and cannot mean and what it must include and exclude. We could, only for convenience's sake, summarize these elements of meaning production as (im)possibility.

The reason why I use this rather ugly word, (im)possibility, is to emphasize the relationality, the co-constitution and dependency of each set of conditions on the other for their existence. More to the point, I want to do this because in order to defend a commitment to universality I need to show that the line between possibility and impossibility is ontologically soft not hard. In contrast, were each set of conditions to name different hard objects of reality, the meaning of each would be dependent on such objects as foundations outside language, and thus the meaning of each term would be entirely independent of the other. What (im)possibility emphasizes then is that independent foundations outside language are not where meaning is generated. However, for (im)possible universality to be the case it would require, as well as the insights of the previous section, that it be shown that the distinction (line) between the possible and the impossible cannot be successfully held.

It is difficult to give an example of (im)possibility without going into great detail of specific cosmopolitan thinkers and their language games.[9] It would be a dreadful injustice to the richness and value of their work to generalize. Generalization is, no doubt, just another version of trying to find elements common to all; something I am seeking to avoid here. However, taking Charles Beitz's cosmopolitanism as an example we can say that the conditions of possibility of what he calls the 'ideal' imply its own conditions of impossibility and, at the same time, the conditions of possibility of what he calls the 'non-ideal' (Beitz 1979, 1983, 2005; Pin-Fat 2010). The important thing to note here is that for Beitz cosmopolitanism is expressed in 'ideal theory'. The conditions for it might be feasible

---

[8] 'Grammatically speaking' is referring to a way of understanding that I have developed called a grammatical reading. There is insufficient space to describe it here, but it can be located in Pin-Fat (2010).

[9] See Pin-Fat (2010) for grammatical readings of the universalisms of Charles Beitz, Michael Walzer and Hans J. Morgenthau.

but do not yet actually exist in the non-ideal world of practice. The features of the non-ideal world, for Beitz then, are the conditions of cosmopolitanism's impossibility. Hence, we can say that for him, the conditions of the non-ideal imply its own conditions of impossibility and, at the same time, the conditions of possibility of the ideal. They are co-dependent and co-constitutive. One cannot be without the other. They include each other by exclusion. So, when Beitz outlines the ideal he is outlining its conditions of possibility for cosmopolitanism, universality and a universal moral subject (humanity). He does this explicitly. It's his global original position. In this hypothetical scenario, Beitz is telling us what conditions need to obtain — veil of ignorance, a moral point of view, etc. — for the ideal to be possible. He's drawing a line around the ideal, around what is possible. As he does draw this line, he is simultaneously offering the line as a marker of conditions of impossibility. He's telling us what must not cross the line and those things are the non-ideal, which are basically all the things that the veil of ignorance screens out, like interests attached to nationality, gender and so on. Not only is he telling us what cannot cross the line as non-ideal, he's also offering the line as a shared boundary with the non-ideal and its conditions of possibility. In this case, that the non-ideal's conditions of possibility are all related to interests, situatedness and so on. And it works the other way round too. For the sake of shorthand, because we need it, I'm calling this (im)possibility to render conspicuous how the drawing of lines (between the possible and impossible) produce meaning and do so in relation to each other and inside language.

I want now to defend universality because it must always fail. That is to say, I want to argue that the line between possibility and impossibility necessarily fails because it is porous. This is what relationality implies here. Having cleared the ground so to speak, and staying firmly on the surface of language, I now want to say more about where I see the space and time for an ethics of universality which I am defending. To argue my answer rather bluntly, I see the space and time for it in failure and as ever present. It isn't anywhere special. There's no digging beneath language and no great search needed. It's right here and now. I want to say we have left everything as it is. It's why I believe that engaging with universality grammatically (that is, superficially on the surface of language) may matter ethico-politically much more than we think. So, two questions: What do the ever-present spaces of the failure of universality look like and why are they so ethico-politically important?

With regard to the first question, they look leaky! Because I see impossibility and possibility including each other by exclusion, each is leaky and bleeds into the other. The line between them is necessarily porous. They can't ever fully keep each other out as each other's absolute other because they internally, as well as externally, belong together in their co-constitution. That's why no exorcism can banish the ghost of the other that haunts it and why universality always fails. If, as I am suggesting, forms of universality are (im)possible, they are always leaky. Practices of universality, even when they try to draw the lines as hard lines, contain within themselves their own failure all the time. That means the invitation I talked of earlier is always there. And, in practice, the invitation is often accepted. The language games around universality always provide the space and opportunity to say, because leakiness/softness makes it so, 'I am not included in your universal' and to unmake it. (Im)possible universalism, then, isn't another form of universality to add to the others. It's just a grammatical remark about universality and its meaning in use (practice).

That the line between impossibility and possibility is porous, and is not anchored to (founded upon) objects which either side of the line name, means that it's not a hard line, grammatically speaking. Turning to the second question then, why is this so ethico-politically important and to be defended as a grammatical feature of universality? It matters because it brings us firmly and inescapably back into the world of ethico-political practice as opposed to abstracted, theoretical, metaphysical digging expeditions. Grammatical questions now become ethico-political practical ones about line drawing: How are lines drawn? Where are they drawn? Who draws them? Who polices them and how? What are the effects of these lines on people's lives and subjectivity? What must be assumed to draw them? And most important of all, how do some answers to these questions add up to a set of practices which draw lines as hard lines, as though they located some inevitable ontological reality?

Viewing grammar this way implies that politics is the practice of drawing lines everywhere. Politics has unavoidable ethical implications because it draws lines (makes distinctions) between what kinds of lives and subjects are politically permitted as possible or impossible: politically legitimate or illegitimate, legal or illegal, human or inhuman, masculine or feminine, normal or abnormal, desirable or undesirable, true or false, and so on (Edkins and Pin-Fat 2004, 2005; Pin-Fat and Stern 2005). When, as all too often happens, such lines are drawn as hard lines, the very possibility for politics is expunged. When a line is taken to demarcate the difference between ontological phenomena (by naming them), the line becomes, seemingly, unquestionable. After all, if such lines really did represent reality, we are faced with a *fait accompli*; a reality that cannot be changed — 'This is how things are' (Wittgenstein 1958: 114). It becomes illegitimate, supposedly, to ask why the lines have been drawn where they have and how they have excluded certain forms of life. Political contestation of the lines themselves is expunged as illegitimate by the very practice of drawing a hard line between legitimacy and illegitimacy (politics) itself. However, if, as I have argued, lines are (im)possible, they cannot be hard in this sense and so the possibility and occasion for politics can never be fully expunged. Ethico-political engagement is always possible because of grammatical leakiness. This is why the significance of grammar has 'roots [that] are as deep in us as the forms of our language and their significance is as great as the importance of our language' and is much more than we think (theorize) it is (ibid.: 111). The 'more' is the world we live in with other people. This grammatical reading of universality has tried to show that the surface of language is ethico-political because it traces the contours of practices that make possible and impossible, rather than name, lives being lived.

Defending universality without foundations is a defence of staying on the surface of language; of challenging the hardness of line drawing. It is a defence of one of the most obviously available practices of politically contesting the drawing of lines because universality draws them so blatantly and grandly. (Im)possible universalism, the porosity of the line between possibility and impossibility, reminds us that attempts at holding the line must always eventually fail. And, ever-present conditions of failure are what make ethico-political contestation and engagement possible. Such a possibility is the ever-present invitation that universality's lack of foundations offers us in practice. Thankfully, such an invitation is often accepted. There exists a rich plurality of cosmopolitanisms simply because the matter of what it can and should be has not been settled. Nor will it ever be since no foundations exist upon which to settle it. I suggest that the continuing ethico-political contestations over the meaning of cosmopolitanism and what it may promise, whether heaven or hell, far from producing incoherent chaos shows that a lack of foundations is what accounts for its present vitality, plurality and dynamism for change.

Mysticism and Humanity

So far I've argued that universality's lack of foundations can be read as ethico-politically desirable. In this section, I want to conclude with a couple of implications of a soft ontology — 'antifoundationalism' — for understanding humanity. The first consists of some meditations on Wittgenstein's enigmatic claim: 'Whereof one cannot speak thereof one must remain silent' (Wittgenstein 1922: 7.0). This is commonly known as his mysticism. The second deploys Lewis Carroll's 'Hunting of the Snark' to suggest the desirability of what might be called 'Boojum ethics'.

Lewis Carroll's poem, 'The Hunting of the Snark: An Agony in Eight Fits', is the tale of a crew of eight men who sail the sea in search of a Snark. A character called Bellman captains them. Bellman has a map. It is a sheet of paper that is 'a perfect and absolute blank'. In the end, the crew don't capture a Snark. It turns out that the Snark was a Boojum. That's the tricky thing about Snarks. Until you encounter them, you can't tell if they are the sort of Snark which are, in fact, a Boojum. And if you do find yourself face to face with a Boojum, 'you will softly and suddenly vanish away, and never be met with again' (Carroll 1891). What I want to talk about in this section are the virtues of blank maps and Snarks being Boojums; the mystical.

Maps, unless they are Bellman's, literally consist of lines that represent the world accurately. So accurate are they that they provide the means to locate one's destination, where one is, and perhaps, most of all, chart the most direct course towards the destination one seeks. What I've tried to show in this chapter is that forms of understanding which rest on language as representation are versions of theory as map drawing, whereby the lines are drawn hard and deep so that a course may be safely charted towards a cosmopolitan destination. I want to suggest that these cartographers won't find what they want (let's call it a Snark) but end up encountering a Boojum instead. The Boojum is the failure of representation, (im)possibility, and it's the Boojum that I am defending as a defence of cosmopolitanism without foundations.

How and why does a hunting expedition for a Snark begin in the first place? I suggest that it all has to do with what we think we're doing when we theorize things like cosmopolitanism, humanity and universality. The idea that language represents reality misleads us here, too. It seduces us into believing that we are mapping reality. Wittgenstein's 'Tractatus Logico-Philosophicus' is the apotheosis of mapping propositions as completely as possible where propositions depict possible states of affairs in the world. It is a picture of reason and is an entirely theoretical endeavour. In the 'Tractatus' he explored only six propositions; the first of which was simply 'The world is everything that is the case' (Wittgenstein 1922: 1.0). That's the world for you right there in one proposition! Wittgenstein's complex numbering system of his remarks is renowned and often times adopted. The number 5.4711, for example, refers to the primary proposition '5', the fourth component of that proposition, the seventh component of the fourth, and the first component of the first component of the seventh component.[10] The numbering system of the 'Tractatus' was designed to represent the intricacies of how elements of reality relate to each other. It amounts to an incredibly detailed map, we might say. The most interesting thing is what Wittgenstein concludes after all this detailed, laborious, cartographic effort. He ends the 'Tractatus' with one last proposition: 'Whereof one cannot speak thereof one must remain silent'; so he does.[11]

What can we make of this? I think the first thing is the failure of theoretical endeavours of this kind of mapping to satisfy our need for an answer to questions of universality and humanity. Wittgenstein invites us to 'surmount' and recognize as 'senseless' the very notion that we might have made a hard connection between propositions and the way the world is and, therefore, successfully mapped

---

[10] 'Propositions are truth-functions of elementary propositions. (An elementary proposition is a truth-function of itself)' (Wittgenstein 1922: 5.0).

[11] My point is not to engage in the thriving academic field of Wittgenstein commentary here, but to render conspicuous what I take to be the relationship between this kind of mysticism and pictures of the subject (humanity).

cosmopolitanism (ibid.: 6.54). He suggests of such a theorist: 'He must so to speak throw away the ladder, after he has climbed up on it' (ibid.: 6.54). Mixing metaphors I want to emphasize that the lines on the map are akin to the rungs of the ladder. Just as the ladder should be thrown away to 'see the world rightly' so too should the map when all is said and done. The argument I am making in defence of universality is not that the theorizing of any of the cosmopolitans mentioned in the first section of this chapter shouldn't necessarily be done. Rather, my argument here is that the ethico-political value of such endeavours does not lie in the success of the endeavour's outcome, the cosmopolis as answer. Nor does it lie in the act of mapping, nor in the lines that have been drawn through the act of mapping. Instead the ethico-political value of language games of cosmopolitanism is that they remind us that we need to throw away something, and that when we do we may see the world rightly. Put simply, I want to emphasize the point that theorizing in ways that assume a representation of the world — how things really are — show us that we have missed the point. This is their ethico-political value and what makes a defence of universality, no matter what its form, defensible, but only once the ladder has been thrown away.

So, proposition 7 of the 'Tractatus' reminds us that we need to throw away something — our belief that theorizing can represent (map) cosmopolitanism, universality, humanity or anything else. We need to lose our desire to understand the world as though language/ ethico-political practice has ontological depth. We have missed the ethico-political point if we hold onto our ladder. Another way of putting it is to say, 'Not how the world is, is the mystical, but that it is' (ibid.: 6.44). The mystical, in this context, is Bellman's blank piece of paper. In the end, the point about theorizing in these ways is that we are no worse off with a blank map; silence.

So much for the mystical in relation to Bellman's blank sheet of paper — but what of Boojums and Snarks? The interesting thing about claims that seek the foundations of cosmopolitanism in its reference to humanity (let's call it a Snark) is that it seduces us into a particular sort of search; a search to capture what is, ethically, most important about being human. Were we able to capture it we would, so the story goes, have hit upon the foundations of our cosmopolitanism. After all, for whom is cosmopolitanism designed to deliver the universal promises of the cosmopolis if not for the whole of humanity equally? We can simply say, foci of this kind send us on a hunting of the Snark (humanity). Lewis Carroll's poem tells us that if we encounter a Snark that is Boojum we 'will softly and suddenly vanish away, and never be met with again'. There is virtue in encountering a Boojum I wish to suggest.

The belief that we can capture the most essential features of humanity — what makes us human (Snark) — by representing it arises from the misinterpretation of our forms of language as deep (Wittgenstein 1958: 111). I've already argued that when we do we encounter the failure of the endeavour and a reminder that we need reminding of what it is that we've done. Humanity cannot be fully captured by language because, whatever it might be, language does not serve to name or locate what is essential/deep about us. Attempts at capturing subjectivity simply remind us that our mistaken attachment to the notion that we *are*, universally, that which has been represented is an opportunity to make such representations of humanity 'softly and suddenly vanish away, and never be met with again'. Rather than seeing the lines that form representations of humanity as hard, deep lines, we would see them for what they are, as soft. So soft, in fact, that their significance to us as markers of what ontologically divides us from one another and/or from what is possible and legitimate may vanish never to be encountered as such a 'thing' again. It's an opportunity to kick away the ladder once and for all and do something else that 'may in no way interfere with the actual use of language; it can in the end only describe it. For it cannot give it any foundation either. It leaves everything as it is' (ibid.: 124).

Just as the world is superficial/mystical, so too is humanity. To paraphrase Wittgenstein, it's not how we are that is the mystical but that we are. There are so many ways of being in the world; so many ethico-political language games of humanity, so many overlapping practices of subjectivity that each person enacts and is subject to, so many experiences of being human beyond representational capture that to map them all and the details of their terrain is an impossible endeavour, let alone finding the elements which are common to all. And as I've tried to argue, we're missing the point when we try to. We can stay on the surface of language and engage with the ethico-political practices of representations of humanity and their effects — 'Boojum ethics'. We can trace how attempts at universally capturing (representing) 'us' are missing the point and are instead practices of determining the possibility and impossibility of specific people living in specific ways. Given that, I have next to nothing to say about humanity, in itself, except that there is nothing to be said. To remain silent about that should return us to giving due attention and moral consideration to the multiple, ethico-political practices of attempts to say something as the drawing of hard lines.

⤸

Acknowledgements

Thanks to Routledge for permission to reproduce parts of my book, *Universality, Ethics and International Relations: A Grammatical Reading* (2010).

References

Archibugi, Daniele. 2008. *The Global Commonwealth of Citizens: Towards Cosmopolitan Democracy*, Princeton University Press, Princeton, NJ.

Archibugi, Daniele and David Held (eds). 1995. *Cosmopolitan Democracy: An Agenda for a New World Order*, Polity Press, Cambridge.

Beck, Ulrich. 2006. *The Cosmopolitan Vision*, Polity Press, Cambridge.

Beck, Ulrich and Natan Sznaider. 2006. 'Unpacking Cosmopolitanism for the Social Sciences: A Research Agenda', *The British Journal of Sociology* 57(1): 1–23.

Beitz, Charles R. 1979. *Political Theory and International Relations*, Princeton University Press, Princeton.

———. 1983. 'Cosmopolitan Ideals and National Sentiment', *Journal of Philosophy* 80(10): 591–99.

———. 2005.'Reflections', *Review of International Studies* 31(2): 409–23.

Çali, Başak. 2006. 'On Legal Cosmopolitanism: Divergences in Political Theory and International Law', *Leiden Journal of International Law* 19(4): 1149–63.

Carroll, Lewis. 1891. *The Hunting of the Snark: An Agony in Eight Fits*, Macmillan, New York.

Edkins, Jenny and Véronique Pin-Fat. 2004. 'Life, Power, Resistance', in Jenny Edkins, Véronique Pin-Fat and Michael J. Shapiro (eds), *Sovereign Lives: Power in Global Politics*, Routledge, New York.

———. 2005. 'Through the Wire: Relations of Power and Relations of Violence', *Millennium: Journal of International Studies* 34(1): 1–24.

Fine, Robert. 2003. 'Taking the "Ism" out of Cosmopolitanism', *European Journal of Social Theory* 6(4): 451–70.

Fossum, John Erik. 2011. 'Review Essay: A Cosmopolitan Constellation?' *European Journal of Social Theory* 14(2) : 235–48.

Holton, Robert J. 2009. *Cosmopolitanisms: New Thinking and New Directions*, Palgrave Macmillan.

Pogge, Thomas W. 1992. 'Cosmopolitanism and Sovereignty', *Ethics* 103(1): 48–75.

Pin-Fat, Véronique. 2000. '(Im)possible Universalism: Reading Human Rights in World Politics', *Review of International Studies* 26(4): 663–74.

———. 2010. *Universality, Ethics and International Relations: A Grammatical Reading*, edited by Jenny Edkins and Nick Vaughan-Williams, Routledge, London.

Pin-Fat, Véronique and Maria Stern. 2005. 'The Scripting of Private Jessica Lynch: Biopolitics, Gender and the "Feminization" of the US Military', *Alternatives: Global, Local, Political* 30(1): 25–53.

Rorty, Richard. 1980. *Philosophy and the Mirror of Nature*, Basil Blackwell, Oxford.

Wittgenstein, Ludwig. 1922. *Tractatus Logico-Philosophicus*, trans. C. K. Ogden, Routledge & Kegan Paul, London.

———. 1958. *Philosophical Investigations*, trans. G. E. M. Anscombe, edited by G. E. M. Anscombe and R. Rhees, 3rd edition, Basil Blackwell, Oxford.

Wonicki, Rafal. 2009. 'Cosmopolitanism and Liberalism: Kant and Contemporary Liberal Cosmopolitanism', *Synthesis Philosophica* 48(2): 271–80.

5

Who are the People of the World?

Sudhir Chella Rajan

Political theory has from the start been troubled by tensions between the 'I' and the 'we', the latter imputing a collective will and identity, the former associated with individuality, rights or heroism. While I might recognize myself as a political agent and leader, it is 'we the people' who have the greater mobilizing force of political action, and never more explicitly than in the formation of constitutions. But constitution-making ironically starts by calling forth the name of the people and almost immediately subsumes their identity within the dominion of individual rights and duties, on the one hand, and the protective sphere of the state, on the other (Lefort 1988). As such, the meaning of the people stays ambiguous. In one interpretation, they are collectively the agents of political change; in another, they are a diffuse mass signifying a particular cultural practice and a mood (for example, nationalism) that drives political action. Alternatively, they are the 'subalterns' who are affected by political change, who occasionally forge weapons of the weak, but whose force is unpredictable and occasionally violent. In most of these meanings, there is an undercurrent of anxiety that political theory expresses towards the very idea, which reaches its apogee in democratic theory. After all, when the people are the sovereign power in whose name politics is enacted, then a lack of clarity about who they are is especially disturbing.[1]

---

[1] While I recognize the new interest in the multitude against the people (Virno 2003; Hardt and Negri 2004), I also share Malcolm Bull's (2005) contention that there is a conceptual confusion in this argument, which ends up pitting two sides of the same category, without addressing the more important problem of political agency. A lexical shift from people to multitude may seem attractive, but it does not fundamentally resolve the problem posed for democratic theory.

Throughout the history of democratic thought, this question has been resolved in different ways, with varying results and residual tensions. Some of the earliest inklings of the political significance of the people appear in Homer, who had three words for them — *laos, demos* and *plethos* — although, even here, the ambivalence in definitions is salient. The *laoi* refer to the followers of a leader, whereas a *demos* is a group of individuals that share a name and a common territory and are aware of their identity as a community. The *plethos*, in contrast, is the undifferentiated multitude, except that all three terms, according to Dean Hammer (2009: 27), could 'refer to the mass of disorderly people . . . and the *plethos* are some-times portrayed sympathetically'. The people might have a certain heroism associated with them or could be passive and silent when required to take action. What remains constant is the notion that they belong to a community and have the ability to play a part in legitimating or even directing decisions, while at the same time disclosing a recurrent volatility.

In modern political theory, the category of the people assumes an imagined identity which is analogous to and coeval with that of the nation. For Machiavelli, both in *The Prince* and *Discourses on Livy*, the mass of the people provide the reason of state to the republic and, correspondingly, their site of political engagement is a given social imaginary within the territorial entity of a state. Machiavelli's people are truest to the classical traditions, whereas Hobbes and Locke, notwithstanding their different political phi-losophies, consider the people as un-tethered and uncoordinated individuals in the state of nature until hypothetical contracts bring them into a confined political society that then forms a collective identity. By then the people appear both as political actors *qua* citizens and as a mass to be manipulated; yet they have significance only in relation to the hyphenated city-state or nation-state. As such, politics proceeds with the idea of popular sovereignty adjust-ing with the prevailing circumstances and aiming to sort out the legitimacy of political action along with normative expectations on the people. For liberals, a sovereign people that plays by the rules is not only a strong and capable political entity; it is by definition also a morally right one, although the resulting institutional forms may be elaborated in multiple ways. For Marxists, too, there are rules, but these imply action to achieve social justice, although the means for achieving this is material/historical rather than reason/ contract. All in all, the people are broadly identified as those who can practise 'good citizenship', whatever the character of the polity itself. In modern times, territory and nationalism have typically served to clarify and limit the otherwise substantial challenges of political agency and action but need not be universal conditions for citizenship.

One might therefore reasonably ask the question: In a cosmopolitan democracy, the people are sovereign, but who are the people of the world? Partly because of cosmopolitanism's liberal origins, its version of the global people does not seem to find easy traction within any of these traditions of political theory and is often loosely transmuted into the more ambiguous and apolitical idea of humanity, or takes on a minimalist position around human rights, or is forced to concede ground to the conception of a plurality of 'peoples' living in harmony with each other. More often than not, the background political identity of a global people as such is elided in most forms of cosmopolitanism, indeed, even more so than in state-centred theories of the people, where at least the territorially bound community is also a political association that has a specific meaning and purpose. Cosmopolitans seem to believe that the 'overlapping communities of fate' provide reasons but not the intention for the political identity of a global people as such, although I want to argue otherwise in this chapter, in which I try to explore some of the theoretical loose ends implied in the cosmopolitan aspiration towards a global politics. I contend that there may be some conceptual confusion as a result of arbitrary criteria for membership in a people, which recent theorists on multiculturalism have already helped to displace. The notion that the political identity of a people implies long-term commitments as a collective, as well as common historic memories, customs and beliefs, is problematic if we are to fold multiculturalism integrally into the body of democratic theory, rather than as the appendix of an already existing nation. Cosmopolitanism's aporia in this regard is understandable but awkward, especially if it needs to make claims to provide a liberating framework for realizing not merely justice beyond borders, but a political society that is global.

The term 'people' may indeed exist, as Lefort (1988: 109) has argued, only 'by virtue of the speech [as] an arbitrary name which is assumed to emanate from within them and which at the same time names them', yet with the birth of democratic politics, speech and naming are virtually everything. Cosmopolitan political theory, as an extension of democracy, cannot therefore ignore the question; rather, it is the elephant in the room that will not be named, but must be if a de-territorial political community is to be mobilized. My limited contribution towards resolving this conundrum is as follows: while the notion of a global people with a single social imaginary may be utopian, post-national politics involving multiple and overlapping political identities have already come into view at different scales. If these transient post-national collectivities were successfully to engage with global power more effectively than ever before and thereby constitute a political will of the people of the world, their repeated acts of power could potentially bring to vision their identity and expand their authority iteratively. Such reflexive exercises on the parts of many may well make up the identity of the people of the world.

Peoples or One People?

For liberal political theorists, Immanuel Kant's moral cosmopolitanism, emphasizing the universality of shared values, generates a challenge, which has frequently been elided since the 18th century, with the rise of nation-states in Europe and North America. For Kant himself, in his famous 'Perpetual Peace' essay, a tension arises between *ius cosmopoliticum* and *ius civitatis*, between the 'law of world citizenship, so far as men and states are considered as citizens of a universal state of men, in their external mutual relationships' (2007: 26), on the one hand, and the civil law governing men in a nation, on the other. States provide the internal scaffolding for giving individual members their domestic moral and legal order, but relations among states and towards individuals ought to be governed on the basis of universal hospitality. But eventually, 'the human race can gradually be brought closer and closer to a constitution establishing world citizenship' (ibid.: 22). After all, 'originally, no one had more right than another to a particular part of the earth' (ibid.: 21).

If world citizenship is in the offing, preparation for it, in Kant's view, ought to be through the development of a federation of free states, each constituted as republics. Nevertheless, what we finally end up with is not a single state of all of humanity, because:

> That would be contradictory, since a state implies the relation of a superior (legislating) to an inferior (obeying), i.e., the people, and many nations in one state would then constitute only one nation. This contradicts the presupposition, for here we have to weigh the rights of nations against each other so far as they are distinct states and not amalgamated into one (Kant 2007: 17).

The nation, then, defines a people, and herein lies an uneasy relationship with Kant's universalist impulse. Where the individual has inviolable natural rights and a violation of right in one part of the world is felt all over it, these rights can only be enforced by individual sovereign states, not on the basis of a universal law and a common political and legal framework. The only possible resolution is that peoples are not organic units as such but accidental associations that are in various stages of development towards civilization. Over time, one might then be tempted to imagine, such a universal framework will in fact arise. In fact, Kant's 'Fifth Thesis' in the *Idea for a Universal History from a Cosmopolitan Point of View* (1784) is quite explicit on this point: 'The greatest problem for the human race, to the solution of which Nature drives man, is the achievement of a universal civic society which administers law among men' (Kant 1986: 254). But even so, Kant is quite insistent that only a given people can conceivably form a political community and that the problem concerning all of humanity concerns building a moral rather than political community. A world state would create a 'soulless despotism', since every existing state already has an internal constitution, which one could interpret as its political culture. And yet one cannot but ask the question as to whether or not it is conceivable that a worldwide political culture might arise from this very diversity. That is a question that Kant surprisingly does not veer towards.

In John Rawls' formulation, a more robust attempt is made to create an ideal structure of a people, separate from a state and having 'their own internal governments, which may be constitutional liberal democratic or non-liberal but decent governments' (Rawls 1999: 2). But these domestic societies are essentially 'closed and self-contained' (ibid.: 86) and, in his framing of the principles of relationship even among liberal democratic peoples, Kant's position on the undesirability of a world government is simply restated without further justification:

> These principles will also, I assume, make room for various forms of cooperative associations and federations among peoples, but will not affirm a world-state. Here I follow Kant's lead in 'Perpetual Peace' (1795) in thinking that a world government — by which I mean a unified political regime with the legal powers normally exercised by central governments — would either be a global despotism or else would rule over a fragile empire torn by frequent civil strife as various regions and peoples tried to gain their political freedom and autonomy (ibid.: 36).

Moreover, for Rawls, no matter how arbitrary the history of the formation of a people's territory might be, it is imperative that their government, as their representative agent, take responsibility for protecting the asset.

> It does not follow from the fact that boundaries are historically arbitrary that their role in the Law of Peoples cannot be justified. On the contrary, to fix on their arbitrariness is to fix on the wrong thing. In the absence of a world-state, there must be boundaries of some kind, which when viewed in isolation will seem arbitrary, and depend to some degree on historical circumstances (ibid.: 39).

Here, again, since the world-state is an absurdity, or at best a recipe for global despotism, it is the relationship within and among peoples that Rawls is interested in pursuing, not the existence and structure of a global people as such. What largely seems to clinch this position is the way the world is divided up in his idealization between liberal and non-liberal peoples. While the former have an obligation of being tolerant towards the latter, it is limited to those non-liberal peoples who Rawls characterizes as 'decent', which is to say, their religious, philosophical doctrines relate to a 'reasonable political conception of justice and its public reason' (ibid.: 59). In a world so divided, one cannot ensure that reason will prevail and that either liberal or decent non-liberals will be dominant in a world government; hence, it is best to leave things alone.

I shall return to this argument shortly, but it is useful to note some obvious challenges even with the domestic characterization of Rawls' people. As Seyla Benhabib and others have pointed out, ignoring the history of formation of actual peoples is problematic, given that their so-called moral and political culture is in fact shaped on the basis of power, oppression and ideology, and contested domestically along axes of gender, class and ethnicity. Liberal peoples need not always be decent in the Rawlsian sense if, for instance, the undercurrent of racial or gender injustice prevails, notwithstanding institutions of public reason, such as courts and legislative action, which might only serve to blunt its edge slightly. It is the quality and outcomes of internal political negotiations relating to both cultural and political identity as a 'we'-people that appears to be at risk. It seems unlikely that a contingently formed community through the logic of liberal or decent non-liberal political self-legitimation would function as a relatively homogenous group, at least in terms of their commitment to public reason of a particular sort.

> "We, the people," is a tension-riven formula, which seeks to contain the universalizing aspirations of rights claims and democratic sovereignty struggles within the confines of a historically situated collectivity. Such a collectivity has its "others" within and "without" (Benhabib 2004: 89).

In terms of the 'without', Rawls' special idealization of liberal and decent non-liberal peoples is that they are membership societies that are not only closed to new members but also comprise solely workable types of people; workable for their ability to engage with each other through public reason from their isolated corners of the world. What about the aliens: strangers, refugees, stateless people and other drifters that enter into the people's lives and whose engagement may serve to go against the grain of a people's republican ideals? And, worse, what if their discourse and practice grate against liberal principles within liberal democratic societies? Benhabib does not really tackle this last possibility, but it is worth noting that these questions collectively create some awkwardness in that foregrounding the long-term stability of existing peoples implies attributing to any given people a strong cultural or social 'glue', but that may in fact have gotten unravelled through the course of history. Indeed, it may even be the case that political 'glue', in terms of a common framework of political goals, may be lacking notwithstanding strong institutions. What that means is that the best way to construe these peoples is in terms of already existing states, whose contingent and troubled histories would have produced equally accidental successes or failures.

Another Possible People

That much of liberal political theory should find it necessary to forego a universal ideal of a political community and hamper itself by focusing on the particular features of historically contingent peoples might itself seem odd, considering its otherwise grandiose theoretical sensibility. For the purposes of this chapter, I choose to leave that question aside, assuming that postcolonial theory has a rich array of explanations for this apparent dissembling. Instead, I choose to explore whether it is possible to construe the people differently and thereby make some allowance for considering the standing of a global political community.

First, both Kant and Rawls seem to have treated political communities as needing a strong sense of *communitas* in order for individuals to bind themselves to each other in a given territory and thereby endure as a people (cf. Turner 1995). This view suggests that individual members form bonds, such as nationalism or republicanism, through rituals and powerful liminal experiences, and that the more poignant these experiences, the more likely it is for their political union to be stable. But both also seem to indicate that it is only a people thus formed who are legitimate, and that the sovereignty they claim on this basis is inviolate. Yet, they would probably want to insist that it is the impersonal institutions of the state, its civic order, as it were, that keep a people's politics functioning, not the cultural ties of *Gemeinschaft*.

If tying the legitimacy of a people to its cultural identity is anti-liberal, basing it on some specific historical origin that creates a societal and even political identity is equally problematic, as both Benhabib (2004) and Sofia Näsström (2007) have argued in different ways. After all, new individuals are continually born into a society, are free to move out and, especially in liberal societies that seek to embrace multiculturalism, it is quite likely that their very composition and character will change over time. The original, defining identity of a people is never constant, even in the most conservative societies; in fact, it is the remarkably recent origins of the self-fashioning of reactionary forms of nationalism (for example, Islamists, Hindutva activists) that have caught the attention of political theorists everywhere. The legitimacy of a people has to be reaffirmed recurrently, but there are only contingent reasons why such affirmation needs to take place among the same territorially bound group. In Nancy Fraser's formulation, the 'Keynesian-Westphalian frame ... gerrymanders political space at the expense of the poor and despised' (Fraser 2005: 78), which suggests that a different districting is possible and along with it the constitution of different peoples.

If the arbitrariness of the peoples' origins as well as the illiberal tendencies at their core were to be acknowledged, then liberal theorists would really have to consider in what ways our 'overlapping communities of fate' could be organized into a much larger political community. The fact that modern political theory has at its genesis a focus on the *polis*, which was later extended to the larger territorial state only on the basis of the historical gerrymandering accidents of various sorts, suggests that we perhaps ought to understand the character of the *polis* that constitutes a people. Modern urban theory since Henri Lefebvre and Jane Jacobs provides us some answers: cities generate synekism because of spatial proximity, which in turn stimulates the rich social life of an urban collectivity.

At the other end of the spectrum, it may well be argued that in a practical sense actually existing states represent the largest possible social imaginaries, so that one could at best speak of the Russian, Chinese or Indian people, but not of larger units with much coherence. Indeed, the current difficulties with the European imaginary may fit into this logic. Nevertheless, I still believe it is possible to identify a global people who serve as a referent for the many transnational social movements that mark our times. One might be tempted to take Lefebvre's statement seriously, and thereby to its logical limit, that 'society has been completely urbanized' (Lefebvre 2003: 1), and postulate that our globalized metropolitan society constitutes the people of the world. But this would simply serve to raise further questions about the character of our so-called global metropolis that are beyond the scope of this chapter.

Instead, I argue that the most fecund approach to identifying the people of the world may actually be to weaken the onus placed on the people, from having a specific identity as a collectivity with a definite history and culture to having particular domains where such social imaginaries are constructed at transnational scales. Such a concept, which is not as dependent on the existence of homogenizing or, for that matter, hegemonic tendencies that appear in much of liberal political theory, may lead us to a more internally consistent cosmopolitical understanding and action that is likely to meet with greater success. Three examples may provide some illustration of this approach.

The first is the movement to establish a Global Parliament, expressed by several civil society organizations and given a somewhat clearer focus in an influential article by Richard Falk and Andrew Strauss (2001). Falk and Strauss propose that an assembly of representatives from around the world be established primarily by civil society or through a formal treaty process. While the assembly would not be formally sanctioned by states, any opposition from governments could potentially be countered with sufficient media and grassroots support.

> Citizens in favor could make their voices heard through popular, fair, and serious elections ... Because its authority would come directly from the global citizenry, it could refute the claim that states are bound only by laws to which they give their consent. Henceforth, the ability to opt out of collective efforts to protect the environment, control or eliminate weapons, safeguard human rights, or otherwise protect the global community could be challenged (ibid.: 215).

I interpret Falk and Strauss' argument to be that the activity of actually developing a global parliament as a parallel (not mock) transnational representative body with inclusive participation from 'people power' from around the world can prove that legitimate and effective policies can be formulated without having to rely on international negotiation. More significantly, the activity need not require the formation of a single political community as such, but invokes the *idea* of a global people as an entity that could actually enjoy some semblance of political representation from them. The actual power of the parliament may not be manifest at once, but its demonstration effect could be considerable and lead to the construction of a global social imaginary, much like any other nation building exercise.

The second is Anne-Marie Slaughter's (2004a) concept of 'disaggregated sovereignty', which she describes as an already existing set of global networks, both formal and informal, of government officials, legislators, judges, and others who appear to be developing alternative modes of governing, drawing on lessons from each other, but also exchanging decisions, providing technical assistance and developing joint strategies.

> As commercial and civic organizations have already discovered, their networked form is ideal for providing the speed and flexibility necessary to function effectively in an information age. But unlike amorphous 'global policy networks', in which it is never clear who is exercising power on behalf of whom, these are networks comprised of national government officials — appointed by elected officials or directly elected themselves. Best of all, they can perform many of the functions of a world government — legislation, administration and adjudication — without the form (ibid.: 160).

Disaggregated sovereignty provides a glimpse again into the potential formation of another people on behalf of whom these legislators and officials are taking action. Indeed, Slaughter suggests that as formal principles are developed to build in safeguards against lack of loss of accountability, they could themselves be understood as part of what she terms a 'global trans-governmental constitution', much like what one may associate with something created by a global parliament. The creation of virtual information spaces and the creation of global policy networks together with transnational civil society organizations, corporations and other private networks are in many ways emerging from these developments, further blurring the single-identity requirement of the people on whose behalf their activities are forming.

Since around the time of the Bretton Woods agreement, the world has seen several international regimes to which countries cede their sovereignty. Thus, the Nuclear Non-Proliferation Treaty (NPT) has required all but eight countries (three that did not sign it plus five that were 'grandfathered' as nuclear powers) around the world to be subject to what might ordinarily be called intrusive regulations. More recently, the World Trade Organization (WTO) has routinely developed rulings that even the most powerful countries in the world have been forced to comply with. The European Union (EU) is yet another example of rule-making at the supranational level, a concession that was agreed to by the member states on the understanding that it was of advantage to all to have a continent-wide regime to govern certain issues like standards for education, health and the environment. It is not that these institutions are not resisted; there are of course bitter conflicts related to all the examples mentioned above. But the commitment of national leaders to maintain them is sufficiently strong that it seems unlikely that they will unravel easily. Moreover, in each case, their legitimacy has already been sealed by the countries themselves, whose legislatures ratified them in the past. In other words, the political question of whether or not to allow outside institutions to play a role in domestic affairs has already been addressed historically, arguably in a reasonable way, inasmuch as the parties that took the decision were legitimate representatives. Barring the rare case of a later government backtracking on an international agreement formed by a previous one, many supranational regimes seem surprisingly durable.

National governments are themselves forming a variety of networks while recognizing the need for broader strategic cooperation on critical issues. Examples can be found in the Alliance of Small Island States, which is focused on addressing the impact of climate change, and the G20, which is developing a concerted developing country trade strategy. Sometimes, these networks are less formally defined and comprise government officials and legislators. For instance, the Global Legislators for a Balanced Environment (GLOBE) was founded in 1989, primarily in the form of an environmental non-governmental organization (NGO) with parliamentarians who seek to share information and potentially develop coordinated policy on the environment. There are several other networks of legislators, judges and bureaucrats through which the participants formulate new ideas together and pursue common goals.

In general terms, the tendency is for these types of institutional arrangements to confer rights and solicit responsibilities at different levels based on the principle of subsidiarity, where governing bodies perform tasks that are best suited to their scale of operation. Thus, local authorities may be associated primarily with the management of the local economy, policing functions and service provision of education, housing, transportation, and health care; eco-regional governments would be responsible for the planning aspects of many of these same concerns within the context of ecosystem demands and constraints; continental scale administrations and global politics would be relevant for resolving inter-regional conflicts and managing commerce, and relate generally to matters of worldwide concern.

The last example, which I describe in a little more detail than the other two, relates to the notion of a Biome Stewardship Council (BSC) (Rajan 2008), a transnational governance form that seeks to promote and maintain ecosystem integrity. A biome is a natural ecological unit that is derived from the understanding that forms of life associated together in a similar physical natural environment, latitude, altitude, and terrain share certain common elements by virtue of belonging to a single habitat. While any group of living and non-living things interacting with each other can be considered as an ecosystem, biomes can be understood simply as large ecosystems comprising habitats of similar climate and vegetation. The close linkages and interdependencies among the soil, flora and fauna within a biome can produce homeostasis, an open system whose structure and functions are maintained through multiple equilibriums. Historically, humans have adapted best to their biomes whenever they have engaged in mutually supportive interactions. But to say this is not to reduce the complexity of social organization into biological terms involving the mere extraction of economic value from natural capital. It is, rather, to acknowledge that the prospects to enhance human well-being over the long term depends crucially on the ability of societies to shift their practices towards sustainable forms after recognizing the constraints that their natural environment places on them as well as the opportunities it affords.

There are fifteen biomes identified around the world, if one includes coastal and marine and coastal fisheries.[2] To the extent that each biome shares roughly similar types of life forms, soil and climate, it is fair to assume that in their geographical extent they would provide comparable forms of ecosystem services. Undoubtedly, the forms and rates of extraction of social and economic value will vary widely within the same biome, depending on the way the societies are organized, their technological capabilities and wealth, policies with regard to environmental protection, and lifestyles. In other words, while it is true, for instance, that montane grasslands and shrublands in the Andes and East and Central Africa share similar ecological features and climate, there are significant differences in social and economic conditions, not to mention political systems and cultural practices. Given the similarities in natural

---

[2] See http://www.worldwildlife.org/science/ecoregions.cfm.

capital, however, it is quite likely that residents in both parts of the world will share many living and working conditions related to farming and crop type, livestock, housing construction, access to water, etc., although the differences in the ecological efficiency of the use of natural capital will largely be a function of the existing human, institutional and technological capital. In short, there will be many significant opportunities for social formations within a given biome to learn usefully from each other on best practices to obtain ecosystem services.

The governance framework I propose is to develop a BSC for each of the fifteen biomes, each in charge of managing a single global biome. To begin with, each BSC would consist of a group of individuals elected or nominated by local community organizations that reside in the regions making up a biome, including a few government officials who are deemed to be particularly sensitive to ecosystem protection. To ensure public confidence, the rules for developing BSCs would need to come, after extensive consultation, from stakeholders who may, for instance, decide that a 'biomic constitution' is warranted. Whatever the final outcome of these consultations, it is important that certain key principles be adhered to, namely that the council members (*a*) be properly representative of the stakeholder groups resident to the biome, (*b*) function through internal rules of legitimacy, and (*c*) uphold basic values of ecological stewardship.

Each of these principles can be satisfied in multiple ways, but the most effective solution would be one that has simple rules developed through stakeholder input that are then consistently applied. For instance, within each biome, the numbers of council members could be in proportion to the corresponding populations, with additional representatives from the member governments. Thus, if there are 200 million people resident in Biome A and there are twenty countries intersecting the biome, one model would have a single popular (for example, elected) representative for every two million residents plus one government (for example, nominated) representative for each country, resulting in 120 council members. Initially, at least, it is conceivable that the popular candidates are proposed by local community organizations within the sub-regions on the basis of their service to the community and involvement with promoting sustainability. Thus, here again, the people in whose names the BSCs would function would have global character, but their social imaginary, as it were, would be organized around their allegiances to their biome rather than to some specific cultural or national interest.

The BSCs would review existing assessments that are relevant to the respective biomes and enhance them with local knowledge to understand threats, opportunities and best practices. Subsequently, they would develop guidelines and capacity building exercises that seek to tap into the self-interest of local residents to become custodians of their local surroundings. These early tasks will be useful in building trust in the organization, and help the BSC itself develop its own institutional capacity. While it would not really have political authority in the sense of being able to enforce changes in practices, its quasi-public role as an elected body would provide it with the legitimacy needed to advise national and local governments as well as local residents on how to improve the environmental efficiency of extracting ecosystem services. Its muted though discernible presence as a responsible and elected body will in turn provide multilateral organizations and national governments with the confidence to cede new functions to them, much the same way that public–private partnerships (PPPs) are developing between governments and NGOs and profit-driven entities.

Over a period of time, the BSCs themselves would authorize performance-based incentives to local community groups in order to maximize ecosystem protection without diminishing services. For instance, much like utility commissions that are mandated to set rates for water and electricity services, the committees set up by the BSCs would be able to set up a system of rewards and penalties depending on how ecosystem services are managed for, say, a given watershed or coastal zone. The authority for such rule-making would be contingent on two crucial, though not unrealistic, legal and political steps taking place. The first is the negotiation of an international treaty based on the Convention on Biological Diversity to provide BSCs with the authority to form transborder rules relating to ecosystem protection. The second is the ratification of the treaty, which would entail the loan of member government resources and personnel for enforcement of the BSCs rules.

To the extent that the rule-making power of the BSCs will be limited to adaptive and flexible forms of performance-based pricing and regulation of services tied to such issues as the prevention or management of floods, drought and land degradation without causing direct interference in more politically sensitive concerns, such as land-tenure or water rights, it seems likely that they will have effective authority to implement their policies. But also because they would have gained legitimacy as elected bodies and through their performance and stakeholder involvement during their formative years, as it were, they would face less resistance from individual governments than would, say, civil society organizations that operate on a global scale. Similarly, by learning from existing participatory forms of ecological stewardship, such as joint forest management, the BSCs will also gain legitimacy and political power 'from below', especially if they continue to ensure room for participatory mechanisms to filter up into their rule development.

The relatively unobtrusive framework of the BSC proposal may also work in its favour. Because of its phased introduction, it should be unthreatening in the early years precisely because no government function would be replaced. Rather, it would operate through a series of learning steps and confidence building measures, developing trust both from its constituency and from government agencies and the executives in the countries it operates in. To the extent that its subsequent development would itself be contingent on an international agreement being drawn, the BSC would not be threatening to national governments. Furthermore, since the precise boundaries of biomes are fuzzy and because they are non-contiguous across continents, the BSC need not ever be viewed threateningly as a political unit having territorial borders, but rather as a functional governance entity concerned with particular types of ecosystems. Conversely, a single country may have many biomes, so that the national government may justifiably think of itself as literally 'outsourcing' its ecosystem management functions to multiple BSCs.

While traditional concepts of sovereignty emphasized separation into territorially independent groups, the newer versions focus on the positive capacity to participate collectively in international institutions to address global and regional problems collectively by accepting mutual obligation (Chayes and Chayes 1995; Slaughter 2004b). In this context, the BSCs can be seen as constituting yet another network that has the unique feature of strengthening existing ad hoc transnational arrangements among governmental and non-governmental agencies, but with the additional legitimacy of democratic input. Nevertheless, in some ways the BSC involves a more radical shift in sovereignty than, say, climate treaties, whose enforcement would take place primarily at the national level. For even if national governments were to provide support for enforcement capability, the BSCs would have the ultimate authority to penalize and reward parties under its jurisdiction, albeit on a narrower basis.

A pluralistic conception of the people and, by implication, the people of the world then appears to be more useful than one that is identified traditionally as a constituted amalgamation that expresses a single will and upon this basis directs political action. Cosmopolitans must surely be right in envisioning a global polity that goes beyond the standard picture of distinct societies, cultures and publics having (relatively) self-contained obligations towards each other and our environment. But in ignoring the question of the people of the world in whose name such a polity can act, they miss a crucial part of the vision and its ensuing politics. The challenge of identifying a global political community is indeed daunting, especially if one thinks of it as all of humanity bound by a single contract that can express collective action as a people. One might instead construe the category differently, as incremental and overlapping political engagements that appear in different arenas of the global theatre, but whose repeated points of entry can potentially build legitimacy. The '99%!' in whose name such repetitive acts take place, from Cairo to Rio via Milwaukee, do not need to have a single coherent will or even identity, but to the extent that they build a collective memory and a history about themselves, they can constitute a people in whose name subsequent acts of institution building can develop.

~

References

Benhabib, Seyla. 2004. *The Rights of Others: Aliens, Residents and Citizens*, Cambridge University Press, Cambridge and New York.

Bull, Malcolm. 2005. 'The Limits of Multitude', *New Left Review* 35: 19–39.

Chayes, A. and A. H. Chayes. 1995. *The New Sovereignty: Compliance with International Regulatory Agreements*, Harvard University Press, Cambridge, MA.

Falk, Richard and Andrew Strauss. 2001. 'Toward Global Parliament', *Foreign Affairs* 80(1): 212–20.

Fraser, Nancy. 2005. 'Reframing Justice in a Globalizing World, *New Left Review* 36(Nov–Dec): 69–88.

Hammer, Dean. 2009. 'Homer and Political Thought', in Stephen G. Salkever (ed.), *The Cambridge Companion to Ancient Greek Political Thought*, Cambridge University Press, New York, 14–41.

Hardt, Michael and Antonio Negri. 2004. *Multitude: War and Democracy in the Age of Empire*, Penguin Press, New York.

Kant, Immanuel. 1986. *Philosophical Writings*, Continuum International Publishing Group, London.

———. 2007. *Perpetual Peace*, Filiquarian Publishing, Minneapolis, MN.

Lefebvre, Henri. 2003. *The Urban Revolution*, University of Minnesota Press, Minneapolis.

Lefort, Claude. 1988. *Democracy and Political Theory*, Polity Press, Cambridge.

Näsström, Sofia. 2007. 'The Legitimacy of the People', *Political Theory* 35(5): 624–58.

Rajan, Sudhir Chella. 2008. 'Meeting the Millennium Ecosystem Assessment Challenge: The Case for Biome Stewardship Councils', in Janet Ranganathan, Mohan Munasinghe and Frances Irwin (eds), *Policies for Sustainable Governance of Global Ecosystem Services*, Edward Elgar, Cheltenham, UK, 315–28.

Rawls, John. 1999. *The Law of Peoples: With 'The idea of Public Reason Revisited'*, Harvard University Press, Cambridge, MA.

Slaughter, Anne-Marie. 2004a. 'Disaggregated Sovereignty: Towards the Public Accountability of Global Government Networks', *Government and Opposition* 39(2): 159–90.

———. 2004b. *A New World Order*, Princeton University Press, Princeton, NJ.

Turner, Victor. 1995. *The Ritual Process: Structure and Anti-Structure*, Aldine, Chicago.

Virno, Paolo. 2003. *A Grammar of the Multitude*, Semiotext(e), Cambridge, MA.

6

Cosmopolitanism, Liberalism and Citizenship

Arvind Sivaramakrishnan

The broad area of cultural and political theory known as cosmopolitanism has been extensively developed in the last fifteen years or so, partly in response to the apparent end of the dominant ideological polarizations of the post-war period and partly in response to what may well be new forms of globalization. To start with, I outline certain forms of cosmopolitan theory and some of the responses; I then try to show that certain tendencies which have given rise to contemporary cosmopolitanism require a more detailed and more cautious response than they seem to have had. Secondly, I argue that some of the positions on which cosmopolitanism relies, such as rights and rights instruments in international law, will not serve to achieve many of the undoubtedly laudable aims that various cosmopolitan theorists hope they will achieve; I attempt to show that this is mainly because those aims were derived from or based on liberal or neoliberal theory and are subject to the same problems, which in effect render both cosmopolitanism and liberalism incoherent. If cosmopolitan is to stand as a set of theoretical approaches to our condition, it must then find alternative foundations. I do not investigate the question of whether foundations are needed at all in social or political theory.

Several very eminent theorists, among them Gerard Delanty, David Held, and Daniele Archibugi, have provided detailed arguments for conceiving our contemporary condition to be a cosmopolitan one (Archibugi 2008; Delanty 2009; Held 2010). Delanty, for example, identifies three main strands in cosmopolitanism, namely the moral, the political and the cultural. Moral cosmopolitanism, which — following an earlier work by Martha Nussbaum — is based on a 'common loyalty to humanity', requires among other things a cosmopolitan education, which will help us to see that we live in a 'connected world requiring greater international cooperation', that we have moral obligations to the rest of the world, and that moral obligations do not stop at national borders. Delanty identifies a resonance with Jürgen Habermas's communication theory, to the effect that the communicative process, the process of dialogue and debate, itself enables participants to subject one another to critical judgement, with the result that all cultural assumptions come to be critically examined (Delanty 2009: 54–55).

Political cosmopolitanism, which according to Delanty is stronger than its moral counterpart, has, according to its proponents, been brought about empirically by globalization, which has created a new political context. The cosmopolitan or cosmopolitanist response has been to articulate some of the resulting or consequent political requirements, such as the need to respond to crimes against humanity, or to crimes committed in the name of states. Such crimes require, at the very least, the creation of a cosmopolitan legal order; and the idea and the fact, for example, of the international criminal court, are now much less strange than they might have seemed even two decades ago. Both conceptually and empirically, too, such developments imply the possibility of what Delanty calls a transnational development which goes beyond the juridical borders of the nation state as inherited from the Treaty of Westphalia (ibid.). David Held, for his part, identifies the creation of multilateral bodies, including supranational ones, as part of the process. The United Nations (UN) and its many agencies, and the European Union (EU), are among the most obvious examples of this kind of development, but Held also includes bodies like the World Trade Organization (WTO), associations of central bankers, networks of non-governmental organizations (NGOs) — many of which now routinely participate in the formulation of domestic and international legislation — under what he calls networks of global governance (Held 2010: 34–35).

These factors in the creation of a cosmopolitan climate are paralleled or complemented by the extension of rights under, broadly speaking, the welfare state — a phenomenon by no means confined to the industrial world or the Global North — to include a form of cultural cosmopolitanism. More specifically, we are now familiar with claims to the political recognition or legal incorporation, or both, of cultural rights; the idea that we live in culturally and ethnically diverse milieux, and that we ourselves draw upon such milieux or embody such diversity, is also relatively commonplace today, with the implication that this was not the case some unspecified time ago (Delanty 2009: 58–59; Held 2010: 110–12). In effect, conceptions of membership, and in particular those of citizenship as articulated by, say, T. H. Marshall, for whom the achievement of welfare rights was the achievement of citizenship, now have to encompass issues such as those of ethnicity and nationality in addition to those of formal citizenship and the legislated confirmation of access to the public benefits and services of the democratic state (Delanty 2009: 58–59). Indeed, one result is a cultural cosmopolitanism characterized by multiple attachments and attachments at a distance. That distance is at once geographical, cultural, and political; our condition is, therefore, one of hybridity, in which meanings are negotiated and even managed all the time. This conception of cultural cosmopolitanism is not without its critics, who remind us that we must neglect neither its material base nor the risks it carries that we shall end up ignoring the kind of popular nationalism that inspires emancipatory movements in the Global South (ibid.). Delanty also points out here that if everything is hybrid, then nothing is hybrid; it becomes impossible to distinguish that which is hybrid from that which is not (ibid.: 59–60).

Even allowing for the problems inherent in the idea that our condition, whether cosmopolitan or not, has a material base or that it must have one, the criticisms of cultural cosmopolitanism for seemingly neglecting our economic condition identify a significant issue within cosmopolitanism, namely, the place of free-market economics or, more precisely, neoliberalism, within it or in relation to it. Held, for example, seems largely to accept the arguments advanced by Friedrich von Hayek in the 1970s to the effect that the market system is better than any other known system for 'coordinating the knowledgeable decisions of producers and consumers over extended territories' (Held 2010: 61). Held, nevertheless, recognizes major problems here, namely those of the often very damaging externalities of the market system, such as its consequences for health, welfare, income distribution, and the environment, and he advocates a form of rights-based intervention in, or regulation of, market systems in order that — at the very least — the basic conditions for human autonomy be established and maintained.

The importance of this approach to the way we conceive the cosmopolitan condition must not be underestimated, and certain significant reservations about it have already been stated. For example, the globalization which Delanty contends has engendered contemporary cosmopolitanization is not necessarily benign, and could be just the opposite, in that it promotes the expansion of dominant economic forces and the capitalist market (Balibar 2012: 292–93). Seen in that light, cosmopolitanism today may well be only an extension of the bourgeois internationalism of the age of empire. That makes it a new form of imperialism, one based on 'financial domination, commercial hegemony, the messianic propaganda of an individualistic model of political democracy, diplomatic influence and humanitarian interventions' (ibid.: 293).

Attempts have been made to reshape this form of globalization, and one example of this is the articulation by the World Social Movement of alternative globalization or *altermondialisme* (ibid.: 293–94). These, however, may not quite serve to address the problems inherent in liberal cosmopolitanism, in view of the difficulties posed by the idea of world citizenship, which would be detached from a *polis* in the general sense, and would also require the conceptual undermining of the ideas behind certain cosmopolitanist doctrines.

Within cosmopolitanist thought, these kinds of problems have been acknowledged, though, as I shall show, these do not address key problems in liberalism and the idea of rights. If a form of world citizenship embodying cosmopolitan social principles is to prevail, new terms of reference, new rules, procedures, and structures, have to be introduced into the ground rules or basic laws of the free-market system, and have to become the 'very *modus operandi*' thereof (Held 2010: 62). This is a modified form of liberalism, which according to one account is of itself a progressive force; on this account the global spread of market mechanisms is necessarily accompanied by the 'spread of the rule of law and democratic culture', and is therefore conducive to the institutionalization of human rights on a worldwide scale (Beck 2012: 313).

Yet any new cosmopolitan order or state of affairs would be significantly incomplete unless what Held calls the enormous social inequalities which coexist with liberal democracy are diminished by systematic economic intervention. Those inequalities are growing, both between and within states; the North American Free Trade Association (NAFTA), the EU, and Japan together account for between two thirds and three quarters of the world's economic activity. This has further consequences beyond the immediately economic; for example, Edward Herman and Robert McChesney have noted that for the largely corporate-owned mass media, over six hundred million of the world's poorest people — who, unsurprisingly, largely inhabit the world's poorest regions — barely exist. The mass media are indifferent to them, because as non-participants in mass consumption they are of no interest to advertisers, and so the media, if they notice them at all, treat them mainly as objects of occasional curiosity when millions of them die in famines and natural disasters (Herman and McChesney 1998: 64–65).

Held's conclusion here is that the cosmopolitan commitment to impartial treatment for all humanity has consequences for our global economic arrangements (Held 2010: 108). He also deals with the objection that the main principles of cosmopolitanism are no more than another expression of a Western project to dominate the rest of the world. The principles he cites are those of equal consideration, equal liberty and human rights, or, in another of his own formulations, egalitarian individualism, reciprocal recognition and impartialist reasoning (ibid.). Held's response, drawing upon work by Albert Weale, is that the origins of principles should not be confused with their validity; this reminder that the historical record does not exhaust the possibilities in ideas or systems of ideas is of some significance, not least in former colonial territories. For example, Abel has pointed out that those who established British rule in India also created enough of a recognizable state, which functioned at least in part on principles that assisted Indians to challenge both imperialism and the more oppressive features of their own society (Abel 2005).

It is certainly crucial to cosmopolitanism that the idea of rights as having universal validity be established. There is no denying the importance of the kinds of work rights are intended to do. Even some who have started off by regarding rights as ideological distractions from questions of the material relations of production have later come to see rights as essential forms of protection. One such is Albie Sachs, who himself says that his move from the United Kingdom to Mozambique, which was then in the grip of a terrible civil war, showed him the value of rights. It was the poorest and the most vulnerable who most needed and wanted the law, particularly justiciable rights stated in the law, to be applied to all and followed by all.

> It was they, people with no contacts and connexions, who could not telephone a minister or a senior officer late at night to get an innocent friend or relative released from arbitrary arrest or detention, could not gain redress for abuses of power, and could not find out what happened to loved ones who disappeared (cited in Sivaramakrishnan 2000).

In this context, a further and central connection emerges, namely that between democracy and fundamental rights:

> In a society divided by huge inequalities, it turned out that the majority — the poor — would accept the idea of fundamental rights if the principle of one person, one vote was protected; similarly the minority, the wealthy, would accept one person, one vote, if fundamental rights were protected (ibid.).

We are also familiar with the transformations wrought by the creation of many other kinds of rights all round the world. The United States Supreme Court ruling in *Roe v Wade* in 1973, which gave women in the United States a right to abortion in the first three months of pregnancy, is just one such example, and the ruling still stands, despite the limitations and qualifications introduced by the respective rulings in *Casey* and *Webster* (United States Supreme Court 1989, 1992). In other areas of public policy, various forms of rights-based anti-discrimination legislation in the United Kingdom — to name but one country — have substantially altered the gender composition of various sections of the workforce; the legislation prohibiting discrimination on the grounds of disability has even brought about significant changes in the physical spaces, including the layout and construction of buildings, bridges, stations, and roads, which are used and occupied by ordinary people in their everyday lives.

The impact of rights and rights instruments also has an international dimension, which is widely noted by cosmopolitan theorists. International law since the Nuremberg trials has maintained and developed the principle that except in situations of severe coercion, such as having a gun held to our heads, we as individuals are obliged to disobey state law or state orders rather than commit war crimes, genocide or other crimes against humanity; Held notes the establishment by the United Nations Security Council (UNSC) of war crimes tribunals for the former Yugoslavia and for Rwanda (Held 2010: 120–21). In addition, we are now familiar with the modification of domestic law in accordance with adverse rights rulings in multilateral, let alone supranational, jurisdictions. The United Kingdom banned corporal punishment in schools after losing a case in the European Court of Human Rights (ECHR), and introduced the ban despite the fact that it had not at that time incorporated the bulk of the Convention into domestic law.

In another case, the United Kingdom also tried to argue — as recently as July 2011 — that its troops in Iraq, particularly those who had been involved in the deaths of several Iraqi civilians, were not bound by the European Convention on Human Rights, as they were outside United Kingdom jurisdiction at the time; but it lost the case. In effect, as Richard Wolin points out, the UN human rights declarations and agencies have helped make individuals bearers of rights in a way that transcends, and possibly subverts, the 'traditional prerogatives' of state sovereignty (Wolin 2010: 147–48). Wolin here cites the development of new criminal law via institutions such as the ECHR and the International Criminal Court (ICC). He includes the European Court of Justice in the list, but that court has so far been granted only civil jurisdiction, which for its part obtains only in matters of EU law, though the procedure requires that cases be heard under EU law in the domestic courts first and referred to itself only via the highest domestic court if appeals go that far. The Court has nevertheless significantly extended the kinds of rights available to individuals and groups against member states of the European Union, for example, under the EU's existing anti-discrimination legislation and under the earlier Equal Treatment Directive (European Union n.d.).

The idea of a cosmopolitan international condition, or as some prefer it, international order, supported or protected by rights or systems of rights has its attractions. Cosmopolitan theorists also, and rightly, acknowledge that the record of implementation or protection of rights is far from perfect, not least because very powerful corporate and other economic interests are involved. This goes beyond economic results per se, because conditions such as poverty, hunger and sickness severely limit individual autonomy, which is one of the founding principles of cosmopolitanist theory. So what is needed, according to cosmopolitanism, is some kind of constraint on the operation of markets so that they do not destroy individual autonomy, which in turn is subject to constraints of community and interdependence within communities (Held 2010: 108).

The proposed constraints on the operation of markets require a bridge between international human rights law and the global economic order so that we can create some form of economic cosmopolitanism. The specific arrangements, as Held says, would include things like global taxation mechanisms, presumably on the lines of a Tobin tax; they would also require procedures for the transfer of resources to the most vulnerable in order that their autonomy be preserved, as well as greatly expanded representation for developing countries in international financial institutions (ibid.).

These are not necessarily conceptual innovations, and therefore do not connote a new kind of international or global condition, though their effective creation, or the improvement of the existing systems which purport to serve the necessary ends, would no doubt enhance our condition greatly. That, however, runs the risk of failing to address the question of whether or not the proposed bridge between human rights law and the global economic order is even needed. We owe to Raymond Plant, among others, the insight that there is no difference in kind between such things as human rights and economic rights, however different those two things might seem to be at first sight. If the kinds of things encompassed by civil rights and human rights are to have any effect, then they must be enforceable; enforceability in turn needs institutional arrangements, staffing, and the like, which, of course, needs funding As a consequence, such procedural rights are as much a matter of economic rights as, say, rights to material goods.

The difference between civil and political rights on the one hand, and economic or material rights on the other, is not one of kind but one of degree; therefore, there is no difference between procedural and material rights or between positive and negative rights (Plant et al. 1980: 73–97; Bellamy 2000: 146–47; Plant 2002[1]). The further implication arises here that reasoning decisions on the extent to which we support particular rights have to be settled not under the

---

[1] Cited here with permission from the author.

rubric of rights but under or within the ambit of some other kind of discourse. In practice, the untenability of the distinction between so-called procedural rights and so-called material rights is implicitly, and often very grudgingly, accepted by many states, particularly in the Global North, in the form of unemployment benefits systems and various forms of public health care provision, though the public discourse around those tends to take place in largely utilitarian terms of alleged affordability or otherwise, or in managerialist terms of effectiveness, targets reached, and so on. And for its part, the United Nations has gone some way towards accepting the untenability of the distinction between civil and political rights on the one hand and social and economic rights on the other (Wolin 2010: 151). Specifically, at its Vienna Conference in 1993, the UN refused to distinguish between the two kinds of rights (ibid.).

Liberalism's problems, nevertheless, are not ended even if a modified form of it, such as the form of cosmopolitanism I am analysing here, accepts the need for minimal or basic material provision as a precondition for individual autonomy. First, it has to establish limits to our range of autonomous choices if we are not to make choices which violate others' right to make autonomous choices. Secondly, it cannot, on its own principles, offer any resources whereby we might decide whether the choices themselves are made in genuinely free conditions:

> How can we know, prior to substantive inquiry into the whole fabric of life within a given society, whether individuals are self-determining or brainwashed, manipulated in subtle and incalculable ways, and locked into forms of false consciousness by social forces (aside from the coercive powers of the state) (Beiner 1992: 27).

Liberalism, therefore, cannot give us the resources we need in order to reach reasoned decisions about what is to count as a sufficiency of material provision, precisely because that would require substantive inquiry into the ways of life within a society, and because liberalism itself cannot adjudicate between rights without accepting that rights are subordinate to the discourse in which we reach such adjudication.

In respect of liberal cosmopolitanism's reliance upon the market, the problem here is that the requirement for rights-based constraints on the operation of the market relies on the tenability of the very idea of rights. One issue is that of conflicts of rights, and we are familiar with public controversies around such matters as, say, the rights of a mother as against the rights of a foetus. Similar problems arise over what are sometimes called group rights, or rights accruing to individuals as a result of their membership of any particular group. In such instances, group rights pose problems if practices within a group violate other rights, such as those of individual members or rights of other groups or individuals (Sivaramakrishnan 2007). My point is that conflicts of rights are irresoluble if rights are absolutes and are to be inviolable; furthermore, in practice, the very fact of negotiated or reasoned settlements of conflicts of rights means that rights are not the absolutes they have to be if they are to have their intended force.

The discourse of rights tends to exclude the content of whatever is claimed as a right. To be fair to cosmopolitanist arguments, they do not in general seem to imply that anything and everything can be claimed as a right. The problem, however, is that questions of the content of rights, and the justifiability of the content of rights, have to be addressed if we are not to end up unable to adjudicate between rights claims, or, worse still, if we are not to end up accepting that almost anything can be called a right.

A similar point about the content of rights is made by Alasdair MacIntyre, who has pointed out that there is no sense in claiming a right to, say, an education which it is worth nobody's while to have (cited in Beiner 1992: 37). This does not eliminate the possibility of credentialism, in which the possession of a certificate is more important than any of the knowledge the certificate is supposed to certify, but that turns the purported right to an education into a claim to a right of access to institutions which are licensed to provide certification. This is, in effect, a process whereby the certificate becomes a commodity, a unit in a market or other system of exchange, and ceases to be a signifier of knowledge or capacity to perform an activity. The commodification or marketization involved has changed the very meaning of the certificate, in a process identified by, for example, Michael Sandel (2012). At worst, if the holder has actually learnt nothing, the certificate becomes a signifier of nothing, and both the education they have undergone and the certificate become meaningless, if not downright dangerous. Yet the right of access to the certifying institution still stands.

I have spent some time on the problems of rights and rights discourses, because cosmopolitanism relies on the idea of rights as placing limits on conduct by individuals, states, and other types of bodies, and also because within liberal political thought, rights seem to provide an essential protection against the worst effects of the free market, not to mention the abuse of autonomy. The question then arises of the soundness of liberal theory, and in particular liberal economic theory or economic liberalism. This has been the subject of much examination, and for the sake of brevity I shall focus on neoliberalism specifically, as expressed in the work of Hayek; I have already noted, for example, Held's apparent approval of Hayek's demonstration of the efficiency of the market in coordinating decisions by producers and consumers.

Hayek's argument is that we cannot know the overall results of our actions; one of his concerns here is the distribution of goods throughout a society and whether or not this can be brought under or organized according to principles of justice. For Hayek, only intentional actions can be just or unjust, and he sees organizations and governments as intentional in the particular sense involved. He does, however, exclude society, because he considers society and its workings to constitute a spontaneous order, the results of which therefore cannot be just or unjust. The same goes for the unintended consequences of just actions (Hayek 1976: 32–33). According to Hayek, no one individual can encompass all the practical knowledge on which individuals in society act. This knowledge is fragmented and dispersed, and so any social order which arises as the aggregate result of our individual actions is spontaneous and not the result of any one individual's efforts. Exactly the same holds for groups of people acting in concert, because by this logic no group can encompass all the relevant knowledge; a group's knowledge is incomplete in the same way an individual's is. This may amount to a form of democracy without rights, even if Hayek's own conduct shows considerable disregard even for the imperfect and flawed democracies in which we live; he is recorded as telling his acolytes not to go in for politics, as it would take too long to change people's minds, but instead to achieve political change or perhaps even control by dominating the minds of intellectuals (Miller 2010: 27–28, 37–38; Birch and Tickell 2010: 48–56).

The premise that we cannot know the aggregate or perhaps long-term or remote effects of our actions is plausible enough, but

Hayek concludes thence that the overall arrangements of society can be neither just nor unjust, because they are the unforeseeable and aggregated outcomes of very large numbers of individual decisions made in the possession of incomplete knowledge. The results of the 'impersonal processes of the market' are neither intended nor foreseeable, irrespective of the justice or otherwise of individuals' intentional actions (Hayek 1976: 69–74). For Hayek, it also follows that politically or morally motivated attempts to alter the economic condition or position of people *en bloc* or *en masse* are radically misconceived, because we cannot possess the kinds of knowledge required in order to make the necessary judgements with regard to policies or other principles for action.

This, as has been noted by economists as well as political theorists, amounts to a very substantial claim about the nature of knowledge itself (Bellamy 2000: 133; Plant 2009: 159–62). This epistemological claim means that we may act as individuals or groups in the market, but that the outcomes or results of our actions are unknowable to us and that where we end up in society, as well as the shape of society as a whole, are beyond our or anyone else's control. According to Hayek, we are, therefore, misconceived in thinking that our position in life is the result of our talent, knowledge, or judgement, and equally misconceived in thinking we can organize society or facilitate its organization to deliver a just state of affairs.

Hayek does recognize that among those who did well out of the market order as it emerged in the early modern period, a belief grew that individuals' well-being depended above all on their own efforts, and he adds that this belief has been of the greatest importance in motivating people to be 'energetic and efficient'. But he is adamant that this belief is erroneous; he says it is 'probably a misfortune' and 'bodes ill for the future of the market order', that such a belief 'seems to have become the only defence of it which is understood by the general public' (Hayek 1976: 74).

Hayek's response to this, however, is extraordinary. He says:

> It is therefore a real dilemma to what extent we ought to encourage in the young the belief that when they really try they will succeed, or should rather emphasize that inevitably some unworthy will succeed and some worthy will fail — whether we ought to allow the views of those groups to prevail with whom the over-confidence in the appropriate

reward of the able and industrious is strong and who in consequence will do much that benefits the rest, and whether without such partly erroneous beliefs the large numbers will tolerate actual differences in rewards which will be based only partly on achievement and partly on mere chance (ibid.).

This has two very serious consequences. First, if we cannot know the principles governing our conduct and we cannot know what results our actions will have, then the very idea of intentional action, of doing things and getting and evaluating results, collapses altogether. Hayek himself shows some sense of this possibility in the passage I have quoted here, where he acknowledges that if we expose the fiction of desert then people will lose their incentive to act, which by implication means whatever incentive they might think the market gives them.

The second consequence is that Hayek has frankly admitted that the free market can be sustained only if large numbers of people — indeed most of humanity — remain in ignorance of its real character. That in turn could well imply systematic censorship, on a global scale, of any literature, talk or news that indicates the contrary. This admission also amounts to the abdication of Hayek's own insistence that the free market is the paramount principle of social organization. For with this utterance Hayek has admitted that the market can survive only if we take other, and supervening, principles as the crucial principles of social or political organization.

Hayek offers no argument whatsoever as to why such a gigantic lie should be maintained solely so that a system in which reasoned judgement can play little or no part can be kept functioning, if indeed functioning is even an intelligible term in light of the inherent instability and tendency to catastrophe of the unrestrained market. Bellamy likens Hayek's requirement for a foundational or founding lie to Plato's Noble Lie, whereby the true organizing principle of a hierarchical society is concealed lest its exposure cause discord or rebellion (Plato 1955: 159–63; Bellamy 2000: 128). Bellamy's analogy, however, needs to be handled with caution, as Plato's lie was intended for the maintenance of stability and order in a society in which the authority of the Guardians was founded on superior, if not comprehensive, forms of knowledge, while Hayek's epistemology would be completely incompatible with the very idea that anyone could possess that kind of knowledge, indeed that such knowledge might even be possible. What is also rendered impossible is the idea of any reasoning justification of our attitudes, intentions and actions. All of those, if we take Hayek seriously, collapse into some form of radical individual preference, or radical ethical or moral subjectivism (Sivaramakrishnan 2012: 79–80).

This, however, does not exhaust the problems Hayek causes for himself. This goes beyond the fact that Hayek himself seems not to see that his account of action — the key feature of which is that we cannot know in advance the outcome or result of what we do — renders intention and action all but unintelligible. Whatever Hayek leaves us with will not be human beings; they will barely be agents at all, let alone free ones. Hayek may not be aware of that consequence of his epistemology, but it remains the case that he knowingly and comprehensively sinks his own ship (ibid.).

It remains the consequence that if we go by what Hayek holds, we must not interfere with people's ends or decisions, whether or not they know or can know the consequences of their actions. It follows that any kind of planning, whether by an individual, a large organization, or perhaps by a society as a whole, becomes impossible. For the cosmopolitanist project, which requires the creation and maintenance of spaces for the reasoning exchange of ideas as well as for the pursuit of cultural and aesthetic activities, and which also requires a reasoning and well-informed global commitment to long-term stewardship of the natural environment, it is hard to see how Hayek can be anything other than a very uncomfortable bedfellow, if not something worse.

Clashes of rights are inevitable, precisely because rights themselves amount to a way of preserving the good — which in turn cannot be characterized except in the context of ways of life and shared cultures and languages, however loosely they may be shared. Now neither of those is self-sealed, or probably has ever been self-sealed, and all cultures have probably always had to negotiate and revise conceptions of the good in whatever respects the relevant issues have arisen. My point here is that clashes of rights are likely to be no less severe in a cosmpolitanized world than they are within any one state or society; indeed it is quite likely that the very idea of rights could be contested by those who might allege that it is a concept alien to their cultures. In effect, such arguments are arguments for the right not to have rights, but I shall not go any further down that road.

In sum, I have tried to argue that liberal conceptions, and in particular those of rights, cannot help us to achieve or embody cosmopolitanism, and that, therefore, we might well need to consider cosmopolitan citizenship in other terms, though of course there is nothing in what I have said to curtail or obstruct the task of establishing cosmopolitan institutions. My argument might, however, imply that the task needs to be undertaken in terms and in a language different in kind from that which seems to constitute much of its contemporary currency.

≈

References

Abel, M. 2005. *Glimpses of the Indian Nationalist Movement*, ICFAI University Press, Hyderabad.

Archibugi, Daniele. 2008. *The Global Commonwealth of Citizens*, Princeton University Press, Princeton.

Balibar, E. 2012. 'Citizenship of the World Revisited', in Gerard Delanty (ed.), *Routledge Handbook of Cosmopolitanism Studies*, Routledge, Abingdon, 291–301.

Beck, Ulrich. 2012. 'Global Inequality and Human Rights: A Cosmopolitan Perspective', in Gerard Delanty (ed.), *Routledge Handbook of Cosmopolitanism Studies*, Routledge, Abingdon, 302–15.

Beiner, Ronald. 1992. *What's the Matter with Liberalism?* University of California Press, Berkeley.

Bellamy, Richard. 2000. *Rethinking Liberalism*, Pinter, London.

Birch, Kean and Adam Tickell. 2010. 'Making Neoliberal Order in the United States', in Kean Birch and Vlad Mykhnenko (eds), *The Rise and Fall of Neoliberalism*, Books for Change, Bangalore, 42–59.

Delanty, Gerard. 2009. *The Cosmopolitan Imagination: The Renewal of Critical Social Theory*, Cambridge University Press, Cambridge.

European Union. n.d. 'M. H. Marshall *v* Southampton and South-West Hampshire Area Health Authority (Teaching)', http://eur-les.europa. eu/smartapi/cgi/sga_doc?smartapi!celexplus!prod!CELEXnumdoc&lg =en&numdoc=61984J0152 (accessed 27 November 2011).

Hayek, Friedrich A. 1976. *Law, Legislation and Liberty, Volume 2: The Mirage of Social Justice*, RKP, London.

Held, David. 2010. *Cosmopolitanism: Ideals and Realities*, Polity Press, Cambridge.

Herman, Edward S. and Robert W. McChesney. 1998. *The Global Media: The New Missionaries of Corporate Capitalism*, Madhyam, Delhi.

Miller, David. 2010. 'How Neoliberalism Got Where It Is: Elite Planning, Corporate Lobbying and the Release of the Free Market', in Kean Birch and Vlad Mykhnenko (eds), *The Rise and Fall of Neoliberalism*, Books *for* Change, Bangalore, 24–41.

Plant, Raymond. 2002. 'Can There Be a Right to a Basic Income?', Paper presented at the Ninth International Congress of the Basic Income European Network, Geneva, 12–14 September, http://www.etes.ucl. ac.be/BIEN/Files/Papers/2002Plant.pdf (accessed 3 March 2008).

———. 2009. *The Neo-liberal State*, Oxford University Press, Oxford.

Plant, Raymond, Harry Lesser and Peter Taylor-Gooby. 1980. *Political Philosophy and Social Welfare*, Routledge and Kegan Paul, London.

Plato. 1955. *The Republic*, trans. H. D. P. Lee, Penguin, Harmondsworth.

Sandel, Michael. 2012. *What Money Can't Buy: the Moral Limits of Markets*, Allen Lane, London.

Sivaramakrishnan, Arvind. 2000. 'Creating the Culture of a Constitution', Report of the Fifth Gabriele Ganz Lecture in Public Law, delivered by Justice Albie Sachs, University of Southampton: *Viewpoint* 410, 16 November, http://www.viewpoint.soton.ac.uk/Viewpoint/410/ (accessed 5 July 2011).

———. 2007. 'Minority Education: Group Right or Otherwise?', in Tahir Mahmood (ed.), *Politics of Minority Educational Institutions: Law and Reality in the Subcontinent*, imprintOne, Gurgaon, 240–54.

———. 2010. 'How the Neoliberal State Sinks Itself', *Economic and Political Weekly*, 45(22): 24–26.

———. 2012. *Public Policy and Citizenship: Battling Managerialism in India*, Sage Publications, New Delhi.

United States Supreme Court. 1989. 'Webster *v* Reproductive Health Services', http://caselaw.lp.findlaw.com/cgi-bin/getcase.pl?court= US&vol=492&invol=490 (accessed 27 November 2011).

———. 1992. 'Planned Parenthood of Southeastern Pennsylvania *v* Casey', http://caselaw.lp.findlaw.com/cgi-bin/getcase.pl?court= us&vol=505&invol=833 (accessed 27 November 2011).

Wolin, Richard. 2010. 'The Idea of Cosmopolitanism: From Kant to the Iraq War and Beyond', *Ethics & Global Politics* 3(2): 143–53.

7

Diasporas, Cosmopolitanism and Post-territorial Citizenship

Francesco Ragazzi

Citizenship has undergone dramatic changes over the past forty years. The conception and practice of citizenship based on mutually exclusive, territorial homogeneous states has come under severe attack. Contrary to the wishes of states, codified in international agreements in the 1930s, and reaffirmed until the European Convention on Nationality of 1997, dual citizenship has been sharply on the rise. Amid a sample of fifteen countries, fewer than 5 per cent allowed dual citizenship in 1959; this figure is now about 50 per cent (Sejersen 2008: 531). According to a larger study, in 2009, out of 189 countries, only 53 (28 per cent) did not accept any form of dual citizenship (Blatter et al. 2009: 10). This phenomenon is only one of the indicators of the progressive institutionalization of transnational communities, diasporas, or what could be broadly defined as transnational forms of identification and belonging. From the standpoint of citizenship, there is increasing evidence that citizenries are more and more overlapping, ever less constrained by state-defined territorial limits.

These developments do not go without questioning some of the most fundamental assumptions of the Westphalian project of the territorial state, as well as the liberal theories of representative politics on which modern democratic regimes are premised. More precisely, transformations, such as the tolerance towards dual citizenship, the possibility of obtaining citizenship abroad or voting and being represented as a constituency abroad, challenge the traditional assumptions of a match between identities, borders, and social and political orders (Albert et al. 2001). They assume and enact the conception that the 'domestic' is not necessarily within the borders of the nation state, but can in fact be a 'domestic abroad' (Varadarajan 2010).

What is the meaning of these transformations, and what have been the main interpretations of it? Over the past twenty years, 'globalization' as a distinct economic and social phenomenon, has carried with it the hopes of a political order that would overcome the traditional frontiers of the nation state. The end of the Cold War has in particular generated a renewed interest in ideas of cosmopolitanism and brought into existence a vibrant interdisciplinary field of study concerned precisely with the possibility of thinking citizenship beyond the territorial state. And so it is not surprising that diaspora policies have been interpreted within this framework.

The aim of this essay is however to question this optimist reading of diaspora policies. I will contend that if cosmopolitanists are right in finding in these developments the emergence of political spaces beyond the territorial state, it is however a mistake to conflate them with manifestations of progressive or cosmopolitan politics. It is indeed important to distinguish the post-territorial nature of diasporic practices of citizenship — what I term post-territorial citizenship — with the misleading, normatively charged assumption that they are necessarily a form of cosmopolitan resistance to an exclusionary or repressive order. In fact, most of the time, the opposite is true: diasporic citizenship has been ethnicized from the onset and has gone hand in hand with exclusionary practices of citizenship towards non-ethnics on the territory, organizing what Igor Štiks and I have defined as the 'ethnic engineering of citizenship' (Ragazzi and Štiks 2009).

I develop in this essay a double argument. I claim that after a historical period of intense territorial securitization of citizenship, which has forced both immigration and emigration states in a territorial straightjacket, the current developments have not meant a desecuritization of migrant citizens, or the advancement of post-national/cosmopolitan values, but the opposite. The current evolution of citizenship has to be understood as a progressive bifurcation of the logics of managing migration, between immigration and emigration logics. In terms of immigration — and despite the current political discourse on the supposed demise of multiculturalism (Vertovec and Wessendorf 2010) — immigrants are ever less required to assimilate in order to gain access to denizenship or citizenship. This, however, does not mean they are less subject to practices of control and surveillance. The imperative of mobility and the management through community are two of the contemporary faces of neoliberal government through risk (Hindess 2002, 2004; Walters 2002; Nyers 2003; Isin 2004). What has rarely been analysed in the literature, however, is the other side of citizenship practices in relation to migration; and the constitutive relationship between immigration and emigration contexts for the shaping of contemporary citizenship.[1] In emigration contexts, indeed the loosening of the straightjacket has meant the appearance of what could be defined as forms of post-territorial citizenship: policies of diaspora inclusion or 'global nations' premised on a deterritorialized, ethnic conception of citizenship, and a novel exclusion of unwanted territorialized ethnic groups.

Cosmopolitan, Post-national or Post-territorial Citizenship?

Why are governmental enactments of diasporic citizenship — that is, practices of extending civic, social and political citizenship rights to populations abroad — not necessarily markers of cosmopolitan citizenship? At first sight, diasporic citizenship seems to have many affinities with cosmopolitan citizenship. As Andrew Linklater argues, the cosmopolitan conception of citizenship stands against 'traditional perspectives [which] maintain that modern conceptions of citizenship are anchored in the world of the bounded community; [which] contend that it loses its precise meaning when divorced from territoriality, sovereignty and shared nationality' (Linklater 1998: 22). It puts forward a notion of citizenship that takes into account the changes brought about by the flows of people, capital and ideas that cross national boundaries at an increasing pace and therefore posits a global sense of entitlement and responsibility that is not and should be bound by the territorial borders of the state (ibid.: 23). In this framework, migrants and diasporas are the primary political subject of cosmopolitan change and hybridization (Gilroy 1994; Appiah 2006). In the normative opposition between a closed, exclusionary nation state and an emancipatory transnational alternative, diasporas are the ontological contenders, the cosmopolitan challengers of the nation state (Appadurai 1991).

---

[1] Important exceptions are, among others, Spiro (1997), Isin (1999), Hindess (2001), Koslowski (2005), and Guillaume (2007).

And so, rather unsurprisingly, cosmopolitanists have located state-backed diaspora policies in this framework. As Seyla Benhabib puts it:

> Today nation-states encourage diasporic politics among their migrants and ex-citizens, seeing in the diaspora not only a source of political support for projects at home, but also a resource of networks, skills and competencies that can be used to enhance a state's own standing in an increasingly global world (Benhabib 2007: 24).

Transnational migrations, Benhabib explains, foreground the 'pluralization of sites of sovereignty' in that diasporas live across multiple legal systems and jurisdictions, under the protection of cosmopolitan norms enforced by human rights treaties, and in struggle with a system of state sovereignty which privileges national citizenship and restricts dual and multiple citizenship (ibid.). Hence diaspora policies support the 'cosmopolitan argument', namely that:

> [W]orld citizenship can be a powerful means of coaxing citizens away from the false supposition that the interests of fellow citizens necessarily take priority over duties to the rest of the human race; it is a unique device for eliciting their support for global political institutions and sentiments which weaken the grip of exclusionary separate states (Linklater 1998: 22).

Aihwa Ong has already produced an extensive critique of the 'innocent concept of the essential diasporan subject, one that celebrates hybridity, "cultural" border crossing, and the production of difference in the work of Gilroy, Hall, Clifford and Bhabha' (Ong 2000: 13). I will therefore not repeat it here. The main issue I take with existing explanations is what we could define as the spectrum of 'methodological post-nationalism'.[2] The 'post-national' argument has been popularized, among others, by the work of Yasemin Soysal.[3] Soysal argues that migrants and diasporas increasingly escape the statist conception of the nation through sub-national,

---

[2] This play on words has also been used by Cauvet (2011).

[3] For variations on the concept of post-nationalism, see Jacobson (1996) and Habermas and Pensky (2001). For a different take on post-nationalism, see the concept of 'denationalization' as developed by Bosniak (2000) and Sassen (2006).

supranational or transnational forms of belonging, anchoring their rights as citizens no longer in the institutions of the state, but through forms of 'universal personhood' embedded in novel human rights norms and treaties which came to force after World War II (WWII). In doing so, they are 'post-national' and, therefore, cosmopolitan.

By 'methodological post-nationalism' I therefore want to suggest, as the proponents of 'methodological nationalism' do,[4] that much of the literature on citizenship and diaspora politics has been permeated by an untold, unconscious set of normative and methodological assumptions that need to be made explicit in order to be overcome.

The first problematic assumption lies in the conflation of the 'national' with the 'territorial'. All that is 'national' — and, therefore, nationalism — can only be territorial. Anything that goes beyond the territory is, therefore, to the opposite, post-national. Thus, transnational practices are interpreted as necessarily undermining the logic of nationalism and its exclusionary effects — and, therefore, a sign of resistance or cosmopolitanism. The second problematic assumption is that state power is exclusively territorial. Processes that go beyond the territoriality of the state are assumed to somewhat escape its power — and therefore solely ruled by individual (ethical) or global (human rights) norms. The conflation of the nation and territory, on the one hand, and state and territory, on the other, paradoxically reproduce, in reverse, the ontological bias of methodological nationalist social science. Mine is therefore not a statist critique of post-nationalism, but a critique of the core assumption of the territorial boundedness of governmental power in explaining the attention of governments to their populations abroad.

What is the alternative? Elsewhere, I have proposed to look at diaspora policies as a shift in the geography of the practices of

---

[4] 'Methodological nationalism' has been developed as a concept to argue that most of the contemporary social science has, from Weber and Durkheim up until recent years, taken for granted the ideas that 'societies' are almost naturally contained by the territorial boundaries of the state, and hence has been blind to social and political processes taking place at the interstice of these frontiers, or simply beyond them. For an in-depth study of the literature of methodological nationalism, see Chernilo (2006).

governmental power (Ragazzi 2009, 2014), by drawing on a large literature in sociology (Hindess 2001; Sassen 2006), political geography (Agnew 1994) and international relations (Ruggie 1993; Bigo and Walker 2007), which has now shown that the state is neither resisting nor being undermined by processes of transnationalization. It is in fact becoming transnational itself. And while a sub-field of diaspora studies now acknowledges the importance of diaspora policies and emigrant citizenship, only a few locate them in a process of transnationalization of state practices.[5]

Building on the work of this latter group of scholars, I suggest conceptualizing state practices of extending citizenship to its citizens beyond the traditional borders of the nation state, forsaking territorial criteria of belonging — such as birth or residence — as practices of 'post-territorial citizenship'. In my understanding — contrarily to most authors who have used the term so far — post-territorial citizenship is not a handy synonym of post-national citizenship; it is a term that undermines its very assumptions.[6] The characteristic of this new form of post-territorial citizenship is indeed to abandon the territorial referent as the main criteria for inclusion and exclusion from citizenship, focusing instead on ethnocultural markers of identity, irrespective of the place of residence. Post-territorial citizenship is hence closely linked to, and partly overlaps with, what Riva Kastoryano (2007) or Nina Glick Schiller and Georges Fouron (1999), among others, have defined as transnational forms of nationalism.

This chapter will argue that as a historical phenomenon, post-territorial citizenship is not new. The territorialization of citizenship — which we take for granted as the normal relation between territory and belonging — spans a brief historical period.[7] In the first section, I show that while states did enact early forms of

---

[5] See Delano and Gamlen (2014) and Ragazzi (2014) for overviews of this literature.

[6] In most of the literature on citizenship and cosmopolitanism, post-national and post-territorial citizenship are used interchangeably. See, for example, Squire (2009), and from a standpoint critical of the concept, see Chandler (2007, 2009), Baker (2007) and Pugh et al. (2007: 107). My goal here is to carve out a different understanding of the term.

[7] I would like to thank Guido Tintori for highlighting the importance of this point.

post-territorial citizenship in the late 19th century, they met repeatedly with two strong territorializing processes. First, since the Bancroft Treaties of the 1860s, and the European Convention on Nationality up to 1997, international agreements actively discouraged dual nationality, the sources of which were precisely practices of post-territorial citizenship. Second, for the most part of this period, even when the nation was conceived in ethnic terms, such as in Italy, Germany or Israel, the political goal up until the past few years was always to 'territorialize' it or 'populate the land'. The nationalities of the Soviet Union, even if conceived in ethnic terms, also had to be territorialized in order to be recognized as such.[8] In the second section, I show that throughout the 20th century, whether civic or ethnic, nations were therefore *territorialized*, and the resolution of issues linked to national heterogeneity of citizenship were perceived as a security threat to the cohesion and survival of the nation or the 'race'.[9] It has led to the enforcement of the principle of mutually exclusive, homogeneous citizenries on territorially defined states. Finally, in the third section, I show how the evolution in the contemporary rationality and practices of government have brought about a bifurcation between immigration and emigration contexts in the relation between citizenship and security: in the former context it is progressively becoming one element among others for the management of populations; in the latter it is becoming the technology of choice to enforce forms of what I term as post-territorial citizenship.

From Perpetual Allegiance to Territorial Citizenship

Thinking of these practices as post-territorial allows two conceptual moves. First, it allows a move from a topology of levels (the subnational, the national, the global) to a topology of transnational, overlapping social spaces (Faist 2004). Practices that cross territorial boundaries create a transnational site of contestation — and therefore politics — and there is certainly no ontological necessity for these practices to be invested in a particular normative position. Second, this space is not a separate, free-floating space

---

[8] See the history of the Jewish autonomous region Birobidhzan in Levin (1990).

[9] What has been debated in critical security studies under the label 'societal security' (Wæver 1993; Roe 2005).

of ideas and cosmopolitan norms, but to the contrary, a space saturated with a multitude of relations of power, legislative systems and bureaucratic routines in which several actors — governments, associations, individuals — are in permanent competition for a material and symbolic definition of the included and the excluded. Analyzing enactments of citizenship as post-territorial therefore allows an exploration of how these open or close down these political spaces.

If we consider the emergence of modern citizenship as resulting from the development of an international society of states in Western Europe roughly around and after the peace of Westphalia,[10] the first logic of citizenship that comes to the fore is the one in which state sovereignty is the ultimate concern, not citizens nor populations themselves. Michel Foucault showed how the practice of power had to be relocated within the broader taken-for-granted assumptions of the time. More precisely, Foucault showed how mercantilism was more than an economic doctrine but a specific programme of government that focused on monetary accumulation and population growth destined at strengthening the power of the sovereign. It carried with it many assumptions about how a state should be ruled. In this perspective, the loss of subjects-citizens was equated with the loss of power for the sovereign in its competition with other powers (Foucault 2004: 7).

Grounded in natural law and encoded in English common law, the principle of perpetual allegiance between the sovereign and its citizens is, throughout feudal Europe, what best illustrates the practice shared by European states. Subjects-citizens had no control over their citizenship; they needed to obtain the consent of the sovereign to renounce it (Spiro 1997: 1419; Legomsky 2003: 109). The sovereign–subject relationship was understood as 'the one of parent and child: a product of nature, hence indissoluble' (Spiro 1997: 1417). It is around this principle that most of the international citizenship battles will be played out until the end of the first half of the 20th century.

---

[10] The peace of Westphalia (1648) serves in this regard more as a symbolic and conceptual reference than an historical and linear starting point, as often assumed in most international relations literature. For a critique, see Osiander (2001).

Throughout most of the 19th century, the freedom to decide one's citizenship waxed and waned according to the political circumstances and more often than not to military preoccupations. France, for example, with the 1803 civil code, was among the first states to give citizens the freedom to move abroad and acquire a foreign citizenship.[11] At the eve of the war with Austria, Napoleon, however, overturned the provision and required that even those who had already naturalized (acquired a new citizenship) in another state to come back. On 26 August 1811, it became illegal to acquire foreign nationality without the permission of the emperor (Weil et al. 2010: 7). In 1889, this again became possible, except for men in age of military service, who had to ask permission (ibid.).

In many states adhering to notions of perpetual allegiance, naturalization (the acquisition of another citizenship) was perceived not so much as an act of treason, but rather as a direct offence to the sovereign. The most telling example of the tension between perpetual allegiance and the new individual freedoms is, in the Anglo-Saxon context, the British policy of forced enrolment (impressement) of US-naturalized subjects of British origins into its Navy, one of the factors that led to the War of 1812. The prince regent captured the view of the time when stating:

> There is no right more clearly established that the right which a sovereign has to the allegiance of his subjects, more especially in time of war. Their allegiance is no optional duty, which they can decline and resume at pleasure. It is a call which they are bound to obey; it began with their birth and can only terminate with their existence (Feldman and Baldwin 2007: 142).

Similar measures existed in Turkey or in China, where, as of 1815, expatriation was punished with death and banishment of the entire family (Spiro 1997: 1420). Throughout the 19th century, the conflict continued between new immigration states, such as the United States, Argentina, Australia or Brazil,[12] which pushed

---

[11] This, in return, entailed the loss of French citizenship (Weil et al. 2010: 6).

[12] 'Brazil, in particular, included in its 1891 Constitution (art. 69) automatic naturalisation of all people resident on 15 November 1889, the day on which the Republic was proclaimed. Renunciation within six months was legally allowed, but strongly discouraged by the public authorities' (Zincone and Basili 2010: 6).

for the release from previous citizenship of their new citizens, and which most (emigration) European states denied, or severely restricted the right of expatriation, facilitating at the same time re-naturalization.

As a reaction to the increased outflow of their population and the naturalization of their citizens in immigration countries, emigration states navigated the ambiguities of citizenship laws and relaxed in practice the requirement of exclusive citizenship. Pre-World War I (WWI) Italy, for example, gave priority to article four of the 1865 code (*ius sanguinis* for children born abroad) over article 11 which did not allow dual citizenship, creating de facto an important number of dual nationals (Tintori 2009: 746). Similarly, the 1913 German citizenship law replaced previous provisions of citizenship loss based on residence and allowed for the preservation or reacquisition of German citizenship regardless of naturalization (Brubaker 1992: 115). A similar trend was found in several other states across Europe and in the world, the result being an exponential increase in dual citizenship. Dual nationals not only created an anomaly that did not fit the strict principles of territorial sovereignty; their progressive increase raised diplomatic tensions. Of particular concern was the military conscription of naturalized immigrants upon their return to their homelands, which happened frequently (Legomsky 2003: 89).[13]

Citizenship laws of emigration countries throughout the 19th century were therefore an indirect diplomatic negotiation with immigration countries over the 'property' of populations, what Koslowski defines as a 'tug of war' between receiving and sending states (Koslowski 2001: 215). It was principally fought over a population conceived as the measurement of the strength of the sovereign power that had nothing to do with the point of view of the populations themselves. As Spiro puts it:

> In this frame, actual sentiments of allegiance on the part of subjects were of an import equivalent to sentiments of allegiance on the part of, say, cannonballs. Expatriation represented an intolerable loss of strength to the birth sovereign, in something of a human equivalent of mercantilist paradigms (Spiro 1997: 1422).

---

[13] Legomsky documents cases in France, Spain, Prussia, and other German states, noting that even today certain citizens of such countries as Turkey, Greece or Iran might face such situations (Legomsky 2003: 89).

Over the years, the conflict, however, settled in favour of the new immigration state; and therefore generalized the freedom to choose one's citizenship. In the US, the spark that pushed for international negotiation concerned the arrest and trial of naturalized US citizens as British subjects in relation to the uprising in Ireland in 1868. They were denied a trial procedure reserved to aliens. Following public outrage, the US Congress passed a law reaffirming expatriation as a fundamental right (ibid.: 1428, 1430). In a series of bilateral treaties passed between the US and countries from Old Europe known as the Bancroft Treaties, emigration states eventually recognized their citizens' right to expatriation. The conflict of migrant population's allegiance between emigration and immigration states was therefore progressively solved through bilateral agreements. Dual nationality had clearly been designated as a problem to solve, and was dealt with by the agreement that diplomatic problems created by dual citizenship would be resolved by policies of simultaneous freedom of expatriation on the emigration end and naturalization on the immigration side.

Yet, the First World War showed the limits of the system. Despite the agreements, many states had claimed their nationals abroad. In the framework of the League of Nations-sponsored International Codification Conference, the regulation of nationality — the success of which was conceived as a solution to future conflicts — became central (Koslowski 2001: 207). The 1930 Convention on Certain Questions Relating to the Conflict of Nationality Laws established that 'it is in the interest of the international community to secure that all members should recognise that every person should have a nationality and should have one nationality only'.[14] A Protocol Relating to Military Obligations in Certain Cases of Double Nationality regulated military matters. The principal measures were to ascertain the automatic expatriation of naturalized citizens, and to reinforce the principle of freedom of renunciation of one's nationality (Legomsky 2003: 92). The Bancroft Treaties, along with the Hague convention, therefore, marked a certain generalization of the principle of free choice of one's citizenship, but also established the juridical framework and the symbolic encoding in international law of the principle of exclusivity of territorial

---

[14] League of Nations 1930, Preamble.

citizenship, which remained mostly untouched until the last three decades.

We can therefore draw a few preliminary remarks. In the relationship between immigration and emigration states, the literature often emphasizes the opposition between *jus sanguinis* and *jus solis* as the main principle of tensions in regard to dual or multiple citizenship. Of course, these regulatory mechanisms played a role in the incorporation of immigrants and their involuntary preservation of citizenship as emigrants. Yet, until at the end of the 19th century, the turning point is the freedom of choice of one's citizenship. This freedom is intended to suppress medieval affiliations with the former country and allow the principle of territorialized and mutually exclusive citizenship to function. Yet, through the principle of strict mutually exclusive citizenship, it is state security that is sought after and guaranteed.

Territorialized Citizens must be Defended

Whereas, in Foucaldian terms, the previous section has mostly been concerned with questions pertaining to forms of sovereign rationality within which the relationship between migration, citizenship and security is articulated, the 19th century marks the progressive emergence and dominance of another rationality of government: territorially-based national homogenization.

As Brubaker noted, 'national homogenization is not simply a political project but a social process that can occur within the institutional and territorial frame of the state even when there is no specifically nationalizing political intent' (Brubaker 2009: 205). National homogenization, is directly linked to the irruption of 'the people' as a source and an object of government; first, the 'race' or 'the nation' and, later on, 'society'. Even though 'the nation' and 'society' quickly became sedimented to the point of becoming taken-for-granted dimensions of the conditions for governmental action, Jacques Donzelot shows how, historically, the question of 'the social' and governing from 'a social point of view' emerged from the contradictions of the democratic promises of the French Revolution of 1789.

Donzelot shows how the notion of 'solidarity' and the progressive establishment of the welfare state allows for a third way between the two conflicting political economical consequences of the revolution: the state's entire withdrawal from the question of redistribution of resources among citizens (radical liberalism) or its entire control of the redistribution of resources (Communism or planned economy) (Donzelot 1994: 157–77). Drawing on this, Nikolas Rose argues:

> [T]he political rationalities that have played so great a part in our own century — socialism, social democracy, social liberalism — may differ on many things, but on this they agreed: the nation must be governed, but one must pose the question of how to govern from "the social point of view". "The social" became a kind of "a priori" of political thought: order would have to be social or it would cease to exist (Rose 1996: 329).

In addition to the logic of exclusive citizenship described in the previous section, the idea that national societies were to be ethnically or culturally homogeneous on a given territory hence became the second dominant set of underpinning assumptions of much of the politics of citizenship in the first half of the 20th century. The ways in which nationalism operated through citizenship to homogenize populations in immigration countries have been well studied, and it is not the purpose of this chapter to revisit these studies. Rather, I would like to highlight the process through which immigration and emigration countries have converged in outlining common problems and finding mirror-like solutions to ensure the national and territorial homogeneity of their states' citizenry.

Let us look at how migration has been conceptualized as a security problem to 'the nation' of citizens. Starting at the end of the 19th century, national diversity was progressively framed as threatening two aspects of political life. First, heterogeneity on the national territory came to be considered, not without complex political struggles (see, for instance, Shain 1999: Ch. 2; Noiriel 2005: Ch. 4), as a problem of allegiance and loyalty. For immigration countries, it became the fear of the 'fifth column': the idea that certain ethnic groups, by preserving their ethno-national identities, posed a threat to national security (Cohen 1996). This is well captured in a discussion on the French nationality law of 1889, in which Maxime Lecomte, a *député* from the north, argued that the highest danger was to 'keep with us men who are not attached to any homeland (*patrie*), who do not like France, whom we did not manage to conquer, and therefore to let ... different nations in the French nation to be created' (Noiriel 2007: 183). This fear was mirrored on the emigration side: the loyalty of those leaving or staying abroad was considered equally suspicious (Shain 1990). A second fear, characteristic of the beginning of the 20th century, was the fear of the corruption of the culture, the nation or the 'race'. Through biological metaphors, only the adequacy between nation and territory came to be considered as a healthy form of political existence, the others as pathologic and therefore threatening. Both immigration and emigration states devised solutions to these fears framed as political problems, and these all pointed to territorial, nationally homogeneous citizenries. Both problems called for responses to ensure the territorial and homogeneous existence of nations.

A first set of practices aimed at creating national homogeneity was based on the premise that migrants could become nationalized citizens. For the immigration states, ethnocultural diversity could be resolved through naturalization and assimilation. The acquisition of citizenship therefore became progressively associated with the acquisition of national features, be it for Jews in Europe (Frankel and Zipperstein 2004), European immigrants in the US (Glazer and Moynihan 1963) and generally foreigners in most immigration countries of South America or Australia. This sparked a parallel reaction among the emigration states: the fear of assimilation of their nationals abroad stimulated cultural policies to prevent it. In Germany, for example, the 1889 'All-German School Association' and post-WWI German Academic Exchange[15] were both conceived as ways to gather the 'nation' across borders and prevent it from dissolving abroad. Similarly, the Dante Alighieri institutes were famously implemented during the 1920s to spread 'national culture' and fascism amongst the Italian emigrant population (Totaro-Genevois 2005: 30). These anti-assimilationists 'aim[ed] to prevent expatriate or same-language communities from being integrated with foreign states, and to maintain them as potential foreign policy instruments, either in relation to territorial claims or to the procurement of economic and political advantage' (Paschalidis 2008: 4).

Yet, starting in the interwar period, assimilation policies were questioned, and with them the idea that those not belonging to

---

[15] Deutscher Akademischer Austausch Dienst (DAAD), the German Academic Exchange Service, was founded in 1925.

the main ethnicity could be turned into loyal citizens. It is in this context that a second set of practices appeared: removing or transferring populations. One particular practice was seen in deportations on an ethno-national basis, from the forced removal of Slovenians and Croats from Italy in the 1930s and the 1940s up to the expulsions of Palestinians from Israel after 1948 (Walters 2002). On the emigration side, this translated in active policies of return: only within its territorial borders would the home state be able to guarantee the security of its citizens. Yet, the return was to be only for a certain ethnicity or religion. In Turkey, for example, Armenians and Greek Orthodox minorities who had left the country during the way of independence were excluded from citizenship by the law of 1927. In 1933, the 'Statute of Travelling' further regulated the return of Anatolian Christians (Kadirbeyoğlu 2010: 2). The complementarity of these two logics is best exemplified in the practice of mutual transfer of populations, in which two states conceive it as their best interest to both deport and import populations, for instance, during the 1923 Greek-Turkish population exchange of about 1.5 million individuals (Hirschon 2003: 3) or the infamous India–Pakistan exchange of more than 12.5 million people (Khan 2007). It is also in this logic that the final solution can be understood. As it is now documented, the idea of the extermination of Jews was seriously considered only after all options for a 'territorial final solution' had been discarded. Eichmann himself built his entire career as a specialist of forced emigration (of Poles and Jews) before becoming an exterminator. At least in two documented occasions in 1936–37 and in 1942, he came into contact with Zionist organizations to facilitate the departure of Jewish German citizens to Palestine. During his trial in Israel in 1961, he went as far as claiming to have been 'the new Herzl' (Cesarani 2004: 9). The collaboration between the Nazi regime and the Zionist organizations reveals the most tragic and most improbable coalition of interests created by the shared desire for homogeneous, territorial citizenries. One side saw it as a condition to preserve the purity of the race and assure it its Lebensraum, the other as the condition of its physical and national survival.

Third, the pervasiveness of the territorial logic is found in practices when populations are not moved over borders, but borders over populations. At the peak of the expansion of nationalist ideas and practices, after the fall of the Ottoman and the Austrian empires, the model of the territorial federation emerges as one of the best blueprints to solve questions of ethnic heterogeneity in the Balkans or Central Europe (Bianchini 1996). Within these federations, the principle of territorial homogeneity remains the organizing principle, as in Yugoslavia or the Soviet Union. The short-lived Soviet Jewish autonomous province of Birobidzhan best exemplifies this conception of the territory. Another practice, the incorporation of missing parts of the national population left abroad in the citizenry by incorporating it territorially, is exemplified by the long history of more or less successful irredentist projects, from the Italian claims over Trieste, Trentino, Istria, and Dalmatia to the 1936 Anschluss or the long list of Great Albania, Serbia, Croatia, Romania, Hungary, Greece which marked the 20th century, as well as the lesser known contemporary claims of the Greater Nagaland and Chinland.

A final set of practices can be found in the resistance of the excluded. In the immigration contexts of the 20th century, migrants and minorities mostly aimed at assimilating and fought for the recognition of their rights, with various degrees of success, in what Engin Isin defined as acts of citizenship (Isin 2002). Yet, when this goal seemed out of reach, the alternative was more often than not equally territorial: if citizenship was endangered in a territorial state, then another nation state had to be created. This was the underlying logic of the Black emigrationist movement in the early 20th century in Jim Crow Southern US, which anticipated Marcus Garvey's Back to Africa slogans (Sundiata 2003: 11–48). The paradigmatic model, and source of many other movements of the kind, remains Zionism. The state of Israel can be seen as the most accomplished result of this practice within which a secure citizenship is conceived as possible only through the territorialization (and therefore refusal) of the diaspora. As an emigration state in which the emigration preceded the creation of the state, it has most zealously enforced the principles of territorial homogeneity as a precondition for security, at least until the 1990s. As Yfaat Weiss convincingly argues, the political context of the early years of Israel, when the Law of Return and the Law on Citizenship were designed, was marked more by the Zionists' memory of interwar Eastern Europe than anything else. Among other factors, the ethnic understanding of citizenship, and, more importantly, 'the adoption of a new spatial-land policy' focused on territorial security and agricultural development, provided the basis for the latest project of European territorial 'nationalizing state' (Weiss 2002). The territorializing project of the state of Israel can therefore be understood as one of the last contemporary attempts and (partial) successes at bringing a large population 'back to the land', in great part in the name of security.

Securing Post-territorial 'Communities'

The previous section has shown how the sovereign and territorial rationalities of power have structured the rationalizations through which threats to and from citizenship have been formulated. The widespread territorial rationality brought together immigration and emigration states in securing their citizenries in mirror-like practices of homogenization. Yet, two important changes have come about with the overall decline of the welfare state and the failure of socialist economies and the related progressive diffusion of what is commonly called a neoliberal or 'advanced liberal' form of governmentality, intended not only as an economic doctrine but as a form of government (Barry et al. 1993; Rose 1999). First, the economic frame of reference for what it is to be governed is no longer thought of purely in terms of national territories; that is, competition is no longer predominantly international, but local, regional and transnational. Hence, policies oriented towards providing welfare are progressively dismantled and become segmented in service to particular professional sectors, geographic locales or types of activity. Second, the 'advanced liberal' political economy brings about the idea that individuals are no longer to be passively and collectively governed through the impersonal figure of the state (through health care, social security, etc.), but that instead they should be active in their own government. Forms of allegiance and responsibilities are therefore oriented towards the local, and circles of solidarity are increasingly located in the community. By defining this process as the 'the death of the social', Nikolas Rose remarked that 'such virtual communities are 'diasporic'; they exist only to the extent that their constituents are linked together through identifications constructed in the non-geographic spaces of activist discourses, cultural products and media images' (Rose 1996: 333).

It is in this context that we are currently witnessing a progressive bifurcation between immigration and emigration contexts. First, and despite the current political discourse on the supposed demise of multiculturalism (Vertovec and Wessendorf 2010), immigrants are ever less required to assimilate in order to gain access to full or partial citizenship. Citizenship is ever less a marker of exclusive ethnic identity or national allegiance. Dual nationality is not only on the rise, but the undesirability of multiple citizenships has been removed from international agreements (Hailbronner 2003: 21). This, however, has not meant a de-securitization of migrant citizens, but the opposite. Migrants, foreigners and minorities are increasingly policed and surveyed independently of their paper identity.

Second, and this has received less scholarly attention, the loosening of the territorial grip has meant, in emigration contexts, the appearance of what could be defined as forms of post-territorial citizenship: policies of diaspora inclusion or 'global nations' premised on a de-territorialized, ethnic conception of citizenship, and a novel exclusion of unwanted territorialized ethnic groups.

Immigration Contexts: The Decreasing Relevance of Citizenship

Within the frame of mobility, the first evolution should be considered in the context of the contemporary imperative of circulation imposed by political economic ideas and practices of *laissez-faire, laissez-passer*. The era of disciplinary economic and political protectionism in which the territorialization and homogenization of citizenship took place is past (Sassen 2006). Immigration governments have by and large acknowledged the necessary mobility of capital and labour, and have acknowledged the illusion constituted by closed territories and societies. Of course, the borders of immigration countries are still violent, as exemplified along the US-Mexican border (Doty 1999) or by the external border of the European Union (EU) (Jeandesboz 2008). Yet, despite the increasing number of deaths at the borders of the US, Australia or Europe, and without diminishing the tragic individual fates behind statistical figures, these deaths represent a numerically small number of individuals in relation to how many of the world's migrants are indeed able to travel, circulate and develop transnational affiliations (Bigo 2010). As studies have documented, the concern of most immigration states and institutions has now moved from stopping and checking all, to assessing the risk of illegal migration, of terrorism, of human smuggling, or organized crime (Aradau and Van Munster 2007; Aradau et al. 2008).

In this process, citizenship is certainly an important feature, but it has increasingly become only one criterion among many to determine the potential threat posed by mobile citizens (Bigo et al. 2011). Biometric data held in travel documents, connected to a growing number of databases, are indeed increasingly complexifying the modalities of control and surveillance, through the progressive constitution of 'smart borders' (Salter 2004; Muller 2008). The logic behind these forms of control has substantially altered the previous ways in which the relation between diasporas, security and citizenship has been articulated. More specifically, it has almost entirely abolished the suspicion of allegiance and loyalty towards a foreign state. Instead, citizenship has become mostly an indicator of geographic provenience, to be correlated with other elements such as travel record, age and sex or dietary preferences (Amoore 2006). In a sense, the belief in biometrics and the anticipation of the future is giving less and less importance to alleged feelings of foreign loyalty and increasingly inscribes practices of security in the body of travellers and their data double, rather than in formal marks of belonging and citizenship.

Concerning the populations that are 'already there', post-nationalists are certainly right when they point out the fact that over the past forty years, immigration states have substantially toned down projects of national homogenization and assimilation of ethno-linguistic minorities and diasporic groups (despite the revival of assimilationist political discourses). Communities have been brought to the fore and are more in line with modalities of government that have abandoned 'the social' as an object of government (Donzelot 1994). The neoliberal reaction to the contradictions of the welfare state has been to shift the management responsibility from the social to 'communities' as 'a new plane or surface upon which micro-moral relations among persons are conceptualised and administered' (Rose 1996: 331). As such, multiculturalism has replaced the previous models of incorporation, precisely constituting communities as a new object of government for politicians, psychiatrists, healthcare professionals, and security forces. The move to communities therefore does not provide us with more evidence of a de-securitization of movement and mobility; instead, it provides us with a re-articulation of the object of policing and surveillance. Rose reminds us that community, as a concept, emerges in part from sociological and bureaucratic sources, but that it is rapidly picked up by the police to talk about things such as the West Indian community. Rapidly, communities became new objects to be 'investigated, mapped, classified, documented, interpreted' (Rose 1996: 331). Similarly, communities have progressively been asked to police themselves, as in programmes of community policing which have flourished in North America, Europe and Australia. While the social was essentially territorial and constituted by individuals captured by the political form of citizenship, communities define a new object of government in which the distinction between citizens and non-citizens is made irrelevant. What is at stake, instead, is the quality of opportunity and risk constituted by the communities, both for the individuals who compose them and for the states that govern them. So while the question of loyalty of certain citizens might still be posed, it is currently posed mostly in relation to their perceived or alleged belonging to a risk community. The category of Muslim has, for example, emerged in the UK and many European countries as a 'suspect community', irrespective of the actual religious practice or political views of its members (Pantazis and Pemberton 2009).

The Emigration Context: Post-territorial Citizenship

On the emigration side, the passage from welfarism or developmental policies to neoliberal conceptions of government has similarly brought about significant change. In this case, however, it has reinforced the importance of citizenship. States with a large population abroad have increasingly used citizenship or para-citizenship[16] to solve the tension between economic growth strategies demanding a circulation of its population and the fear of a brain-drain and dispersion of resources. Citizenship here serves as the main tool through which a population residing abroad is perceived and included as useful for the economic or political interests of the state. The specificity of this new form of citizenship is that it is no longer tied to residential or territorial constraints; rather than a post-national modality of citizenship, it can be defined as post-territorial.

These symbolic politics first started with a major relabelling of groups abroad, from 'immigrants', 'refugees', 'political exiles', or

---

[16] By para-citizenship, I refer to all sorts of symbolic documents and cards delivered to emigrants with the purpose of giving them a special status. These are, for example, the Person of Indian Origin (PIO) card, the 'Pink Card' in Turkey or the 'CRO Card' in Croatia.

'guest workers' they are now officially 'diasporas', 'global nations' or 'nations abroad' (Schnapper 2001; Smith 2003; Brubaker 2005). Previously pejorative terms become the object of stigma reversals, for example, the valorization of the 'pochos' (a pejorative term for emigrants in Mexico) by the Programme for Mexican Communities Abroad (Smith 2003: 728). Heads of states increasingly embrace populations that were previously forgotten. While Zionism was based on a negation of the diasporic existence, Ariel Sharon announced in 2002 that he understood his mandate as unifying not only Israel but 'Jews worldwide' (Shain and Bristman 2002: 77); Mexico's president, Vicente Fox, announced in 2000 that he would 'govern on behalf of 118 million Mexicans', 18 million of whom are living in the US (Varadarajan 2010: 3). Similarly, diasporas are increasingly becoming a specific 'state category'. This has translated into administrative modifications of sending states and a multiplication of 'diaspora' ministries and agencies; be it the Ministry of Diaspora in Serbia or in Armenia, the Institute for Mexicans Abroad in Mexico, the Irish Abroad Unit in Ireland, the Ministry of Italians Abroad in Italy, the Commission on Filipinos Overseas, the Overseas Employment Office in China and a broad range of 'diaspora' ministries across the Middle East and Africa. In this context, sending states' citizenship laws have increasingly been amended in favour of dual citizenship: a specific legal status and identification documents are often given to expatriates, for instance, non-resident Indians (NRIs) and Persons of Indian Origin (PIOs) in India, or 'Matricula Consular' in Mexico. Similar types of status exist thus far in Argentina, Colombia, Salvador, Honduras, Peru, Morocco, Pakistan, and Turkey.

The institutionalization of diasporic citizenship has however not meant an opening up or a move towards a more cosmopolitan conception of belonging, as post-nationalists would argue. In most emigration countries, the extension citizenship to co-ethnics outside the territorial borders of the state goes with exclusionary practices towards the non-ethnics on the territory. The ethnicization or re-ethnicization of citizenship can be seen in the re-emergence of essentialized conceptions of belonging, such as *italianità* (Italianness), *mexicanidad* (Mexicanness), *Hrvatsvo* (Croatianness), and *Hindutva* (Indianness). These conceptions allow the repackaging of heterogeneous national constructions into a homogeneous essence, and, more importantly, as a feature that is independent from the territory. Italianità, for example, can be used to refer to a hypothetical national character shared by all Italians, no matter where they live. It, therefore, becomes a mobile criterion of belonging through which institutionalized state practices can be deployed. Similarly, the Croatian Law on Citizenship of 1991 is explicitly aimed to include Croats everywhere in the world, and exclude as many non-Croats (that is, Serbs) (Ragazzi and Štiks 2009). Comparable developments have taken place in Serbia and Macedonia in which the aim has been explicitly to exclude Albanians from the national population (Ragazzi and Balalovska 2011). The debate around the Status Law in Hungary, which extends citizenship to Hungarians abroad, revolves around similar patterns of inclusion and exclusion (Waterbury 2006). Examples can be found in several other emigration countries outside Europe. Israel's recent reconsideration of its relation with its diaspora is similarly grounded in the ideal of a non-Palestinian and non-Arab citizenry (Levy and Weiss 2002). India's diaspora policy promoted by the Bharatiya Janata Party (BJP) has run parallel to a discourse of exclusion of the Muslims from Indian citizenship (Jaffrelot and Therwath 2007). In sum, the inclusion of co-ethnics abroad has meant, in several contexts, the simultaneous exclusion of non co-ethnics on the territory. Rather than a form of inclusion, diaspora policies have therefore meant a redefinition of the borders of the nation and a renewed modality of discrimination.

Conclusion

In our most recent history, diasporic and transnational forms of identification, mobilization and belonging have been constituted as a question of security in a context in which the homogenization of citizenship was the governmental project. As this chapter has argued, this project has been linked mainly to specific rationalizations as to how wealth is concentrated and organized, and how loyalty and security can be best assured and organized. In this sense, a history of citizenship cannot be separated from the history of the different rationalities of power within which it has been deployed (Isin 2002). The contemporary era is marked by the progressive unbundling of territory, identities and political orders. Yet the consequences of this process for citizenship should not be interpreted as the emergence of cosmopolitan norms of citizenship, but rather as a redistribution of the features of citizenship. On the one hand, it continues to be a tool for governments to distribute and organize practices of control, surveillance and exclusion. On the other hand, citizenship always potentially enables acts of citizenship that bear the promise of further inclusion. I have shown how the neoliberal production of community 'as a logic of governing that migrates and is selectively taken up in diverse political contexts' (Ong 2007: 3) appears to be translated in the terms of communitarian citizenship in immigration contexts and in the forms of post-territorial citizenship in emigration contexts. These are two sides of the same coin, and mark a deep shift in the rationalities of citizenship, increasingly oriented towards privileging the criteria of race, religion or ethnicity to the detriment of those of territoriality and residence (Glick Schiller and Fouron 1999). These practices do not go unchallenged, and the contemporary evolution of citizenship does not go without generating its new modalities of resistance.

≈

References

Agnew, John A. 1994. 'The Territorial Trap: The Geographical Assumptions of International Relations Theory', *Review of International Political Economy* 1(1): 53–80.

Albert, Mathias, David Jacobson and Yosef Lapid. 2001. *Identities, Borders, Orders: Rethinking International Relations Theory*, Borderlines, University of Minnesota Press, Minneapolis.

Amoore, Louise. 2006. 'Biometric Borders: Governing Mobilities in the War on Terror', *Political Geography* 25(3): 336–51.

Appadurai, Arjun. 1991. 'Global Ethnoscapes: Notes and Queries for a Transnational Anthropology', in Richard Fox (ed.), *Recapturing Anthropology: Working in the Present*, School of American Research Press, Santa Fe, 191–210.

Appiah, Anthony. 2006. *Cosmopolitanism: Ethics in a World of Strangers*, 1st edition, W.W. Norton & Co, New York.

Aradau, Claudia and Rens Van Munster. 2007. 'Governing Terrorism Through Risk: Taking Precautions, (un)Knowing the Future', *European Journal of International Relations* 13(1): 89–115.

Aradau, Claudia, Luis Lobo-Guerrero and Rens Van Munster. 2008. 'Security, Technologies of Risk, and the Political: Guest Editors' Introduction', *Security Dialogue* 39(2–3): 147–54.

Baker, Gideon. 2007. 'Commentaries: Debating (De)Territorial Governance: Post-Territorial Politics and the Politics of Difference', *Area* 39(1): 109–12.

Barry, Andrew, Thomas Osborne and Nikolas Rose. 1993. 'Liberalism, Neo-liberalism and Governmentality: Introduction', *Economy and Society* 22(3): 265–66.

Benhabib, Seyla. 2007. 'Twilight of Sovereignty or the Emergence of Cosmopolitan Norms? Rethinking Citizenship in Volatile Times', *Citizenship Studies* 11(1): 19–36.

Bianchini, Stefano. 1996. *Sarajevo, Le Radici dell'Odio — Identità e Destino dei Popoli Balcanici*, Edizioni Associate, Roma.

Bigo, Didier. 2010. 'Freedom and Speed in Enlarged Borderzones', in Vicky Squire (ed.), *The Contested Politics of Mobility. Borderzones and Irregularity*, Routledge, New York.

Bigo, Didier, Julien Jeandesboz, Francesco Ragazzi, and Philippe Bonditti. 2011. 'Borders and Security: The Different Logics of Surveillance in Europe', in Saskia Bonjour, Andrea Rea and Dirk Jacobs (eds), *The Others in Europe*, Editions de l'Université de Bruxelles, Brussels, 77–89.

Bigo, Didier and R. B. J. Walker. 2007. 'International, Political, Sociology', *International Political Sociology* 1(1): 1–5.

Blatter, Joachim, Stefanie Erdmann and Katja Schwanke. 2009. 'Acceptance of Dual Citizenship: Empirical Data and Political Contexts', *Working Paper Series Global Governance and Democracy*, University of Lucern, Lucern.

Bosniak, Linda. 2000. 'Citizenship Denationalized', *Indiana Journal of Global Legal Studies* 7(2): 447–509.

Brubaker, Rogers. 1992. *Citizenship and Nationhood in France and Germany*, Harvard University Press, Cambridge MA.

———. 2005. 'The "Diaspora" Diaspora', *Ethnic and Racial Studies* 28(1): 1–19.

———. 2009. 'National Homogenization and Ethnic Reproduction on the European Periphery', in Marzio Barbagli and Harvie Ferguson (eds), *La teoria sociologica e lo stato moderno: Saggi in onore di Gianfranco Poggi*, Il Mulino, 201–21.

Cauvet, Philippe. 2011. 'Deterritorialisation, Reterritorialisation, Nations and States: Irish Nationalist Discourses on Nation and Territory Before and After the Good Friday Agreement', *GeoJournal* 76(1): 77–91.

Cesarani, David. 2004. *Eichmann: His Life and Crimes*, W. Heinemann, London.

Chandler, David. 2007. 'Commentaries: Debating (De)Territorial Governance: The Possibilities of Post-Territorial Political Community', *Area* 39(1): 116–19.

Chandler, David. 2009. 'Critiquing Liberal Cosmopolitanism? The Limits of the Biopolitical Approach', *International Political Sociology* 3(1): 53–70.

Chernilo, Daniel. 2006. 'Social Theory's Methodological Nationalism', *European Journal of Social Theory* 9(1): 5–22.

Cohen, Robin. 1996. 'Diasporas and The Nation-State: From Victims to Challengers', *International Affairs* 72(3): 507–20.

Delano, Alexandra and Alan Gamlen. 2014. 'Political Geography', *Political Geography* 41: 43–53.

Donzelot, Jacques. 1994. *L'invention du social: Essai sur le déclin des passions politiques*, Vol. 287, *Points*, Seuil, Paris.

Doty, Roxanne. 1999. 'Racism, Desire, and the Politics of Immigration', *Millennium: Journal of International Studies* 28(3): 585–606.

Faist, Thomas. 2004. 'Towards a Political Sociology of Transnationalization: The State of the Art in Migration Research', *European Journal of Sociology* 45(3): 311–66.

Feldman, David and M. Page Baldwin. 2007. 'Emigration and the British State Ca.1815–1820', in Nancy L. Green and François Weil (eds), *Citizenship and Those who Leave: The Politics of Emigration and Expatriation*, University of Illinois Press, Urbana, 135–55.

Foucault, Michel. 2004. *Naissance de la biopolitique: Cours au Collège de France (1978–1979)*, Coll. *Hautes Etudes*, Gallimard, Seuil, Paris.

Frankel, Jonathan and Steven Zipperstein. 2004. *Assimilation and Community: The Jews in Nineteenth-Century Europe*, Cambridge University Press, Cambridge.

Gamlen, Alan. 2008. 'The Emigration State and the Modern Geopolitical Imagination', *Political Geography* 27(8): 840–56.

Gilroy, Paul. 1994. 'Diaspora', *Paragraph* 17(1): 207–12.

Glazer, Nathan and Daniel Moynihan. 1963. *Beyond the Melting Pot*, MIT Press, Cambridge, MA.

Glick Schiller, Nina, and Georges Fouron. 1999. 'Terrains of Blood and Nation: Haitian Transnational Social Fields', *Ethnic and Racial Studies* 22(2): 340–66.

Guillaume, Xavier. 2007. 'Unveiling the 'International': Process, Identity and Alterity', *Millennium: Journal of International Studies* 35(3): 741–58.

Habermas, Jürgen, and Max Pensky. 2001. *The postnational constellation political essays*. 1st MIT Press ed, *Studies in contemporary German social thought*, MIT Press, Cambridge Mass, London.

Hailbronner, Kay. 2003. 'Rights and Duties of Dual Nationals: Changing Concepts and Attitudes', in David A. Martin and Kay Hailbronner (eds), *Rights and Duties of Dual Nationals. Evolution and Prospects*, Kluwer Law International, The Hague (Netherlands).

Hindess, Barry. 2001. 'Citizenship in the International Management of Populations', in Denise Meredyth and Jeffrey Minson (eds), *Citizenship and Cultural Policy*, Sage, Thousand Oaks California and London, 92–103.

———. 2002. 'Neo-liberal Citizenship', *Citizenship Studies* 6(2): 127–43.

———. 2004. 'Citizenship for All', *Citizenship Studies* 8(3): 305–15.

Isin, Engin F. 2002. *Being Political: Genealogies of Citizenship*, University of Minnesota Press, Minneapolis.

———. 2004. 'The Neurotic Citizen', *Citizenship Studies* 8(3): 217–35.

Jacobson, David. 1996. *Rights Across Borders: Immigration and the Decline of Citizenship*, Johns Hopkins University Press, Baltimore.

Jaffrelot, Christophe and Ingrid Therwath. 2007. 'The Sangh Parivar and the Hindu Diaspora in the West: What Kind of "Long-Distance Nationalism"?' *International Political Sociology* 1(3): 278–95.

Jeandesboz, Julien. 2008. 'Reinforcing the Surveillance of EU Borders: The Future Development of FRONTEX and EUROSUR', *CHALLENGE Research Papers* No. 11, The Centre for European Policy Studies (CEPS), Brussels.

Kadirbeyoğlu, Zeynep. 2010. 'Country Report: Turkey', *EUDO Citizenship Observatory*, European University Institute, Florence.

Kastoryano, Riva. 2007. 'Transnational Nationalism: Redefining Nation and Territory', in Seyla Benhabib, Ian Shapiro and Danilo Petranovic (eds), *Identities, Affiliations, and Allegiances*, Cambridge University Press, Cambridge, 159–80.

Koslowski, Rey. 2001. 'Demographic Boundary Maintenance in World Politics: Of International Norms on Dual Nationality', in Mathias Albert, David Jacobson and Yosef Lapid (eds), *Identities, Borders, Orders: Rethinking International Relations Theory*, University of Minnesota Press, Minneapolis, 203–24.

———. 2005. *International MIGRATION and the globalization of Domestic Politics, Transnationalism*, Routledge, London and New York.

Legomsky, Stephen H. 2003. 'Dual Nationality and Military Service. Strategy Number Two', in David A. Martin and Kay Hailbronner (eds), *Rights and Duties of Dual Nationals. Evolution and Prospects*, Kluwer Law International, The Hague (Netherlands), 79–126.

Levin, Nora. 1990. *The Jews in the Soviet Union since 1917: Paradox of Survival*, New York University Press, New York.

Levy, Daniel and Yfaat Weiss. 2002. *Challenging Ethnic Citizenship: German and Israeli Perspectives on Immigration*, Berghahn Books, New York.

Linklater, Andrew. 1998. 'Cosmopolitan Citizenship', *Citizenship Studies* 2(1): 23–41.

Muller, Benjamin. 2008. 'Governing through Risk at the Canada/US Border: Liberty, Security, Technology', *BPRI Working Paper* (2), Western Washington University, Bellingham.

Noiriel, Gérard. 2005. *Etat, Nation Et Immigration: Vers Une Histoire Du Pouvoir*, Gallimard, Paris.

———. 2007. *Immigration, antisémitisme et racisme en France, XIXe–XXe siècle: Discours publics, humiliations privées*, Fayard, Paris.

Nyers, Peter. 2003. 'Abject Cosmopolitanism: The Politics of Protection in the Anti-deportation Movement', *Third World Quarterly* 24(6): 1069–93.

Ong, Aihwa. 2000. *Flexible Citizenship: The Cultural Logics of Transnationality* 2, Duke University Press, Durham.

———. 2007. 'Boundary Crossings: Neoliberalism as a Mobile Technology', *Transactions of the Institute of British Geographers* 32(1): 3–8.

Osiander, Andreas. 2001. 'Sovereignty, International Relations and the Westphalian Myth', *International Organization* 55(2): 251–87.

Pantazis, Christina and Simon Pemberton. 2009. 'From the Old to the New Suspect Community: Examining the Impacts of Recent UK Counter-Terrorist Legislation', *British Journal of Criminology* 49(5): 646–66.

Paschalidis, Gregory. 2008. 'Exporting National Culture: Histories of Cultural Institutes Abroad', Paper read at 5th International Conference on Cultural Policy Research, 20–24 August, Istanbul.

Pugh, Jonathan, Caspar Hewett and David Chandler. 2007. 'Commentaries: Debating (De)Territorial Governance: Debating (De)Territorial Governance', *Area* 39(1): 107–9.

Ragazzi, Francesco. 2009. 'Governing Diasporas', *International Political Sociology* 3(4): 378–97.

———. 2014. 'A Comparative Analysis of Diaspora Policies', *Political Geography* 41: 74–89.

Ragazzi, Francesco and Kristina Balalovska. 2011. 'Diaspora Politics and Post-Territorial Citizenship in Croatia, Serbia and Macedonia', *CITSEE Working Papers Series* 2011/18, Edinburgh.

Ragazzi, Francesco and Igor Štiks. 2009. 'Croatian Citizenship: From Ethnic Engineering to Inclusiveness', in Rainer Baubock, Wiebke Sievers and Bernhard Perchinig (eds), *Citizenship and Migration in the New Member and Accession States of the E.U.*, University of Amsterdam Press, Amsterdam, 339–63.

Roe, Paul. 2005. *Ethnic Violence and the Societal Security Dilemma*, Routledge, London and New York.

Rose, Nikolas S. 1996. 'The Death of the Social? Re-figuring the Territory of Government', *Economy and Society* 25(3): 327–56.

———. 1999. *Powers of Freedom: Reframing Political Thought*, Cambridge University Press, Cambridge UK and New York.

Ruggie, John Gerard. 1993. 'Territoriality and Beyond: Problematizing Modernity in International Relations', *International Organization* 47(1): 139–74.

Salter, Mark B. 2004. 'Passports, Mobility, and Security: How Smart can the Border be?', *International Studies Perspectives* 5(1): 71–91.

Sassen, Saskia. 2006. *Territory, Authority, Rights: From Medieval to Global Assemblages*, Princeton University Press, Princeton.

Schnapper, Dominique. 2001. 'De l'Etat-nation au monde transnational (Du sens et de l'utilité du concept de diaspora)', *Revue Européenne des Migrations Internationales* 2(17): 9–36.

Sejersen, Tanja Brondsted. 2008. '"I Vow to Thee My Countries" — The Expasion of Dual Citizenship in the 21st Century', *International Migration Review* 42(3): 523–49.

Shain, Yossi. 1990. *The Frontier of Loyalty: Political Exiles in the Age of the Nation-state*, Wesleyan University Press, Middletown, CT.

———. 1999. *Marketing the American Creed Abroad*, Cambridge University Press, Cambridge.

Shain, Yossi and Barry Bristman. 2002. 'Diaspora, Kinship and Loyalty: The Renewal of Jewish National Security', *International Affairs* 78(1): 69–95.

Smith, Robert C. 2003. 'Diasporic Memberships in Historical Perspective: Comparative Insights from the Mexican, Italian and Polish Cases', *The International Migration Review: IMR* 37(3): 724–59.

Spiro, Peter. 1997. 'Dual Nationality and the Meaning of Citizenship', *Emory Law Journal* 46(4): 1412–85.

Squire, Vicki. 2009. 'Migration, Minorities, and Citizenship', *The Exclusionary Politics of Asylum*, Palgrave Macmillan, Basingstoke and New York.

Sundiata, I. K. 2003. *Brothers and Strangers: Black Zion, Black Slavery, 1914–1940*, Duke University Press, Durham.

Tintori, Guido. 2009. 'Nuovi italiani e italiani nel mondo. Il nodo della cittadinanza', in Paola Corti and Matteo Sanfilippo (eds), *Storia d'Italia — Annali, Migrazioni*, Giulio Einaudi, Torino, 743–64.

Totaro-Genevois, M. 2005. *Cultural and Linguistic Policy Abroad: The Italian Experience*, Multilingual Matters Limited, Clevedon.

Varadarajan, Latha. 2010. *The Domestic Abroad: Diasporas in International Relations*, Oxford University Press, Oxford.

Vertovec, Steven and Susanne Wessendorf. 2010. *The Multiculturalism Backlash*, Routledge, New York.

Wæver, Ole. 1993. 'Societal Security: The Concept', in Ole Wæver, Barry Buzan, Morten Kelstrup, and Pierre Lemaitre (eds), *Identity, Migration and the New Security Agenda in Europe*, St Martin's Press, New York.

Walters, William. 2002. 'Deportation, Expulsion, and the International Police of Aliens', *Citizenship Studies* 6(3): 265–92.

Waterbury, Myra. 2006. 'Internal Exclusion, External Inclusion: Diaspora Politics and Party-Building Strategies in Post-Communist Hungary', *East European Politics & Societies* 20(3): 483–515.

Weil, Patrick, Alexis Spire and Christophe Bertossi. 2010. 'Country Report: France', *EUDO Citizenship Observatory*, European University Institute, Florence.

Weiss, Yfaat. 2002. 'The Golem and its Creator, or How the Jewish Nation-state became Multiethnic', in Daniel Levy and Yfaat Weiss (eds), *Challenging Ethnic Citizenship: German and Israeli Perspectives on Immigration*, Berghahn Books, New York.

Zincone, Giovanna and Marzia Basili. 2010. 'Country Report: Italy', *EUDO Citizenship Observatory*, European University Institute, Florence.

8

The 'Domestic Abroad' and the Limits of Cosmopolitanism

Latha Varadarajan

In the heady aftermath of the collapse of the Soviet Union, theorists of international politics, by and large, celebrated what they regarded as an epochal shift. The 'end of history' and the ostensible victory of liberal democracy contributed to a drifting away from archaic notions of territorial sovereignty, and a reassessment of the limits of the nation-state system. Prominent in this theoretical firmament were the heirs of the venerable intellectual tradition of cosmopolitanism, a tradition that seems to have been given a new lease of life by the developments of the past two decades. As scholars were quick to point out, the rapid and intensified movement of people, capital, ideas, and technology was engendering a world in which territorial boundaries no longer had the same meaning they once had. It had become increasingly apparent that sociopolitical, cultural and economic problems were in actuality 'beyond boundaries'. This reality was further reflected in the fact that there were numerous, and growing, transnational movements engaged with issues that cut across boundaries, demarcating distinct ethnic and political communities. In other words, political developments were making obvious that the individual, more than ever before, was a citizen of the world, not just of a narrowly defined *polis*. In the contemporary international system, it no longer made sense to think about the rights and associated duties of human beings primarily in terms of bounded, territorially defined entities. In a world characterized by the declining power of the nation state, citizenship had to be conceptualized in transnational or global terms.

A cursory glance at global politics at the turn of the 21st century gives some credence to cosmopolitan claims. In the past few decades, a large number of countries — the People's Republic of China, Russia, Mexico, Italy, Tunisia, Morocco, India, Jordan, Hungary,

Haiti, the Dominican Republic, and Poland, to name but a few — have been actively involved in crafting policies that seemingly recognize and seek to overcome the territorial limits to political belonging. Attempting to institutionalize their relationship with populations that migrated from their territories, those constituted as 'diasporas', state actors have embraced policies such as granting dual citizenship, creating ministries for diaspora affairs allowing them to participate in domestic elections, policymaking and reserving seats for them in the national legislature. The adoption of what has been characterized as 'transnationally informed policy-making' opens up the realm of domestic politics to groups that were traditionally excluded primarily because of their location 'outside' the territorial boundaries of the nation state. This, in turn, seems to make the distinction between 'inside' and 'outside' — a distinction regarded as a crucial constitutive feature of the international system — increasingly irrelevant. In this context, as states themselves are in the process of recognizing the existence of domestic constituencies living abroad, does it not make sense to conceptualize political belonging in broader, overlapping, and possibly universal terms? Does not the inviting of their diasporas 'back home' by states serve as a striking acknowledgement that, in an increasingly globalized world, the functional correspondence between nation, state and territory can no longer be taken for granted? To put it differently, is not the dramatically changing relationship between states and their diasporas a validation of what cosmopolitan theorists have long argued? Tempting though it might be to answer these questions in the affirmative, I argue in this chapter that a closer look at the actual processes points us in the opposite direction.

The institutionalization of the relationship between states and their diasporas — a process that I have theorized as the rise of the 'domestic abroad' — is indeed a manifestation of transnationalism in the latest phase of globalization. However, it is a peculiar form of transnationalism in that it poses a serious challenge to the predominant conception about the nature and effects of this process on global politics, as understood by cosmopolitan theorists. It is a form of transnationalism that is very much rooted in circuits of global capital, is driven by the state, and is national in origin, character and aspirations. It is aimed at extending not only the boundaries of the imagined community of nation but also the extent of the state's authority. Its paradoxical effect is therefore to strengthen, rather than undermine, the foundations of the nation-state system. In this sense, far from fulfilling the promises of cosmopolitanism, as I argue in this chapter, the domestic abroad serves to reveal its limitations both as theory and as a political project. To make this argument, this chapter is divided into two sections. In the first, I tease out the underlying cosmopolitan logic of diaspora studies, which has led to scholars largely ignoring the role of diasporas in the re-inscription of the existing political order. In the second section, I trace the production of the Indian domestic abroad to illustrate the way in which it represents a powerful (albeit contradictory) reassertion of the nationalist imaginary and state authority in the current stage of development of global capitalism.

Diasporas and the Cosmopolitan Mystique

The movement of people across different localities, not just as 'cultural tourists', but also as migrants who settle in distant lands is, as Kwame Anthony Appiah notes, a central feature of a cosmopolitan world. For it is through travel, through the encountering of the 'other' that an individual learns to go beyond the attachment to a 'home of one's own, with its own cultural peculiarities', and take 'pleasure from the presence of other, different places that are home to other different people' (Appiah 1997: 618). Admittedly, these processes have oftentimes in the past been the product of violent and involuntary resettlements. However, according to Appiah, while far from being ideal, the world that we live in does provide us with the essential elements for the eventual attainment of a cosmopolitan universe, as well as an initial approximation of it. Notwithstanding the lack of free choice in the past, the persistent mobility amongst human beings has led to the creation of a world 'in which each local form of human life [is] the result of long-term and persistent cultural hybridization' (ibid.: 619). It is in this context that the crucial, constitutive role of diasporas in the development of cosmopolitanism comes to the fore.

Cosmopolitan Diasporas and Diasporic Cosmopolitianism

Cosmopolitan theorists discussing international relations have largely ignored the subject of diasporas. Despite this, it is possible to see in diasporas building blocks of a qualitatively different, and progressive, world order, since they are largely treated in the literature as active agents in the processes of hybridization, challengers of notions of cultural purity, and transnational subjects who through their very existence challenge the notion of hermetically sealed political communities. What makes this strange, however, is that this development is not so much the result of the dominance of cosmopolitanism as a theoretical tradition in diaspora studies. It is rather a result of the pioneering work done by scholars such as Stuart Hall, Homi Bhabha, Paul Gilroy, and Arjun Appadurai, writing under the umbrella of cultural studies and firmly situated in the realm of postmodern, postcolonial theory. At one level, postcolonial theory does indeed challenge some of fundamental tenets of cosmopolitanism, be it the ontological primacy of the rights-bearing individual subject or the presumption of teleological progressive movement towards a universal morality. A body of scholarship that is seen more as focused on the celebration of the particular, the local, the 'fragment' as it were, it may seem rather peculiar to insist on it sharing common ground with a theoretical tradition that is committed to the exact opposite. However, when it comes to the way in which diasporas have been studied, understood and analysed, paradoxical though it might seem, it is quite evident that at least one strain of postcolonial thought and cosmopolitanism share a common commitment and outlook.

In an argument that is one of the best-known illustrations of this trend, Appadurai contends that the contemporary world is characterized by a 'rupture' (1997: 9). If the modern world was dominated by the imagined communities of the nation (and its corollary, the territorial state), the contemporary world according to Appadurai is characterized by 'images and viewers' that do not 'fit into circuits or audiences that are easily bound within national, regional or local spaces' (ibid.: 4). In other words, 'the nationalist genie, never perfectly contained in the bottle of the territorial state, is now itself diasporic' (ibid.: 160–61). The task of studying diasporic public spheres becomes then one of spelling out the processes of de-territorialization — the 'unyoking of the imagination from place' — that characterize the present. Despite his occasional protestations to the contrary, Appadurai highlights these relationships and their unforeseeable consequences precisely because he sees in them the potential for ways 'to think ourselves beyond the nation'. The 'modern governmental apparatuses', he argues, 'are increasingly inclined to self-perpetuation, bloat, violence and corruption' (Appadurai 1997: 20). They have persistently tended to use nationalism as an ideological alibi for exclusion and eventually some form of totalitarianism. To be more precise, a singular, official nationalism has generally become the 'ideological alibi of the territorial state' and 'last refuge of ethnic totalitarianism'. Implicit in this process has been a flattening of different kinds of imaginings of political communities that are not necessarily territorially bound. However, in the modern world such alternative imaginaries do exist and can be found mainly in the diasporic public sphere, the groups of mobile populations, connected by mass media and de-territorialized imaginations. It is in them that one can find the possibility of a new post-national world order.

What makes Appadurai's analysis noteworthy is not only its omnipresence in the general literature, but also the fact that one can find similar arguments across the spectrum of loosely defined cultural studies scholarship dealing with the question of diasporas. Paul Gilroy, Homi Bhabha and Stuart Hall, to name a few outstanding examples, deploy tropes of imprisonment and liberation that are featured prominently in their descriptions of the dominance of territorial nation states in modern vocabulary and imagination and the challenge posed by diasporas to that dominance. In fact, the conceptual category of the nation state emerges in these scholarly narratives as restrictive, and fundamentally suspect.

While dominant nationalist discourses try to deny the hybridity that is constitutive of national identity, migrants and diasporic subjects embody the hybrid history of the nation. They are the true postcolonial subjects — 'neither new nor old' — who challenge the construction of a homogeneous national space that travels through empty time from a pristine past (the 'old') to a future (the 'new') unencumbered by external influences. Out of this outlook emerges the celebration of mobility, hybridity and the critical, constitutive role of diasporas in shaping a new, a better post-national political order.

There is undoubtedly something very distinctive about the logic that leads scholars like Appadurai to this particular conclusion. The deep suspicion of nationalism in any form, the disillusionment with the nation-state system, and the conviction that the territorial nation state has played a role akin to a jailer in imprisoning 'alternative geographies of frontiers and borders' have a certain visceral quality that is not necessarily in tune with cosmopolitan scholarship. However, what is not so peculiar to the cultural studies scholarship is what Katharyne Mitchell has aptly called 'the hype of hybridity' (Mitchell 1997, 2004). Take for instance, the efforts of Kwame Anthony Appiah, one of the most prolific advocates of cosmopolitanism. In numerous articles and books published over the past two decades, Appiah has consistently argued against those he sees as presenting a hollow and fundamentally flawed argument defending the presumed purity of native cultures (be it that of the Asante or the American family farm) from the onslaught of globalization. Appiah rightly points out that, quite apart from having 'licensed a great deal of mischief in the past century', these claims of 'purity and preservation' are themselves highly dubious given the history of travel, migrations and conquests that have shaped global culture. Taking this further, he argues that it is this particular history that has enabled an already existing cosmopolitan order characterized by a fundamental belief: 'I am human: nothing human is alien to me' (Appiah 2006a, 2006b). Arriving at this order, according to Appiah, has required a conscious decision to embrace 'contamination', a 'counterideal', if you will, to the notion of cultural purity. It is a 'counterideal' that celebrates the 'hybridity, impurity, mongrelization' coming about as a result of 'intermingling' of 'new and unexpected combinations of human beings, cultures, ideas, politics, movies, songs' — an ideal, in other words that is engendered through, and propped up by what Appadurai in a different context has called 'diasporic public spheres'.

What I have put forth so far is a fairly straightforward though generally overlooked argument: despite protestations of distinct ontological foundations and epistemological outlooks, there exists a common ground between cosmopolitanism and the dominant postmodern, postcolonial perspective on diasporas. This becomes even more obvious when one looks at the manner in which 'postmodern post-nationalism' can, with nary a hesitation, be easily conflated with 'cosmopolitanism'. In a recent analysis of the changing position and role of diasporas, Marco Cuevas-Hewitt argues that to understand diasporic political activism, one needs to take seriously the newly emergent 'cosmopolitan tendencies' that have materialized in the contemporary era of globalization (Cuevas-Hewitt 2009, 2010). Focusing particularly on Filipino-American activists, Cuevas-Hewitt claims that even just a few decades ago, diaspora activism was dominated by organizations like the Union of Democratic Filipinos (KDP) that were shaped by a 'pan-nationalist' epistemology — one that insisted on an orientation determined by political struggles taking place in the 'homeland'. However, the changing 'world-historical context' has revealed the fundamental problem with such an orientation. In a world wrought by the advent and gradual spread of neoliberal globalization, the limits of a bounded nationalist imaginary are readily apparent. Though, as Cuevas-Hewitt readily grants, this does not guarantee a cosmopolitan disposition, it does 'provide much of the raw materials for its possibility'. Out of these raw materials, there have emerged diaspora organizations such as the Filipino/American Coalition for Environmental Solidarity (FACES) that are — unlike their counterparts in the past — very consciously geared towards a 'more cosmopolitan, post-nationalist politics'. What makes this orientation apparent is the commitment of such organizations towards global issues — in this case, the environment — that affect the world at large and not just a narrowly defined national community. Drawing from his own fieldwork with FACES and the work of scholars like Giorgio Agamben, Cuevas-Hewitt goes on to argue that the new cosmopolitanism not only highlights a change in diaspora political activism, but also enables diasporas to see themselves in a new light. No longer the perpetual outsiders, removed because of their location from the inside space of homeland politics, but rather 'a vast swarm', who 'through their riotous mobility, are in fact weaving a new inside: that of the world as a whole'. The analysis ends with the rousing conclusion that in this changing, brave new world of ours, far from being 'mere exiles', diasporas are the new 'global citizens'.

Old Wine in New Bottles: The Foundations of the Cosmopolitan Critique

As even the brief summary of the argument about 'diasporic cosmopolitanism' should make clear, there are certain unstated assumptions underlying these narratives. Not surprisingly, these assumptions are themselves not novel, even when packaged as part of a novel critique of the current world order. Three of them deserve a closer scrutiny. First, there is the notion that the on-going changes in the 'world-historical context' — sometimes described hazily in terms of the end of the Cold War and the victory of liberal democracy, sometimes grouped under the broad category of globalization, and very occasionally spelled out as the spread of neoliberalism — are themselves worthy of scrutiny only to the extent that they help us make sense of the new subjects ('diasporic public spheres') and subject-positions ('cosmopolitans') that are being engendered. Furthermore, these changes (unspecified, and largely ignored though they might be) are at a very minimum, productive of a better, politically progressive global order. Most scholars would of course hedge their bets by pointing out the less progressive elements (such as the more right-wing nationalist tendencies highlighted by Cuevas-Hewitt) that co-exist in the new world order. But, even for those trafficking in ambiguities, there seems to be the idea that the move towards a world in which issues are framed in 'global' terms can only mean something progressive and good.

To make this point about progressive development, many of the exemplars provided of 'diasporic cosmopolitan activism' highlight environmental causes. Admittedly, this is a seductive outlook. After all, who can be opposed to something as benign as wanting to save the planet for future generations by planting trees? In a world as interconnected as ours — a point brought out here most obviously by the fate of the very air we breathe — it does make sense to realize that our futures will not be decided on narrow, bounded national terrain. However, to move from this inescapable conclusion to an unquestioning acceptance of the 'changing world-historical context' is to perform an intellectual sleight of hand that serves a very definite political project. It is one that, for all its emphasis on change and movement, ultimately serves to defend and protect a very specific status quo — that of capitalist social relations. Treating the on-going changes in the nature and scope of capitalism as a more or less taken-for-granted starting point serves the political purpose of bracketing any discussion of alternative political orders that might rest on fundamentally challenging this framework. In this context, for all its commitment to transformation, the cosmopolitan outlook reveals itself to be one that is indelibly committed to the preservation of the existing status quo. Merely categorizing a particular orientation as 'global' becomes more or less a statement of it being progressive and works to foreclose any closer scrutiny of what exactly that might mean. Notwithstanding scholarly diktat, however, questions about what is 'good', 'progressive' or 'desirable' can neither be moved to the terrain of abstract, moral philosophy, nor treated as having already been answered through consensus. They are, for better or for worse, political questions, the answers to which will be arrived at through on-going political struggles on a very material terrain. And while diasporas are certainly important actors in this struggle, there is no immediate or necessary connection between their mobility and their proclivity towards playing an emancipatory role in global politics.

This brings me to the second assumption underlying celebratory narratives of diasporic cosmopolitanism — the idea that diasporas are, for all practical purposes, free-floating agents. This is not to say that scholars do not pay attention to the subject-positions of diasporas. However, what unites most of the scholarship is an understanding that the only position that matters in making sense of diaspora politics is that of their being embodiments of hybridity, of that mobility characterizing human culture. To put it somewhat differently, the only position that matters insofar as diasporas are concerned is that of their being 'outside' of a narrowly conceived *polis*. This is, as I have argued elsewhere, a highly problematic and suspect assumption (Varadarajan 2008). The mere facts of mobility ('riotous' though it might be), of relocation, or even dislocation, do not fundamentally, and in perpetuity, uproot individuals from social relations in general, and in the modern era, capitalist social relations in particular. What this means is that the issue of social class cannot simply, through a more or less unspoken scholarly consensus, be dismissed as passé, as no longer relevant in making sense of contemporary politics. Diasporas, as would be evident by the political activities of different strata of society, are not unified, monolithic entities, whose actions are determined by their positions as 'outsiders'. Within diasporas, there exist different sociological layers with very different interests, which in turn situates them in very specific ways in the existing political order. To understand what kind of political actors members of diasporas could be — reinforcements for the existing status quo, essential elements of a more progressive world order, etc. — we therefore need to go beyond the hailing of hybrid subject-positions and consider seriously the question of what exactly the changing 'world historical context' means in terms of social relations and how that might be affecting the very structure of the nation-state system.

Finally, in the accounts of diasporic cosmopolitanism in general (and to a large extent, cosmopolitanism as well), there seems to always be a certain presumption about the fate, as it were, of the nation state. While few scholars would claim outright that the nation state has ceased to matter, most would congregate around variations of the argument that the authority of the state has been severely undermined in the current phase of globalization, especially due to the rise of a transnational civil society. In large part due to this presumption, the focus of much of the scholarly work in the field has been on the nature and role of these transnational actors in world politics — be it acknowledged institutions of a presumptive global civil society, or diasporas. Consequently, what we have is more or less an erasure of the state from analyses of cosmopolitan developments. This erasure, as I have argued before, is not merely a product of the lack of empirical focus, but also an effect of the sometimes explicitly stated argument that links the territorial nation-state system to all that is politically regressive. While one can sympathize with political commitments that demand a gradual fading away to the territorial limits of our imagination, that unfortunately cannot be achieved through scholarly diktats. For better or for worse, we live in a world where nation states continue to play a critical role not just in global politics in general, but also in the shaping of transnationalism. This is not to deny that in the current phase of globalization the nature of nation states has undergone a change. But, these changes cannot be captured merely by statements about decreasing authority or increased democratization. This, of course, begs the question of how one might understand the dynamic logic underlying the nation-state system and the forms of transnationalism they engender. In this chapter, I contend that the phenomenon of the domestic abroad provides us with an important critical lens to make sense of these transformations. To begin with, the domestic abroad phenomenon helps us put into sharp analytical focus the very transformation of the 'world-historical context' that cosmopolitans take as an unproblematic starting point. In other words, it puts front and centre the question of the development of capitalism on a global scale. Furthermore, it not only reveals the continuing importance of state actors in the shaping of a putatively 'new' global order, but also the ways in which a state-driven transnationalism can be essentially national in origin, scope and aspiration.

Global Nations and the Limits of Global Citizenship

In January 2003, the Indian capital of New Delhi was the site of an event that was touted as the 'largest gathering of the global Indian family'. Organized by the Indian Ministry of External Affairs and the Federation of Indian Chambers of Commerce and Industry (FICCI) at a cost of over ₹22 crore (approximately US$49 million), the event was the celebration of the first ever Pravasi Bharatiya Diwas — literally, the 'Day of the Indians Abroad'. In his keynote address, L. K. Advani, the deputy prime minister, declared that the recognition of the '20 million strong' Pravasi Bharatiya (Indians abroad) community was long overdue. The Pravasi Bharatiya Diwas celebrations, as Advani put it, were an acknowledgement by his government of a new phenomenon: Vishwa Bharati (Global India). The subjects being honoured by his government, he claimed, did not just represent India to the rest of the world — they *were* embodiments of India in the world. As such, the Indian state was willing to turn its back on a policy that had been in place since Indian independence and introduce dual citizenship legislation in parliament, and to set up a separate ministry of non-resident Indians (NRIs)/Persons of Indian Origin (PIOs) affairs to facilitate greater interactions between the Indian nation state and Indians abroad.

In embracing this 'transnationally informed policy-making', the Indian state, as I have already noted, was not unique — it was embarking on a path that seems to be quite popular amongst state actors at that particular historical juncture. Over the past two decades, a large number of states around the world have adopted varying policy initiatives all aimed at constituting their diasporas as part of a territorially diffused, yet politically cogent national communities. At one level, the fact that these initiatives mark an acknowledgement by state actors of the limits of territorial boundaries might tempt one to see it as yet another manifestation of an emergent cosmopolitan world order. After all, if state actors themselves recognize that citizenship cannot be defined in terms of territorial boundaries, does it not send a message? It certainly does, but a closer look reveals that the message being sent is not quite what it might have appeared to be. The rhetoric of 'global nations' far from being similar to the rhetoric of 'global citizens' is, in fact, its exact opposite. While seeming to celebrate a borderless world, it actually hails a bounded political community. While seeming to celebrate an expansive — perhaps even universal — notion of citizenship, it presents new forms of exclusion. In that sense, the domestic abroad phenomenon, in all its glory, challenges the very idea of cosmopolitanism, in general, and diasporic cosmopolitanism, in particular. What makes this striking is that this phenomenon has emerged in the era that has been hailed as the new age of cosmopolitanism, and in fact its rise and its logic can be traced to the very same changing 'world historical context'. The rise of the Indian domestic abroad serves as a great illustration of this point.

Defining the Limits of the 'Polis'

In the aftermath of independence, the diaspora policy of the post-colonial Indian state was framed as a choice that was to be made by the various groups that were then characterized as 'Indians abroad'. Former Prime Minister Jawaharlal Nehru best summed up the policy in a speech given to the Indian parliament a decade after independence. Indians abroad, the Prime Minister asserted, were at an important crossroads. They could choose to claim Indian citizenship, thus officially becoming a part of the independent Indian nation state. In that case, while the Indian state would accept its duties towards them and strive to protect their interests through the means of traditional diplomacy, they could not expect anything other than 'favourable alien treatment' outside of India's territorial boundaries. As for those who chose to accept 'the nationality of the country they live in', the Indian state wished them well, and in that spirit, exhorted them to comport themselves in their new countries as true citizens and not exploitative agents. Despite contestations, it was this overall framework that guided the Indian state's policies for nearly five decades, before it was officially overturned in the early years of the new century.

The Nehruvian policy of emphasizing the territorial basis of the national community was not much of a surprise by the time it was officially articulated a decade after Indian independence. However, within the broader milieu of the anti-colonial nationalist struggle that had led to India's independence, this declaration did mark a dramatic turnaround. The leaders of the Indian national movement had in fact first articulated their demands for complete freedom from British rule by establishing a direct link between the discrimination faced by people of Indian origin in various British colonies to India's lack of sovereignty. In that sense, Indians abroad, had indeed been an essential part of the development of Indian nationalism.

Given this context, it would have been reasonable to expect that once independence was attained, the Indian state would actively protect the rights of 'Indians abroad'. But, the advent of independence brought about something different. India, imagined as a transnational nation during the struggle against colonialism, was reproduced as a bounded, territorially defined community with the state very systematically distancing itself from the concerns of the 'Indians abroad'. To make sense of this shift, as I have argued elsewhere, it is crucial to analyse the historical, political struggles that were productive of particular set of relationships between nation and state in the Indian context. More specifically, it is critical for us to understand the ways in which the sociopolitical agenda of the postcolonial Indian state reflected the successful establishment of the hegemony of a particular class: the Indian bourgeoisie, as it existed in a specific moment in the development of global capitalism (Varadarajan 2010: 78–106).

While space constraints prevent me from going into the details of this argument, it is important to highlight three crucial, broadly accepted facts. First, in the decades prior to independence, the Indian capitalist class emerged as a strong force in the economic realm. Second, this class was, from the early stages, very closely, and organically, connected to the institutional structures of the Indian National Congress (INC). Third, in the period leading up to Independence, the leadership of the INC — which was to form independent India's first government — adopted a socio-economic agenda that was almost exactly the same as that which was proposed by the leading lights of the Indian bourgeoisie. The final point, I have argued, was not a matter of mere coincidence, or because the bourgeoisie became truly national, in the sense of submerging their interests to a larger cause. Through calibrated distancing from the colonial authorities, and occasional sacrifices of narrowly perceived class interests, the Indian bourgeoisie succeeded in staving off the dangers of a true mass movement, strengthening the hands of the Congress right wing and in ultimately managing to frame its interests as being seamlessly integrated with those of the nation-at-large. This, in essence, was the successful establishment of the hegemony of the Indian capitalist class. This success was reflected in the socio-economic platform adopted by the postcolonial Indian state.

As envisaged by the leaders of the Indian bourgeoisie, the state that replaced the colonial state was a highly centralized one, committed to state-sponsored industrialization, and protecting the domestic economy, particularly as the chief financier of the private sector. In addition to these measures aimed at promoting industrial development, the Indian state also played an active role in protecting domestic industries from the potential threat of 'foreign domination', by enacting a series of stringent regulations governing the inflow of foreign capital and investments in India.

The legacy of an anti-colonial movement that had clearly and successfully articulated the connections between the foreign occupation and the exploitation of national resources enabled the ruling class to present Indian capitalists as an intrinsic part of the nation that had to be protected from foreign exploitation and supported by the state. The net effect of these practices was to produce a state that emphasized and upheld the political and economic significance of territorial boundaries.

One of the main effects of the processes of territorializing an independent, modern India was that of situating the Indian diaspora at a distance from the Indian nation state. The constitution of a strong, sovereign nation state rested on the defining of the boundaries that separated the 'outside' from the 'inside', the 'foreigner' (the exploiter) from the 'national' (he who needed to be protected from exploitation). The bourgeois nationalism that lay at the heart of state ideology emphasized the territorially limited, legal-juridical aspect of statehood in making the distinction between those who could be counted as Indian and those who ought not to be. The main argument made by successive Congress regimes after independence regarding the Indian state's attitude towards the diaspora was quite straightforward: members of the diaspora had been given the chance to embrace Indian citizenship which they chose not to accept; under these circumstances, the newly independent Indian state did not have any legal responsibilities towards them. And since as part of the modern system of nation states India respected the sovereignty of other countries (especially the newly independent nation states), it could not intervene in their domestic affairs. Despite intermittent struggles, the logic underlying the drawing of the boundaries of the nation and the delineation of the role of the state remained more or less dominant for over three decades.

Speakers at the 2003 Pravasi Bharatiya Diwas celebrations made constant reference to this official stance, sometimes defensively (especially representatives of the Indian state), sometimes accusingly (as did some of the feted members of various diaspora delegations). But the main point they tried to drive home was that the past was truly over and done with, and a new chapter had begun in the history of the Indian state's relationship with its diaspora. This shift, Deputy Prime Minister Advani explained, had been made possible by the 'happy confluence of two historical developments — the coming of age of India and the coming of age of Indians working and living abroad'. But, what exactly did this 'coming of age' entail and why had it happened at this precise historical juncture? To answer these questions, it is perhaps useful for us to move from the poesy of political rhetoric to the somewhat more prosaic terrain of changing social relations on global and national scales.

The Flexibility of Citizenship

In the prelude to independence, the Indian bourgeoisie had succeeded in establishing its hegemony in the context of very specific socio-economic and political conditions. This in turn, as I have argued, resulted in a particular defining of the limits of national belonging and shaped the post-independence relationship between the Indian state and the groups categorized as the Indian diaspora. However, these conditions, and concomitantly the policies they helped shape, were hardly set in stone. By the mid-1980s, the possibility of change, if not quite its nature, was becoming increasingly apparent. On the one hand, a wave of post-independence immigrations (both skilled and unskilled) had changed the profile of the 'Indians abroad'. For the first time, there existed immigrants in the West (particularly North America) and West Asia (particularly the Gulf states) who had undeniably close familial ties to the 'motherland', even if that was narrowly understood as the post-independence Indian nation state. On the other, the hegemony of the Indian bourgeoisie had begun to show visible cracks in its façade. The Indian capitalist class, once portrayed as an intrinsic part of the nation, had begun to be increasingly portrayed as a corrupt, bloated group that had benefited from government patronage for way too long. The idea of a closed economy, which rested on a fundamental distinction being drawn between the 'inside' and the 'outside' — an idea that was once seen as an absolute necessity to protect national resources — was largely represented in popular discourse as a conspiracy by the bourgeoisie to hold on to outmoded privileges (Varadarajan 2010: 93–106, 117–19). What numerous scandals made very clear was that even among its political representatives, the Indian bourgeoisie could no longer sustain its claims of representing the interests of the nation-at-large.

To understand how these changes came about, it is useful to turn our attention to developments of the global capitalist economy. Under the Keynesian system institutionalized in the Bretton Woods agreement towards the end of the Second World War, state actors were able to exert a level of control over the functioning of 'domestic' economies. More specifically, it was considered both legitimate and desirable for states to regulate the flow of foreign capital, and invest in the public sector. However, by the late 1970s, the rapid decline in the manufacturing edge of the United States and the collapse of the main elements of the Bretton Woods system announced the passing of the Keynesian model and the beginning of the neoliberal epoch. Under this changed international context, it was no longer possible for states to hold on to the economic strategies that worked in the earlier decades. In other words, purely national bourgeoisies found it virtually impossible to sustain the hegemony on the grounds that had succeeded in the past. In the Indian case, this process was further intensified by changes taking place in the industrial landscape.

While industry in India was still largely dominated by the handful of family-based conglomerates that had long historical roots, the picture was undergoing a gradual transformation by the 1980s. For the first time in post-independence Indian history, technologically advanced segments of industry — be it large, medium or small-scale — began emerging as visible actors. Differentiating themselves from the older, most established ranks of the Indian bourgeoisie, this new faction played up their connections to the modern segment of sunrise industries, presenting themselves not as inheritors of familial legacies, but rather a professionally trained cadre of entrepreneurs who were wedded to technological innovation and economic growth. Represented by the Association of Indian Engineering Industry (AIEI) (renamed the Confederation of Engineering Industry in 1986, and later Confederation of Indian Industry in 1992), this faction deliberately set out to present itself as the face of a modern, progressive industrial sector. It made no bones about the fact that its governing philosophy was one that favoured 'de-regulation, de-control and de-licensing' in all areas, and that it was willing to work in partnership with the Indian government to push for favourable policies (Pederson 2000: 270). The changing 'world-historical context' combined with the rise of this new faction set the stage for the introduction of 'economic reforms' in 1991, on a scale, and in a way, that had not yet been witnessed in India (Pederson 2000). There was, however, a critical issue that could not be avoided.

The hegemony of the Indian bourgeoisie had initially been established in the context of both a particular moment in the development of global capitalism (that is, the onset of Keynesianism), and the historical experience of the struggles against colonialism. This in turn was productive of a state that justified its policies in terms of protecting the domestic economy from foreign exploitation, and steering the productive forces of the nation to promote the welfare of the people. However, the institution of neoliberal reforms implied that the state had officially started the process of dismantling safeguards put in place for this purpose. Furthermore, it was actually inviting foreign investors who could potentially exploit the Indian economy, challenging the very constitutive basis of postcolonial India. In other words, the restructuring of the economy along neoliberal lines marked at a very obvious level the undermining of the raison d'être of the post-independence Indian state. More importantly, given their negation of the foundational socioeconomic agenda of the post-independence Indian state, the institution of these policies marked a significant crisis of legitimacy for the Indian bourgeoisie. The task faced by its dominant faction at this juncture was not merely one of convincing legislators about the necessity of adopting a certain set of economic policies. Rather, it was a larger one of reasserting the connections between their interests (in this case, the liberalizing of the Indian economy) and that of the nation to appear once again seamless and natural. It was this challenge that made imperative the hailing of the diaspora by the Indian state as a natural and, in fact, essential part of India's future. If economic liberalization was not to be seen as an instrumental and calculated attempt by fractions of the bourgeoisie to maintain and perpetuate their privileged status, if it were to be sustainable over a longer period of time, then what was needed was a way to make it seem like an essential step in the path of national progress. To put it differently, what was needed was a subject who could supposedly embody 'national' aspirations, the potential for India to succeed in the global economy, and to reflect between aspirations and the potential. In the context of the neoliberal restructuring of the state, thus, the re-articulation of bourgeois hegemony made essential a diasporic reimagining of the nation. It is these two on-going, simultaneous processes that have resulted in the production of the Indian domestic abroad, centred around the new subject, 'the global Indian'.

But who was this 'global Indian' and what exactly were the characteristics that made him or her both 'global' and 'Indian' at the same time? Various hagiographic accounts from numerous media outlets were quick to provide an answer to this question. The most common response was the kind that could be found in Chidanand Rajghatta's laudatory accounting of the successes of India's 'Silicon Valley Gurus' (Rajghatta 2001). In Rajghatta's narrative, as immigration from India grew in a steady trickle during the 1970s, a number of Indian technology workers (commonly referred to as 'techies') began to emerge as entrepreneurial figures in the Silicon Valley of the United States. Emboldened by the success of pioneers like Narendra Singh Kapany (who arrived in the US as a student from India and set up the first Indian-owned fibre optics industry in 1960) and Dr Amar Bose (the founder of the Bose Corporation, who despite being half-German was appropriated by the Indian immigrant community as a 'cult hero'), a small group of Indian entrepreneurs helped 'jump-start Digital America', while 'becoming bold enough to name companies after themselves'. Educated in some of the best engineering schools in India, these immigrants had moved to the West and, despite numerous setbacks, had within a matter of decades made their mark in Silicon Valley. It was to these narratives that the reformers turned in making their argument that India had proven that it could succeed in the global economy.

In documenting tales of the success of NRIs in science and technology, what was highlighted was not just the training received by the entrepreneurs in India, but also the fact that they had managed to succeed despite the manifold challenges that they faced. As such, the NRI businessman embodied the new type of Indian entrepreneur — no longer just members of storied business families that were tied to the INC, but individuals who through their own merit and professional skills had become successful in cutting-edge industries, while competing on a global playing field. However, if it were to have wider resonance, the official narrative could not afford to merely reiterate the successes of the 'Silicon Valley Gurus', and would in fact have to go beyond and connect it to the broader emigrant experience. It was this task that was taken up with notable enthusiasm in the lead-up to the Pravasi Bharatiya Diwas celebrations.

In a special issue, the popular Indian weekly *India Today* commemorated the 'Global Indian' who was 'Doing us proud'. In his editorial, the well-known journalist Aroon Purie claimed that one did not need the Indian government to tell the world that there was a twenty million strong Indian diaspora. Through a 'quiet, gradual, but relentless' migration, Indians had effected what he called 'a reverse colonization'. Despite arriving in places such as Fiji as indentured labour during the colonial period, Indians had overcome insurmountable odds and 'today, their children are presidents, prime ministers, senators, tycoons and Nobel prize winners'. Echoing a theme that framed the Pravasi Bharatiya celebrations, Purie declared:

> Persons of Indian Origin are impossible to typecast ... They come in all shapes and sizes, fit all descriptions. What links the astronaut on our cover with the Punjabi sheep farmers in New Zealand? What connects white-collar techies in Silicon Valley to the Indians who seem to have a monopoly on 24-hours stores in Britain — or the Patels who so dominate the US motel industry that motels are often referred to as "Potels"? 'It is the will to succeed' [reference to the *India Today* article has not been made].

In other words, what made them 'Indians' was the 'indomitable will' — the spirit of enterprise that was intrinsic to India. Wherever they went, regardless of the passport they carried, it was this spirit that characterized all Indians. For, as Purie concluded quite seriously, 'You can take an Indian out of India, but you cannot take India out of an Indian'. While this 'Indian' was already a member of the 'global Indian family', it was only proper that the Indian state formally acknowledge this relationship by changing its citizenship laws. At the moment of independence, the Indian state had distanced itself from the Indian diaspora, instituting a very limited citizenship policy. But, as supporters of neoliberal reforms argued, at the turn of the century there was a new world and a new India — an India that had finally, and with confidence, opened itself to the challenges of the global economy and taken its rightful position on the global stage. As such, they claimed, it was time for the Indian nation state to acknowledge its presence beyond its territorial limits, and embrace a 'transnationally informed' policymaking. In January 2004, the Indian parliament passed an amendment to the Citizenship Act (1955), recognizing the possibility of dual citizenship for the first time in India's post-independence history. With the production of the domestic abroad, with the recognition of the 'global Indian family', India, it was claimed, had finally 'come of age'.

Conclusion

Claims of an essential Indian-ness that overrode all difference, the imposition of a singular experiential narrative on all sections of the Indian diaspora and the constant reiteration of a 'coming of age' theme have more or less defined the official rhetoric of the Pravasi Bharatiya Diwas in its first decade. While the giddy celebrations that marked the early years of the Pravasi Bharatiya Diwas, with its catchy background slogans of 'India Shining' and 'India Everywhere', have been somewhat tempered by the material reality of the global economic meltdown, the annual gathering itself continues in an abated form. Every January, as representatives of the Indian state and members of various diaspora groups gather in a designated Indian city, they work hard to establish the veracity of a particular set of equations: neoliberal restructuring and the opening of the Indian markets, which served the interests of the dominant faction of the Indian bourgeoisie, actually served the interests of the nation-at-large; the embrace of liberalization was a sign of national self-confidence; the success of the 'global Indian entrepreneur' was the success of the Indian nation state; the Indian diaspora was best represented in the figure of the 'global Indian' who, through a clever sleight of hand, also became the 'global Indian entrepreneur'; and the fêting of the 'global' Indian, the diasporic Indian, was actually the celebration of India as a 'global' actor whose time had finally arrived. The point here is not so much that these are successful articulations. In fact, while the essential hollowness of these claims — and, relatedly, the figure of the 'global Indian' — can be camouflaged under the right conditions, it is fundamentally unsustainable in the long run. Despite this, I have argued that the domestic abroad phenomenon provides us with an important and revealing perspective on the theoretical and political promise of cosmopolitanism.

Take for instance, the idea of an expanding and expansive political community that is central to the production of the domestic abroad. At the obvious level, this seems like a notion quite compatible with cosmopolitan claims of a new world order characterized by increasingly irrelevant territorial borders, and the emergence of global citizens, who are attuned to sociopolitical issues beyond narrowly defined ethnic or political associations. But, as a closer look reveals, the transnationalism manifested in the domestic abroad is of a distinctly different order. To begin with, both *polis* and citizenship, though couched in global terms, are essentially bounded. In that sense, the domestic abroad phenomenon reflects not so much the gradual disappearance, but rather the redrawing of boundaries by the very state actors that are largely neglected by cosmopolitan theorists. Furthermore, as the previous section reveals, the boundaries do not just refer to the distinction between the 'native' and the 'foreigner', for the 'national' community reflected in the domestic abroad is of a very specific sort. In the Indian case, being an 'Indian' implied the 'will to succeed' on a global stage. Couched in terms of the willingness to face the challenges of the global economy, 'Indian-ness' is equated, more or less, to support for free markets in general and neoliberal restructuring in particular. Thus, the institutional acknowledgement of the extension of the *polis* in this context serves the crucial purpose of not only sustaining a particular narrative of nationalism, but also delegitimizing any questioning of the natural-ness or progressive nature of a capitalist global order. In this sense, the political project at stake in the production of the domestic abroad is not some kind of abstract progressive transnationalism, but the very material re-articulation of bourgeois hegemony, the re-inscription of the raison d'être of the state, in the context of changing capitalist relations on both global and national scales. This is, in other words, a project that is concerned not with the fundamental transformation of politics as usual, but rather the perpetuation of the existing systemic status quo. It is in this context, I contend, that the domestic abroad brings to the centre-stage the limitations of cosmopolitanism as a political project.

Cosmopolitanism, especially in its latest guise, presents itself as a political project that has overcome the narrowness of other forms of politics; say, for instance, 'parochial nationalism' or 'proletarian internationalism'. Unlike these other political projects that focus on specific groups (be it the 'nation' or 'the proletariat'), the subject of cosmopolitanism is humanity at large. In this lies its seductive charm. However, I argue that notwithstanding the emphasis on the emergence of new political communities, the embracing of putatively progressive agendas, such as the democratization of global politics, etc., the political project embraced by cosmopolitanism is essentially conservative. As Archibugi admits, cosmopolitanism does not concern itself with any fundamental transformation of existing socio-economic relations. Its goal is to find institutional loci to address and manage existing conflicts. Thus, for all the talk of transformation, it is a project that aims to help perpetuate the existing systemic status quo, albeit a reformed one. In that sense, paradoxical though it might seem, the domestic abroad as a political project does reflect the goals of cosmopolitanism. For it is after all an attempt to develop specific kinds of institutional mechanisms that while couched in terms of transforming and expanding the limits of political community, are actually concerned with the continuation of very specific social relations. Thus, notwithstanding its untenable character, the domestic abroad phenomenon serves as an important illustration of the limitations of cosmopolitanism, both as theory and as a political project.

⌒

References

Appadurai, Arjun. 1997. *Modernity at Large: Cultural Dimensions of Globalization*, University of Minnesota Press, Minneapolis.

Appiah, Kwame Anthony. 1991. 'Is the Post- in Postmodernism the Post- in Postcolonial?', *Critical Inquiry* 17(2): 336–57.

———. 1997. 'Cosmopolitan Patriots', *Critical Inquiry* 23(3): 617–39.

———. 2006a. 'The Case for Contamination', *The New York Times*, 1 January, http://www.nytimes.com/2006/01/01/magazine/01cosmopolitan.html?pagewanted=1; (accessed 23 May 2014).

———. 2006b. *Cosmopolitanism: Ethics in a World of Strangers*. W. W. Norton, New York.

Archibugi, Daniele (ed.). 2003. *Debating Cosmopolitics*. Verso, London.

Archibugi, Daniele. 2004. 'Cosmopolitan Democracy and Its Critics: A Review', *European Journal of International Relations* 10(3): 437–73.

———. 2008. *The Global Commonwealth of Citizens: Towards Cosmopolitan Democracy*, Princeton University Press, Princeton, NJ.

Archibugi, Daniele and David Held (eds). 1995. *Cosmopolitan Democracy: An Agenda for a New World Order*, Polity Press, Cambridge.

Archibugi, Daniele, David Held and Martin Koehler (eds). 1998. *Re-imagining Political Community: Studies in Cosmopolitan Democracy*, Polity Press, Cambridge.

Bhabha, Homi K. 1985. 'Signs Taken for Wonders: Questions of Ambivalence and Authority under a Tree outside Delhi, May 1817', *Critical Inquiry* 12: 144–65.

———. 1988. 'The Commitment to Theory', *New Formations* 5: 5–23.

———. 1995. 'Cultural Diversity and Cultural Difference', in Bill Ashcroft, Gareth Griffiths and Helen Tiffin (eds), *The Postcolonial Studies Reader*, Routledge, New York.

Brennan, Timothy. 2001. 'Cosmo-Theory', *South Atlantic Quarterly* 100(3): 659–91.

Chandler, David. 2003. 'New Rights for Old? Cosmopolitan Citizenship and the Critique of State Sovereignty', *Political Studies* 51(2): 332–49.

Chatterjee, Partha. 1998. 'Beyond the Nation-State, or Within', *Social Text* 56: 57–69.

Cuevas-Hewitt, Marco. 2009. 'From Pan-Nationalism to Cosmopolitanism: Epistemological Tensions in Filipino Diasporic Activism', in Jane Fernandez (ed.), *Diasporas: Critical and Interdisciplinary Perspectives*, Interdisciplinary Press, Oxford (e-book).

———. 2010. 'The Figure of the 'Fil-Whatever': Filipino-American Trans-Pacific Social Movements and the Rise of Radical Cosmopolitanism', WAN e-journal, 5.

Darieva, Tsypylma. 2011. 'Re-thinking Homecoming: Diasporic Cosmopolitanism in Post-Soviet Armenia', *Ethnic and Racial Studies* 34(3): 490–508.

Dirlik, Arif. 1994. 'The Postcolonial Aura: Third World Criticism in the Age of Global Capitalism', *Critical Inquiry* 20(2): 328–56.

India Today (International). 2003. Special Issue, 13 January.

Kaldor, Mary. 2003. *Global Civil Society: An Answer to War*. Polity Press, Cambridge.

Kochanek, Stanley A. 1995–96. 'The Transformation of Interest Politics in India', *Public Affairs* 68(4): 529–50.

Mitchell, Katharyne. 1997. 'Different Diasporas and the Hype of Hybridity', *Environment and Planning D: Society and Space* 15: 533–53.

Mitchell, Katharyne. 2004. *Crossing the Neoliberal Line: Pacific Rim Migration and the Metropolis*. Temple University Press, Philadelphia.

Pederson, Jorgen D. 2000. 'Explaining Economic Liberalization in India: State and Society Perspectives', *World Development* 28(2): 265–82.

Rajghatta, Chidanand. 2001. *The Horse that Flew: How India's Silicon Gurus Spread their Wings*. Harper Collins, New Delhi.

Varadarajan, Latha. 2008. 'Out of Place: Re-thinking Diaspora and Empire', *Millennium: Journal of International Studies* 36(2): 267–93.

———. 2010. The Domestic Abroad: Diasporas in International Relations. Oxford University Press, New York.

Part III
Towards a Postcolonial Critique

9

The Elusiveness of 'Non-Western Cosmopolitanism'

Rahul Rao

In this chapter, I examine four different academic discourses that purport to discuss questions of cosmopolitanism, world order and global justice. I argue that liberal cosmopolitan discourses in political theory and philosophy have tended to theorize global justice without being particularly attentive to global thought produced outside the West. Disciplines other than political theory and philosophy have been more attentive to the cosmopolitical experiences of non-elites, locating these in a range of border-transgressing experiences and ways of life. Yet this 'practice turn' has left obscure the relationship between cosmopolitan experience and moral obligation. The emerging field of comparative political thought (CPT) promises to engage with the question of moral thought produced outside the Western world. However, using recent work on similar questions in global history, I will argue that the ontological premises of much CPT scholarship, with its emphasis on intellectual traditions, lineages and civilizational thought, threatens to obscure the spaces in which, and the encounters through which, cosmopolitan political thought has been produced in the world outside Europe.

Global Justice without the Globe

There is something dismaying about the proliferation of literature on cosmopolitanism and global justice that takes little cognizance of the political thought and aspirations of what is problematically called the 'non-Western' world. In some of the liberal cosmopolitan literature, this inattention to the 'non-West' is a function of perspective and audience. Taking aim at the Western communitarian claim that it is permissible — even obligatory, in some versions of the thesis — to ascribe ethical priority to fellow-nationals over non-nationals (Tamir 1993; Miller 1995; Walzer 1995), the early and hugely influential work of Peter Singer (1972) and Henry Shue (1996) addresses itself largely to Western states and societies with a view to persuading these audiences to accord ethical parity to the stranger. Laudable as this objective is, the very question animating this work — 'What obligations do we owe strangers?' — betrays an elitist conception of its audience. Anyone teetering on the brink of existence, on account of material deprivation or persecution, might be forgiven for not giving the question of their obligations to strangers much consideration. This is not to deny the universal philosophical significance of the question, for even those most marginalized in some contexts will occupy positions of relative power in others in which capacity they will have the potential to harm strangers in their midst. Yet the question fails, politically and psychologically, as an opening gambit, insofar as it aims to provoke a global conversation about global justice. To ask what obligations one owes strangers presupposes an audience that thinks itself able to afford the luxury of thinking about strangers. The political economy of the field of academic cosmopolitanism means that the question is usually posed by Euro-American authors (or those working in Euro-American universities — a category in which I include myself) to privileged Euro-American audiences, with a view to persuading them to treat the 'non-Western' subaltern with respect. Yet this begs the further question of what those who are spoken of as strangers (however conceived), in debates over global justice, make of these conversations in which they are largely imagined as passive recipients of Western largesse.

In other liberal cosmopolitan work, particularly those strands influenced by the thinking of John Rawls, the inattention to the non-West (or to questions of place more generally) seems to be a function of methodology. Taking his cue from the tradition of social contractarian thinking in which society is envisaged as a contract for mutual advantage that human beings will enter into when the 'circumstances of justice' obtain (that is, when it becomes rational for them to exit the state of nature and make a compact for mutual advantage), Rawls offered a procedure by which the principles of a just society might be arrived at. This entails a thought experiment in which members of that society are imagined as gathering together in an 'original position' to contract from behind a 'veil of ignorance' — a state of mind in which they are divested of knowledge of characteristics (such as race, gender, wealth, education, etc.) that are judged to be morally arbitrary from the point of view of determining basic entitlements. Rawls suggested that the result of such a procedure would be agreement on a 'difference principle', according to which inequalities would be tolerated only if they were to the benefit of the least advantaged (Rawls 1971). Although Rawls's work on global justice endorsed more severe inequalities at a global level (Rawls 2001), earning the censure of self-avowed cosmopolitans, his work has been stretched in cosmopolitan directions by a number of theorists who have argued that nationality ought to be considered a morally arbitrary characteristic, from which contracting parties should abstract themselves in the process of devising principles of global justice. The result, cosmopolitans argue, would be the endorsement of the difference principle on a global scale (Beitz 1979; Pogge 1989; Moellendorf 2002; Brock 2009).

What interests me here is less the conclusions to which Rawlsian cosmopolitans arrive, than the way in which an interpretation of methodological imperative has tended to obviate the need for close engagement with what might be called the 'circumstances of injustice' encountered by the stranger. Common to all contractarian approaches is the premise that the principles resulting from the thought experiment described above would be just, given its egalitarian starting point and fair procedure, with the fairness of the procedure relying on an active suppression of self-knowledge on the part of the contracting parties. Yet, as I have argued elsewhere (Rao 2010: 396–97), the emphasis on ignorance of self-interest has occluded the extent to which the fairness of the Rawlsian choosing procedure — on its own terms — is contingent on the acquisition of knowledge about subaltern interests. Only if the contracting parties are able to make the imaginative leap necessary to picture what life might be like for the subaltern, to consider the possibility that they might themselves occupy positions of subalternity, and to reflect on what entitlements should be universally guaranteed so as to reasonably enable the alleviation of subalternity, can the choosing procedure yield principles of justice for the society as a whole. However well intentioned, postcolonial theorists have been warning for considerable time that such imaginative leaps are fraught with the imperialist possibilities of elite theorists speaking for sub-alterns (Spivak 1988). My purpose here is the more modest one of suggesting not so much that Rawlsian methodology is flawed, as that its immanent imperative of acquisition of knowledge about subaltern interests has not been adequately recognized even by its most dedicated practitioners.

David Harvey has suggested that:

> There are ... three ways in which cosmopolitanism can arise: out of philosophical reflection; out of an assessment of practical requirements and basic human needs; or out of the ferment of social movements that are engaged in transforming the world each in their own ways (Harvey 2009: 94).

The Western liberal cosmopolitan literature arrives at its conclu-sions overwhelmingly via the first method, and typically through a narcissistic reflection on Western philosophical thought on the meaning of the good life (Munro and Shilliam 2011: 161). One might see in the capabilities approach of Martha Nussbaum (2006), which attempts to articulate a bare minimum conception of the good life through an intuitive grasp of the goods that are required for human flourishing, an exemplar of Harvey's second, more practical and needs-based approach. Yet even this alternative is grounded in an Aristotelian conception of human flourishing, with modern non-Western thinkers such as Rabindranath Tagore being conscripted into the argument to confirm rather than to challenge the universality of Western liberal thought (Nussbaum 1996).

The charge of Eurocentrism has of course been levelled against the fields of political theory and international relations for some time. Yet this charge acquires a particular intensity and irony when the question under consideration is cosmopolitanism. Lib-eral cosmopolitans claim that the cosmopolitan stance is consti-tuted by three commitments: first, individualism, or the claim that individual human beings are the ultimate units of moral concern; second, universality, or the claim that the status of the ultimate unit of concern attaches to every human being equally regardless of the groups to which they may belong; third, generality, or the claim that individuals are the ultimate units of concern, equally, for everyone (Caney 2001: 977; Pogge 2002: 169). It is the claim to generality that, without a meaningful engagement with the political thought of the 'non-Western' world, renders liberal cosmopolitan-ism's self-understanding untenable. This is theorization on behalf of the globe without the participation of the globe.

Indeed this suspicion is borne out by close attention to the etymological, historical and political provenance of the very idea of cosmopolitanism. As is well know, the term 'cosmopolitan' is of Greek Stoic origin. Bringing together the root words 'cosmos' (world) and 'polis' (city, people), it described a moral stance rooted in a belief in the equal worth of humanity in all persons, in virtue of their capacity for reason (Nussbaum 1997: 28–32). It urged the extension of Greek norms of civility and mutual respect between citizens of the *polis* to all human beings, as if they were members of a common *polis* whose boundaries were those of the cosmos itself. Anthony Pagden has drawn attention to the darker side of this extension, observing with regard to Zeno of Citium, the founder of the Stoic School, that 'in calling upon all men to belong to a com-mon *deme* or polis, Zeno was also ... making all men members of the *deme* or polis to which *he* belonged' (Pagden 2000: 5). Univer-salism did not necessarily imply egalitarianism in this view, for the assumption that the cosmos was permeated and guided by a *logos* or purpose implanted in each human being as the principle of reason did not carry with it the implication that this logos was shared by all persons to an equal degree (ibid.). More broadly, Pagden (2002) has noted that Stoic, Cynic and Enlightenment cosmopolitanisms emerged in tandem with the spread of the Greek, Roman and modern European empires. Analogously, Petter Korkman (2008) has argued that the cultivation of cosmopolitan sociability in the work of early Enlightenment thinkers was motivated in large part by a desire to oil the wheels of global commerce. Taken together with the more recent resurgence of liberal cosmopolitan discourse in the unipolar moment afforded by the end of the Cold War, it is tempting to conclude from this literature that ideas of universal moral community and world citizenship have been championed by elites who have been able to experience a sense of inhabitation of the world as a whole on account of their political and economic power (Calhoun 2002: 872). If the notion of cosmopolitanism has occurred most readily to those in a position to rule the world, might not the search for 'non-Western cosmopolitanisms' in the modern period be a futile endeavour?

The 'Practice Turn': But Can Non-Europeans Think?

Partly as a response to criticisms of the kind levelled above, the literature on cosmopolitanism — particularly in disciplines outside philosophy and political theory, including history, anthropology, sociology, and literary studies — has begun to take what might be called a 'practice turn'. Brue Robbins (1998: 1) has suggested that 'cosmopolitanism should be seen not as a luxuriously free-floating view from above, but should be extended to transnational experiences that are particular rather than universal and that are underprivileged — indeed, often coerced'. This move locates cosmopolitanism not simply in elite utopian thought but also in experience and, moreover, in experience that is partial and particular and that may have been coerced rather than sought after. It suggests that the cosmopolitical is to be found in the consequences of all sorts of border-transgressing practices including conquest, commerce, migration, and carbon consumption, but that the experience of the cosmopolitical will not be the same in any two places.

Moving in this way from a normative to a more epistemological usage of the term, the editors of an influential collection of essays titled simply *Cosmopolitanism* frame their task as one of 'look[ing] at the world across time and space [to] see how people have thought and acted beyond the local' (Pollock et al. 2002: 10). This collection treats phenomena such as the circulation of Sanskrit literature from Central Asia to the South China Sea in the pre-colonial area, or the melange of architectural styles that characterized pre-war Shanghai, as cosmopolitan practices. Rather than referring simply to a moral philosophical stance on the question of obligation, 'cosmopolitanism' in these usages refers to potentially infinite 'ways of living at home abroad or abroad at home' (ibid.: 11). In a similar vein, Arjun Appadurai (1997) has written about how globalization makes 'postnational' forms of belonging possible, including for subaltern subjects. If Benedict Anderson (1991) famously drew our attention to the ways in which patterns of mobility and print capitalism facilitated the 'imagined communities' of New World nations, Appadurai has argued that global migration and global mass media now provide the infrastructural basis for the imagination of postnational communities. Importantly, in Appadurai's view, it is not simply the privileged who are thinking and feeling beyond the nation: the demographic basis for his postnational world is provided as much by the experiences of refugees, migrant labour, trafficked women and illegal immigrants, as by those of wealthy frequent flyers (Appadurai 1997: 21).

Sheldon Pollock's work functions as a useful point of convergence in the political theoretic, anthropological and historical literature on cosmopolitanism. Against communitarians such as Will Kymlicka and Tom Nairn who appear to regard the vernacular as an enduring condition of life standing outside of history and therefore deserving of protection from an encroaching cosmopolitanism, Pollock offers a comparative historical account of the ancient Sanskrit and Latin cosmopolitan worlds outlining the complex processes by which they were fragmented into vernacular linguistic and political entities. In this view, vernacular community is the result of conscious decisions to renounce the larger world for the smaller place rather than something that exists primevally and prior to interaction with others. In Pollock's magisterial argument, we have an account of a 'non-Western' cosmopolitanism — the Sanskrit world — and the ways in which it differed from a contemporaneous Latin cosmopolis. Yet the emphasis on 'conscious decision' notwithstanding, what interests me here is that Pollock understands cosmopolitanism and vernacularism

> as action rather than idea, as something people do rather than something they declare, as practice rather than proposition (least of all, philosophical proposition). This enables us to see that some people in the past have been able to be cosmopolitan or vernacular without directly professing either, perhaps even while finding it impossible rationally to justify either. By contrast, the attempt to vindicate cosmopolitanism or vernacularism — the production of the very discourse on the universal or the particular — seems to entail an objectification and abstraction, and their associated political practices, that have made the cosmopolitan so often take on the character of domination and the vernacular, that of inevitability (Pollock 2000: 593).

The interventions surveyed in this section seek to shift conceptualizations of cosmopolitanism from the realm of ideas and thought to that of experience/practice/action/ways of life. This has the consequence of pluralizing the cosmopolitical and taking it out of the social locations of imperial capitalist elites. Yet there are two problems with the practice turn. The first is that, as many scholars have noted, there is no necessary link between transnational experience and the recognition of cosmopolitan moral obligation, even if the former has the potential to facilitate the latter (Vertovec and Cohen 2002). Diasporas provide a case in point. Far from being harbingers of postnational consciousness, diasporas can in fact exemplify a sort of long-distance ultra-nationalism fuelled by guilt at having abandoned the homeland and fear of assimilation to the point of identity dissolution in the host country (Sud 2008).

A second and more troubling difficulty with the practice turn is that the shift away from 'thought' when one turns to the world outside the West can convey the unfortunate implication that while the West 'thinks', other parts of the world simply 'do'. In a recent polemical intervention, Hamid Dabashi takes to task the writer of a profile on Slavoj Žižek, whose innocuously bland opening paragraph begins with the pronouncement that 'There are many active and important philosophers today', before going on to name Judith Butler, Simon Critchley, Victoria Camps, Jean-Luc Nancy, Chantal Mouffe, Gianni Vattimo, Peter Sloterdijk, and of course Žižek himself (Zabala 2012). Dabashi expresses incredulity at the unabashedly Eurocentric character of what the author calls 'philosophy today', asking rhetorically, in the title of his response: 'Can non-Europeans think?' (Dabashi 2013). I am tempted to pose the same question in response to the practice turn in the cosmopolitan literature.

In doing so, I do not wish to exaggerate the distinction between thought and practice, for all practice is informed by thought at some point in its historical evolution even if not on an ongoing basis in the case of practices that become habits or customs. And it may be that Pollock himself is not vulnerable to the criticism above because he is looking at literary practices, which are especially 'thoughtful' practices centred around reading, writing, reciting, copying, printing, and circulating texts. In his words, literature is an especially sensitive gauge of sentiments of belonging. Practices around literature meant for large worlds or small places are a declaration of affiliation with that world or place, making the production and circulation of literature utterly different from the production and circulation of things (Pollock 2000: 594). This suggests that literary practice might occupy a space between moral philosophical thought and amoral habitual practice — a space of everyday thought, if you like.

Yet even if the turn to literary practice does not quite abandon 'thought', it is nonetheless a departure from the enterprise of grand theorizing around questions of global justice and world order — a departure that Pollock is candid about — leaving these questions to be answered by Western voices alone. While valuable in pluralizing conceptualizations of cosmopolitanism, the practice turn — even of the literary kind — leaves unanswered the question of whether non-Europeans have addressed themselves to questions of world order and global justice.

The Ontology of Comparative Political Thought

If the practice turn has tended to marginalize thought in favour of practice and experience, the recent emergence of the sub-field of CPT offers an opportunity to return to the problem of how one might recognize political thinking outside the West on questions of global order and justice. Early methodological debates in CPT have tended to focus on issues of ontology and epistemology — what should CPT study and how. While promising in a number of respects, I suggest in this section that the apparent ontological presuppositions of some CPT scholarship might work to obscure, rather than illuminate, non-European reflection on the global. I want to be clear that this is not a critique of the usefulness of CPT methodology for the analysis of all possible questions, but a more specific concern that ontological premises in these methodological debates could impede the identification of recognizably cosmopolitan thought outside the West.

Early discussions in CPT have tended to invoke macro units of analysis, such as 'Chinese', 'Indian', 'African', and 'Islamic' thought, for the purpose of comparison, even as some theorists have pointed out the incommensurability of these categories when juxtaposed against each other. Thus of the units mentioned above, the first two are national, the third continental (or pan-national), and the fourth transnational with no categorical territorial dimension. Andrew March has suggested that if CPT is largely concerned with political value conflict, it should take a predominant interest in religious doctrine and political thought (2009: 550–53). Yet a focus on religion would not, by itself, alleviate difficulties of incommensurability. Sanjay Seth has argued that although the category 'religion' takes the form of a genus divided into different species (Christianity, Islam, Buddhism, etc.), thereby appearing sensitive to difference and facilitative of comparative analysis, it is imbued with the idea that 'beliefs' pertaining to the transcendent or 'sacred' define the essence of religions and that different religions might be distinguished by their differing beliefs. Citing scholars of religion, he notes that far from being a universal and trans-historical category, this understanding of 'religion' is in fact a product of rationalist reconstructions of spirituality in 17th- and 18th-century England, making it a Christian theological category. Its export to other parts of the world has tended to produce misunderstandings and unfruitful comparisons when applied to 'religions' that have not been subject to the same interpretive processes shaping them into systems of belief (Seth 2009: 336). In effect, Seth does to the category 'Religion' what Dipesh Chakrabarty (2000) does to 'History', reminding us of its provenance, but in doing so destabilizing its utility as a stable category for comparison across space and time.

More fundamentally, scholars have expressed concern that if CPT were reduced to the study of the 'non-West', it risks becoming a ghetto in which marginalized political thought is sequestered, leaving the mainstream of political theory undisturbed in its Euro-American moorings. Chris Goto-Jones has suggested that the motivation for studying political thought emanating from outside Europe cannot simply be geographical: rather, such thought becomes interesting because of fundamental 'discontinuities' with European thought founded on metaphysical and cosmological differences (2010: 220). The shift of emphasis from geography to conceptual discontinuity has significant implications: it implies, on the one hand, that non-Western thinking that is continuous with European thought is not appropriate subject matter for CPT; conversely, European conceptual innovation that is discontinuous with prior European thought becomes relevant to the study of CPT. In Goto-Jones's view then, the study of CPT should aim, not at comparative 'West v. Rest' analyses, but at the study of discontinuity.

In contrast, Farah Godrej defends the retention of the West/non-West distinction as central to the enterprise of CPT (2011: 13–14). While reframing the distinction as one referring to patterns of historical privilege and exclusion rather than to 'traditions' clearly bounded by geography and culture, she nonetheless continues to invoke the geo-cultural traditions — 'Indian', 'Chinese', 'Islamic' — that seem to have become a staple of CPT discourses. Godrej's text entitled *Cosmopolitan Political Thought* takes note of the burgeoning literature on cosmopolitanism and its problematic

Eurocentrism, but is more concerned with articulating a cosmopolitan method for political theorizing on all sorts of questions including that of cosmopolitanism itself. She argues that while the ultimate aim of a cosmopolitan political thought would be to move beyond binaries of self/other or West/non-West towards a discourse in which coeval engagement between Western, Chinese, African, Japanese, Islamic and other political resources might become possible (without necessary reference to a European 'centre'), the move towards such an eventuality cannot avoid making reference to the dichotomies that have constructed and constrained the world of knowledge production thus far (ibid.: 14).

Godrej's insistence on taking cognizance of such dichotomies and boundaries produces a 'cosmopolitan' political method that is essentially one of careful negotiation between intellectual traditions and lineages. She outlines a three-step method in which the CPT scholar would first dislocate herself from her particular context with a view to entering the world of the text she was studying and immersing herself in the tradition within which that text was produced. She would then have to reconstruct and represent the ideas in that text for an audience outside the tradition being investigated. Finally, she would have to wrestle with the conflicting imperatives of adherence or immersion and critical scholarship. As Godrej puts it, the 'cosmopolitan scholar's task will be to make the transition between deep existential immersion in a particular context, and the importation of its cultural products into another, often radically alien context' (ibid.: 79). Elaborating on the need for these distinct steps, she argues that

> only the scholar who has taken seriously the self-dislocating activities previously outlined can engage in the self-relocating task in a way that carefully navigates [potential problems] . . . This scholar has undergone a process that provides scholarly credibility, for it locates one at a positionality that makes his or her relationship to a set of texts or ideas stand up to the scrutiny of fellow members of that intellectual community. It is not merely that it puts one beyond the reach of Orientalist or Eurocentric reproach and thus provides a 'stamp' of insider approval, but rather that it gives a scholar the tools to treat a subject matter that travels across boundaries with the requisite sensitivity and care. This prior effort of participation in a set of activities and ways of life might confer something akin to an 'insider' status. Creative license is something that implies a permission or authorization to engage in an

act that might otherwise seem problematic, absent this authorization. This replication of 'insider' status, then, acts as our scholar's license to import ideas across boundaries, not in a blindly arrogant or appropriating way, but with the requisite methodological understanding to ensure that such importation occurs with care for the nature of the ideas and texts involved (Godrej 2011: 95).

The emphasis on credibility, positionality, insider status, permission, authorization, and license to import takes us very far from the tropes of borderlessness and voracious cultural mongrelization that have tended to characterize cosmopolitan worldviews (Rushdie 1991: 394). Indeed, the ontological premises of Godrej's methodological imaginary seem to approximate quite closely the gate-keeping, permission-seeking and boundary-producing practices of our actually existing world of sovereign states. Part of the problem here seems to be that the very enterprise of comparison requires the identification of 'units' for comparison, which in turn requires the separation and distancing of discrete artefacts as a prelude to their juxtaposition and comparison (Goto-Jones 2010: 225). Yet I worry that the isolation of something called 'Indian cosmopolitanism' with a view to bringing it into comparison with 'Western cosmopolitanism' might sever it from the intellectual and material exchanges that made it possible. In a later section of this chapter, I will question whether the 'cosmopolitan' method that Godrej advocates reflects the historical processes by which cosmopolitan thought has in fact been produced outside Europe and, more generally, whether the ontological presuppositions of the CPT imaginary might work to obscure the spaces within which such thought was produced.

In Godrej's defence, her concern with outlining the circumstances in which the CPT scholar might earn the prerogative to engage in cultural translation and transmission comes out of an acute awareness of a history in which imperial agents ranged freely across borders without the care and respect that she seeks to foster (Godrej 2011: 96). Yet the weight of this history leads Goto-Jones to argue, in exactly the opposite direction, that 'the key might be to de-privilege regional appellations altogether, rather than to emphasize them, otherwise the spectres of nationalism, patriotism, fundamentalism, and identity politics seem to warp and swamp everything' (Goto-Jones 2010: 224–25).

The awareness of imperial history also produces more nuanced moments in Godrej's text that stand in some tension with the more strongly bordered ontology of the paragraph quoted above. In a move that appears to echo Chakrabarty's characterization of European categories as 'indispensable and inadequate' in the conceptualization of political modernity outside the West (Chakrabarty 2000: 6), Godrej recognizes that imperialism has bequeathed a certain pervasiveness of Eurocentric categories within non-Western traditions, leaving no sites of pristine non-Eurocentric discourse. The task for the CPT scholar, in her view, then becomes one of learning to locate sites of resistance to European categories within these traditions (Godrej 2011: 100). This recognition of the inescapability of Europe provides an interesting contrast with the work of Leigh Jenco, who takes Chakrabarty to task for exactly this claim by providing an account of Confucian scholars who, even as they engaged with the West, did so by drawing on a repertoire of methods internal to their traditions that were not beholden to the West (Jenco 2007). The contrast between Godrej and Jenco may be a function of the historical differences between the intellectual traditions they engage with most closely: the pervasiveness of European categories in modern Indian political thought is unsurprising given the fact and duration of its colonization, contrasted with the semi-colonial experience of China which, in addition, had a consciousness of itself as a civilizational entity for centuries before contact with the West.

These differences apart, for the most part, Godrej and Jenco share a common ontology in which political thinking and innovation takes place from within a set of intellectual traditions and lineages that — with the notable exception of Islam — seem to map on to geo-cultural entities. Such political thought is cognizable by the present-day CPT scholar through immersion in the substantive worldviews but, crucially for Jenco, also in the methodological protocols of these traditions. March has a particular interest in 'religions' — yet here, too, the enterprise of comparison requires the juxtaposition of discrete 'units' that can then be examined for similarity and especially difference.

The Spaces of Global History

The idea that comparison requires separation and juxtaposition might appear too banal and uncontroversial as to be worthy of further comment. But I would like, in this penultimate section, to consider what might be obscured by such an ontological pre-supposition, particularly for those of us with an interest in extra-European thought on the global. Independently of comparative political theorists, global historians have turned their attention to the genealogies of political thought, deploying very different conceptions of space with which to think through the production of cosmopolitan thought outside Europe.

If European empires were global in their extent, anti-colonial nationalists also operated on a global scale, generating a set of moral and political discourses that were invested not only in the winning of independent states for particular national movements but in the re-imagination of a world order in which imperialism was no longer legitimate. These discourses evolved through conversations amongst disparate anti-colonial nationalists over the course of the 19th and 20th centuries in what the editors of a recent collection describe as 'cosmopolitan thought zones': 'shared transnational public spaces . . . generated by the pragmatic need to get things done in communities with highly different others' (Manjapra 2010a: 1). These were certainly not the first cosmopolitan discourses generated by non-European peoples (think here of the religious and linguistic cosmopolitan discourses alluded to earlier), but they are amongst the most significant of the modern period. What is interesting about the global history literature on non-European political thought, and the notion of cosmopolitan thought zones more specifically, is the relationship that is suggested between space and thought. Of significance here is not simply the absolute space in which political thought is produced, but the reciprocal relationship between space and thought, in which space shapes thought but thought also shapes conceptualizations of the space of belonging.

The notion of cosmopolitan thought zones seeks to destabilize two features of the ontologies hegemonic in the social sciences and humanities, including CPT. The first is the ontology of nation states and, on a larger scale, 'regions' constituting 'area studies', that lurks behind the units of analysis deployed in CPT with its emphasis on traditions, lineages, canonical and civilizational thought. Sugata Bose's characterization of the Indian Ocean as an 'interregional' space — one that is neither global nor national, nor regional in the sense in which regions are conventionally demarcated — provides an exemplary instance of the sorts of spaces that are obscured by hegemonic ontologies. Bose regards the space of the Indian Ocean as being held together by myriad political, economic and cultural linkages that predate European domination and are never fully disrupted by it. Importantly, from the point of view of cosmopolitan political thought, the oceanic space becomes a venue for articulating universalisms that are distinct from those of European provenance (Bose 2006: 273).

By way of example, Bose cites the political itinerary of Gandhi who spent nearly two decades in South Africa, crafting the technique of satyagraha from 1906–14, learning to forge solidarity amongst the diverse religious communities that constituted the Indian diaspora as well as making alliances with the Chinese community in ways that were respectful of cultural and religious difference but also transcended them (ibid.: 169–70). These techniques would later be deployed on a larger scale in forging Hindu–Muslim unity in the non-cooperation movement of 1919–22, not least through the championing of the Khilafat movement — an Islamic cosmopolitan movement dedicated to the restoration of the caliphate (see Devji 2008: 125–26, for a non-instrumental reading of Gandhi's enthusiasm for Khilafat). Bose likewise reads Subhas Chandra Bose's travels in Southeast Asia to mobilize Indian expatriates for service in his Indian National Army (as well as his delicate negotiations with governmental authorities in Burma for use of their territory to launch an assault on British India) as remarkably successful efforts in bridging religious and national differences, enabled perhaps by the fact that the question of territory was less salient in diaspora (Bose 2006: 192). Finally, while much has been made in recent years of Tagore's cosmopolitanism (Nussbaum 1996; Sen 2005), Bose demonstrates the ways in which Tagore's universalism was an outgrowth of his experiences of travel within the space of the Indian Ocean. A sea voyage to Java to explore the remnants of Indian cultural influence abroad gives him a firsthand glimpse of 'signs of the history of India's entry into the universal' (Bose 2006: 235). Likewise, a visit to Iran, during which Tagore embraces its rich heritage of Sufi poetry, leads to an appreciation of the historic unity of Indo-Persian culture. Bose's larger point is that the cognizance of this comparative and connective history through the experience of travel within the space of the Indian Ocean is central to the universalism in the political thought of these figures — a universalism that cannot be reductively attributed to the intellectual resources drawn from a territorially defined 'Indian' political thought.

Deploying a more relational conception of space (Harvey 2009: Ch. 7), Nico Slate locates Gandhi within a world of 'coloured cosmopolitanism' constituted in part by Indian and African-American thinkers who regarded themselves and each other as engaged in a shared struggle against racism and imperialism. Once again, rather than placing Gandhi within a distinct intellectual lineage, what is remarkable about the spatial ontology of Slate's argument is the circulation of ideas, practices and people between India and the United States. While his book is peopled with a large number of figures, a focus on Gandhi is illustrative of this circularity. Gandhi draws on abolitionist history, including the thinking of Henry David Thoreau on civil disobedience, in crafting his early views on satyagraha. Importantly, his initial conservative views on race and caste are radicalized as a result of interaction with African-American visitors to India, and particularly through an engagement with the work of Booker T. Washington, from whom he imbibes the importance of rural education and dignity of labour (Slate 2012: 23–24, 94).

Gandhi in turn exercises a major influence on African-American struggles: an early interest in Gandhian spirituality and integrity in the 1920s, morphs into a serious debate in the 1940s about the practicability of Gandhian ideas of civil disobedience in the context of the US South. Interestingly, participants in this debate respond to W. E. B. DuBois's doubts about such applicability with a reminder that Gandhi was himself indebted to US thinkers such as Thoreau, making civil disobedience 'an American original' (ibid.: 214). Gandhian ideas attain what is perhaps the height of their influence during the 1950s civil rights movement under Martin Luther King, before being eclipsed by the Black Power movement, born out of disillusionment with the predominant framing of Gandhi and the civil rights movement as non-violent. Yet Black Power ideas themselves enter the circuits of 'coloured cosmopolitanism', influencing the birth of the Dalit Panthers in Bombay in 1972. While each of these movements was no doubt drawing on a stock of indigenous ideas of resistance, a bordered ontology that fails to theorize this circulation of ideas, practices and individuals between political formations that actively sought to learn from one another would offer a radically incomplete account of cosmopolitan thought.

The notion of cosmopolitan thought zones disrupts a second feature of hegemonic bordered ontologies, namely the assumption that encounters with difference take place solely or mainly along the imperial centre-periphery axis. Edward Said (1994) famously argued that core and periphery are mutually constitutive, an idea that has been taken up in a number of other disciplines including international relations (Barkawi and Laffey 2006). Yet the postcolonial literature has persisted in assuming that the most significant encounters from the view of political thought are those that took place between core and periphery, between imperial states and their colonies or semi-colonized modernizing states. More recent work in global history suggests that cosmopolitan thought zones were as much the product of contact between peripheries.

Nowhere is this demonstrated more clearly than in Kris Manjapra's biography of the Indian communist M. N. Roy (Manjapra 2010b). Steeped in the Swadeshi avant-garde of early 20th-century Bengal, Roy begins a close engagement with Marxism while on a sojourn in the US in 1916–17. Pursued by governmental authorities, he flees to Mexico where he helps to found the Mexican Socialist Party, before being deputed to the Second Congress of the Comintern as the Mexican representative. Here he famously disagrees with Lenin's advocacy of a tactical alliance between bourgeois nationalists and communists in anti-colonial struggles, insisting that Indian peasants already possessed a class consciousness that made them ripe for revolt — and in doing so begins the intellectual project of decolonizing Marxism (Young 2001: 131–34). A stint in Berlin in the 1920s, during which he works closely with the German communist fringe associated with the thinking of Rosa Luxemburg and the Spartakusbund, coupled with his observation of the crushing of Chinese communists by their bourgeois compatriots in the Kuomintang, leads him to become increasingly critical of the Bolshevik leadership of the worldwide communist movement. Out of synch with official communism, Roy is expelled from the Comintern and returns to India. While remaining alienated from the Communist Party of India, Roy also offers fierce critiques of Gandhian nationalism and Bose's neo-Swadeshi internationalism,

continuing to articulate a Marxist vision of international solidarity underpinned by widening alliances of peasants, industrial proletariat and petty bourgeoisie. Towards the end of his life, this
utopian vision becomes one of radical humanism grounded in a
recognition of the universal material interests of a common humanity (Manjapra 2010b). While there is much to say about the cosmopolitan life and vision of Roy, the spatial point that one might
draw out of his biography is that the coeval engagement between
peripheral intellectual formations that Godrej looks forward to as
a utopian destination for her cosmopolitan political method was
already happening in the late colonial world and is in fact obscured
by the ontological premises of her method.

Can one read Roy as a careful traveller between intellectual
traditions in the way that Godrej recommends, immersing himself in the world of the texts he was interpreting and internalizing
their methodological protocols before translating them for his
intended audiences? I would suggest not. For one thing, the Swadeshi
milieu in which his political education began was itself a highly
cosmopolitan formation rather than a bounded 'tradition', deeply
invested in the success of anti-colonial nationalist struggles in other
parts of the world, and envisioning Bengal as part of pan-Asian,
pan-Islamic, proletarian and various other universalist discourses.
Manjapra describes it as a modernist thought zone that emerged
'not genealogically but conjuncturally' with German expressionism
and Italian and Russian futurism (ibid.: 48). Far from internalizing
the methodological protocols of scientific materialism before introducing its precepts to his countrymen, Roy's approach to Marxism,
in Manjapra's description, was one of an exegete approaching a
canon of scripture, not because of methodological imperatives
internal to Marxism but as a result of his historical inheritance of
a Brahmo Samaj hermeneutic tradition (ibid.: 51).[1] These features

---

[1] One could almost say that it is wilful creative mistranslations, rather
than fidelity to one's source material, that introduce innovation in political
thought and enable imported concepts to resonate with new audiences.
In Godrej's defence, perhaps we need to make a distinction between the
techniques deployed by the political *activist* engaged in CPT with a view to
importing concepts that are politically useful for their intended audience,
and the *scholar* of CPT engaged in a politically agnostic comparison of
categories across intellectual formations. Yet a CPT scholar interested in

of Roy's method lead Manjapra to insist that 'the hermeneutic "middle world" in which varied influences meet and fuse is a more appropriate field for situating Roy's ideas, as opposed to attempting to assimilate him to problematically reified categories of either "indigenous" or "Western" thought' (ibid.: 161). Importantly, Manjapra views Roy as worthy of study not because he is exceptional but rather because he is representative of important general features of anti-colonial cosmopolitanism (ibid.: xix).

Conclusion

In this chapter, I have examined four different academic discourses that purport to discuss questions of cosmopolitanism, world order and global justice. I argued that liberal cosmopolitan discourses have tended to theorize about global justice without being particularly attentive to global thought produced outside the West, partly for methodological reasons and partly because of implied audiences and political agendas. The practice turn pursued in discussions of cosmopolitanism in disciplines other than political theory and philosophy has the virtue of pluralizing the social locations in which cosmopolitics is visible, but has left obscure the relationship between border-transgressing practices and cosmopolitan moral obligation. The emerging field of comparative political thought promises to engage with the question of moral thought produced outside the Western world. Yet as recent work on similar questions in global history suggests, the ontological premises of much CPT scholarship, with its emphasis on traditions, lineages and civilizational thinking, threatens to obscure the spaces in which, and the encounters through which, cosmopolitan political thought has been produced in the world outside Europe.

Indeed the discussion in the previous section suggests that there might be something oxymoronic in claiming to have recovered something that might be described as 'Indian', 'Chinese', 'African', or even 'Western' cosmopolitanism. Such geo-cultural referents are meaningful only in the rather banal sense that they might describe the geographical coordinates of the people articulating these

---

the history of cosmopolitan political thought would need to be attentive to the border-transgressing practices inherent in the very production of *cosmopolitan* political thought and to the border-straddling spaces in which such thought is incubated.

discourses (and even that only very incompletely). For if cosmopolitanism is ultimately a discourse about learning to live with the stranger, perhaps it can only ever be produced in conversation with the stranger. In reflecting on the intellectual journey that culminated in her book *Parting Ways*, which explores Jewish philosophical resources for the critique of Zionism, Judith Butler notes a moment of realization of the profound irony of writing a book on co-existence with Palestinians purely with reference to Jewish thought. The realization led her to a deep engagement with the work of Edward Said and the Palestinian national poet Mahmoud Darwish (Butler 2013). If it is true that cosmopolitan discourses can only ever be articulated in conversation with those who are different, then it is also true that cosmopolitanism can never be fully owned by any of the participants in that conversation.

~

References

Anderson, Benedict. 1991. *Imagined Communities: Reflections on the Origin and Spread of Nationalism*, Verso, London.

Appadurai, Arjun. 1997. *Modernity at Large: Cultural Dimensions of Globalization*, University of Minnesota Press, Minneapolis.

Barkawi, Tarak and Mark Laffey. 2006. 'The Postcolonial Moment in Security Studies', *Review of International Studies* 32(2): 329–52.

Beitz, Charles R. 1979. *Political Theory and International Relations*, Princeton University Press, Princeton.

Bose, Sugata. 2006. *A Hundred Horizons: The Indian Ocean in the Age of Global Empire*, Harvard University Press, Cambridge.

Brock, Gillian. 2009. *Global Justice: A Cosmopolitan Account*, Oxford University Press, Oxford.

Butler, Judith. 2013. 'Parting Ways: Jewishness and the Critique of Zionism', conversation with Jacqueline Rose, Jewish Book Week, London, http://www.jewishbookweek.com/past-events/284 (accessed 16 June 2014).

Calhoun, Craig. 2002. 'The Class Consciousness of Frequent Travellers: Toward a Critique of Actually Existing Cosmopolitanism', *South Atlantic Quarterly* 101(4): 869–97.

Caney, Simon. 2001. 'Review Article: International Distributive Justice', *Political Studies* 49(5): 974–97.

Chakrabarty, Dipesh. 2000. *Provincializing Europe: Postcolonial Thought and Historical Difference*, Princeton University Press, Princeton.

Dabashi, Hamid. 2013. 'Can Non-Europeans Think?' *Al Jazeera*, 15 January, http://www.aljazeera.com/indepth/opinion/2013/01/201311414263 8797542.html (accessed 16 June 2014).

Devji, Faisal. 2008. *The Terrorist in Search of Humanity: Militant Islam and Global Politics*, Hurst, London.

Godrej, Farah. 2011. *Cosmopolitan Political Thought: Method, Practice, Discipline*, Oxford University Press, Oxford.

Goto-Jones, Christopher. 2010. 'Comparative Political Thought: Beyond the Non-Western', in Duncan Bell (ed.), *Ethics and World Politics*, Oxford University Press, Oxford, 219–36.

Harvey, David. 2009. *Cosmopolitanism and the Geographies of Freedom*, Columbia University Press, New York.

Jenco, Leigh Kathryn. 2007. 'What Does Heaven Ever Say? A Methods-centered Approach to Cross-cultural Engagement', *American Political Science Review* 101(4): 741–56.

Korkman, Petter. 2008. 'The Vital String of Mankind — Sociability and the Foundation of Natural Law and Universal Rights', in Petter Korkman and Virpi Mäkinen (eds), *Universalism in International Law and Political Philosophy*, Helsinki Collegium for Advanced Studies, Helsinki, 5–34.

Manjapra, Kris. 2010a. 'Introduction', in Sugata Bose and Kris Manjapra (eds), *Cosmopolitan Thought Zones: South Asia and the Global Circulation of Ideas*, Palgrave Macmillan, Basingstoke, 1–19.

———. 2010b. *M. N. Roy: Marxism and Colonial Cosmopolitanism*, Routledge, New Delhi.

March, Andrew. 2009. 'What is Comparative Political Theory?', *The Review of Politics* 71(4): 531–65.

Miller, David. 1995. *On Nationality*, Clarendon Press, Oxford.

Moellendorf, Darrel. 2002. *Cosmopolitan Justice*, Westview Press, Boulder.

Munro, Martin and Robbie Shilliam. 2011. 'Alternative Sources of Cosmopolitanism: Nationalism, Universalism and Créolité in Francophone Caribbean Thought', in Robbie Shilliam (ed.), *International Relations and Non-Western Thought: Imperialism, Colonialism and Investigations of Global Modernity*, Routledge, Oxford, 159–77.

Nussbaum, Martha C. 1996. 'Patriotism and Cosmopolitanism', in Joshua Cohen (ed), *For Love of Country: Debating the Limits of Patriotism*, Beacon Press, Boston, 3–20.

———. 1997. 'Kant and Cosmopolitanism', in James Bohman and Matthias Lutz-Bachmann (eds), *Perpetual Peace: Essays on Kant's Cosmopolitan Ideal*, The MIT Press, Cambridge, 25–58.

———. 2006. *Frontiers of Justice: Disability, Nationality, Species Membership*, Harvard University Press, Cambridge.

Pagden, Anthony. 2000. 'Stoicism, Cosmopolitanism, and the Legacy of European Imperialism', *Constellations* 7(1): 3–22.

———. 2002. *Peoples and Empires: Europeans and the Rest of the World, From Antiquity to the Present*, Phoenix Press, London.

Pogge, Thomas. 1989. *Realizing Rawls*, Cornell University Press, Ithaca.

———. 2002. *World Poverty and Human Rights*, Polity Press, Cambridge.

Pollock, Sheldon. 2000. 'Cosmopolitan and Vernacular in History', *Public Culture* 12(3): 591–625.

Pollock, Sheldon, Homi K. Bhabha, Carol A. Breckenridge, and Dipesh Chakrabarty. 2002. 'Cosmopolitanisms', in Carol A. Breckenridge, Sheldon Pollock, Homi K. Bhabha, and Dipesh Chakrabarty, *Cosmopolitanism*, Duke University Press, Durham, 1–14.

Rao, Rahul. 2010. 'Disciplining Cosmopolitanism', *Transnational Legal Theory* 1(3): 393–420.

Rawls, John. 1971. *A Theory of Justice*, Harvard University Press, Cambridge.

———. 2001. *The Law of Peoples*, Harvard University Press, Cambridge.

Robbins, Bruce. 1998. 'Actually Existing Cosmopolitanism', in Pheng Cheah and Bruce Robbins (eds), *Cosmopolitics: Thinking and Feeling Beyond the Nation*, University of Minnesota Press, Minneapolis.

Rushdie, Salman. 1991. *Imaginary Homelands: Essays and Criticism 1981–1991*, Granta, London.

Said, Edward. 1994. *Culture and Imperialism*, Vintage, London.

Sen, Amartya. 2005. *The Argumentative Indian: Writings on Indian History, Culture and Identity*, Penguin, London.

Seth, Sanjay. 2009. 'Historical Sociology and Postcolonial Theory: Two Strategies for Challenging Eurocentrism', *International Political Sociology* 3(3): 334–38.

Shue, Henry. 1996. *Basic Rights: Subsistence, Affluence, and US Foreign Policy*, Princeton University Press, Princeton.

Singer, Peter. 1972. 'Famine, Affluence, and Morality', *Philosophy and Public Affairs* 1(1): 229–43.

Slate, Nico. 2012. *Colored Cosmopolitanism: The Shared Struggle for Freedom in the United States and India*, Harvard University Press, Cambridge.

Spivak, Gayatri Chakravorty. 1988. 'Can the Subaltern Speak?' in Cary Nelson and Lawrence Grossberg (eds), *Marxism and the Interpretation of Culture*, Macmillan, Basingstoke, 271–313.

Sud, Nikita. 2008. 'Tracing the Links Between Hindu Nationalism and the Indian Diaspora', *St. Antony's International Review* 3(2): 50–65.

Tamir, Yael. 1993. *Liberal Nationalism*, Princeton University Press, Princeton.

Vertovec, Steven and Robin Cohen. 2002. 'Introduction: Conceiving Cosmopolitanism', in Steven Vertovec and Robin Cohen (eds), *Conceiving*

Cosmopolitanism: Theory, Context, and Practice, Oxford University Press, Oxford, 1–24.

Walzer, Michael. 1995. *Spheres of Justice: A Defence of Pluralism and Equality*, Blackwell Publishers, Oxford.

Young, Robert J. C. 2001. *Postcolonialism: An Historical Introduction*, Blackwell, Oxford.

Zabala, Santiago. 2012. 'Slavoj Žižek and the Role of the Philosopher', *Al Jazeera*, 25 December, http://www.aljazeera.com/indepth/opinion/2012/12/20121224122215406939.html (accessed 16 June 2014).

10

Cosmopolitanism and Nationalism: A Re-examination

Sonika Gupta

As a discourse that argues for change in the nature as well as structures of global politics, cosmopolitanism needs to be examined in light of the critique it makes of existing discourses on global politics. Cosmopolitanism's moral discourse places a negative value on nationalism and considers it antithetical to the process and form of constructing a cosmopolitan political community premised on the concept of global justice (Appadurai 1993; Barry 1996; Brock 2002; Nussbaum 2010). I juxtapose cosmopolitanism's moral evaluation of nationalism with the historical project of anti-colonial nationalism. The argument offered is that nationalism in the West and in postcolonial states performs and fulfils different historical functions. Therefore, any evaluation of nationalism as a moral category needs to be grounded in its specific historical context. Specifically, this chapter addresses the universalization of the Eurocentric experience of nationalism and argues that anti-colonial nationalism's moral project is not in opposition to the moral project of cosmopolitanism. However, the philosophical foundations of cosmopolitanism and anti-colonial nationalism respectively draw on their historically antagonistic and mutually constitutive narratives of modernity and coloniality that underlie fundamental inequalities of power and political agency in contemporary global politics. One cannot understand, critique or evaluate the historical–moral impact of nationalism unless one looks at both the experience of the colonizer and the colonized as mutually constitutive.

This chapter makes two claims about anti-colonial nationalism in the context of the Indian National Movement. First, anti-colonial nationalism was not solely a statist discourse limited or dedicated solely to the creation of independent and sovereign territorial nation states, but a larger discourse challenging political, cultural and moral hierarchies of power in the imperial as well as internal spheres. As such, anti-colonial nationalism is not merely about promoting the patriotic discourse of the state, but a universal discourse, morally grounded in notions of equality and freedom for all. This is reflected in social reform movements that co-existed within the broader struggle for independence. While the political struggle of the colonies was oriented towards the creation of sovereign states, the moral impetus for anti-colonial struggles comes from a more universal discourse of equality among races, nations and peoples. Second, nationalism is of intrinsic value to postcolonial societies as the embodiment of their struggle against oppression. Nationalism is the framework within which these states defined their aspirational political community imbued with ideas of justice and equality. In many postcolonial states, national liberation movements underpinned a process of deep social transformations. This process of social transformation is a continuous one, with nationalism still being a relevant location for negotiating ideas of justice and co-existence for postcolonial nations.

The historical trajectory of nationalism in Europe does not share these conditions of anti-colonial nationalism. In contrast, the birth of the nation state in Europe, in the context of the separation of Church and State, provided an essential territorial mapping of nation state, linked intrinsically to the linguistic identity. Arising from this, dominant history of nationalism in Europe is that of statist expansion and colonial exploitation. In addition, unlike in many postcolonial states, social transformation in Europe was grounded not so much in the process of the creation of the nation state, but in the (*a*) separation of the spiritual and temporal spheres of authority and (*b*) the Industrial Revolution's sociopolitical impact. Consequently, the liberal critique of nationalism emerges from the experience of (*a*) incessant nationalistic warfare among European states culminating in the Second World War, (*b*) the accompanying colonialist expansion and (*c*) the experience of the Cold War. Based on this experience, cosmopolitanism considers nationalism to be an inherently divisive (Nussbaum 2010) and dominantly statist (Barry 1996) discourse. Not surprisingly then, much of cosmopolitan scholarship that emanates from historically, philosophically and even geographically European concerns attaches a negative value to nationalism in the search for an aspirational political community beyond the nation state that can deliver on the ideals of global justice (Appadurai 1993; Barry 1996; Brock 2009, 2002). This understanding of nationalism is universalized in the search for a cosmopolitan political community that is essentially beyond the state. This constructs a linear understanding of the nature and direction of a cosmopolitan political community which is based dominantly on liberal values that provides predetermined forms of the 'cosmopolitan' to be emulated. This is a de-historicizing imposition of the 'cosmopolitan' to argue for a 'universal' idea of 'global justice' which is essentially contested.

Presenting a critique of dominant notions of nationalism, Partha Chatterjee has persuasively argued that the history of anti-colonial nationalism does not merely reproduce prototypes of modern nation states as the march of modernity continues into the non-European world (Chatterjee 1992). Chatterjee posits that anti-colonial nationalism has a sovereign narrative of the nation within which the assumptions of modernity are significantly renegotiated. Following from this, I argue that the nature and function of anti-colonial nationalism have given rise to political forms and practices that do not merely replicate the processes of nationalism that created the European nation state. To illustrate this I employ the two following examples of the nation form and of secularism as they unfold in Europe and in postcolonial locations.

I begin with the comparison of the rise of the nation form and democracy in Europe and in the colonized nations. Ranabir Samaddar argues that 'democracy as a process of transformation has been perched on a national template' (Samaddar 2012: 13). Samaddar refers to this as a 'concrete universal' historically equally true of the colonizing states of Portugal, Spain, Holland, France, Britain, and Germany, as well as the colonized nations in Africa, Latin America and Asia. The point of difference between them, I argue, emerges from their respective experiences of colonialism. In Europe, nationalism produced the mutually contradictory processes of democracy at home with imperial missions abroad, whereas in the colonies, democratic aspirations of all people and national assertion were compatible. The history of nationalism in the postcolonial states is tied in with rise of democratic and participatory political form. The success or failure of that political form, as experienced variously across the postcolonial states, is not contested here. While prominent European states saw the simultaneous rise of nationalism and colonial imperialism, anti-colonial nations, even those that did not turn out eventually as democracies, related the rise of nationalism with a struggle for democratic participation challenging imperial and domestic hierarchies of power. In current cosmopolitan literature, there is little historical relevance of nation and nationalism as a liberating discourse for millions of people that experienced the creation of the nation state as the moment of freedom. This moment of freedom carried within it long histories of popular and participatory movements, challenging racial, cultural and political inequalities of colonialism. Therefore, in historical evaluation, nationalism's moral worth is at opposite ends of the spectrum for the colonizer and the colonized. Even as cosmopolitanism critiques the dark side of nationalism, it must simultaneously make room for the positive moral worth of nationalism for postcolonial states.

The rise of the nation form and its relationship with the separation of the church and state is a similar point of difference between European liberal states and many postcolonial states. This chapter explores this relationship in India to argue that liberal definitions of secular that underlie cosmopolitan prescriptions of 'civic nation' do not allow for an examination of the secular state as it emerged in the nationalist struggle in India. This has implications for the mapping of the role of nationalism in contemporary India as discussed ahead.

The separation of religion and politics dominantly informs the Western understanding of 'secular' that advocates distance from religion, rather than accommodation of religion in the state. According to Ashis Nandy, Western definitions of secularism assume that

> [r]eligious tolerance could come only from the devaluation of religion in public and from the freeing of politics from religion. The less politics is contaminated by religion, this argument goes, the more secular and tolerant a state you will have. The word secular here is opposite of the word sacred (Nandy 1995: 35).

Secularism here becomes a coercive category, one that provides an aspirational template for others, not-yet-secularized to follow.

Nandy notes that that this definition of secularism is a product of a 'peculiar form of imperialism of categories' imposed on postcolonial societies under which a 'conceptual domain is sometimes hegemonized by a concept produced and honed in the West' (Nandy 1988: 177). Therefore, the separation of religion and politics as present in Western sociopolitical forms becomes a benchmark for judging the practice of secularism everywhere. This is a de-historicizing and de-contextualizing imposition that disregards different treatments of secularism as they emerge from non-Western locations.

The above examples of nationalism and secularism underline the need to 'decolonize' these categories, as argued by Walter Mignolo (2000). Mignolo argues that it is not enough for cosmopolitanism to be 'critical'; it must first 'dewesternize and decolonize' the cosmopolitan project's epistemological mapping of the world in the context of colonial difference, before it can engage in any meaningful manner with the idea of equal moral worth of all (Mignolo 2011: 258). I take Mignolo's broader argument about the dominance of European historical trajectory in the present cosmopolitan discourse and demonstrate its relevance by critically examining cosmopolitanism's engagement with nationalism.

Evaluating Nationalism

I identify here two main strands in cosmopolitanism's engagement with nationalism. First, there is moral evaluation of nationalism, as reflected in the work of Martha Nussbaum, that sees nationalism and cosmopolitanism as opposing if not adversarial categories (Nussbaum 2010). It is especially useful to look at Nussbaum's work here as she has engaged with the issue of anti-colonial nationalism and has in recent times moved away from a more stringent cosmopolitan position to one that accommodates national identity in the trajectory of creating a cosmopolitan political community. Second, there is an understanding of nationalism as a dominantly statist discourse, as reflected in the work of Brian Barry (1996, 2010) and Gillian Brock (2002), that treats nationality as a morally arbitrary category that is antithetical to the delivery of global justice. In response to the above negation/disregard of nationalism as a location for creating a cosmopolitan political community, there is defence of nationalism by 'communitarians' like David Miller

(2010), Will Kymlicka (2010) and Yael Tamir (1995). These scholars emphasize the ascriptive value of national identity and locate the idea of justice in notions of community. For them nationalism provides the context for actualization of the cosmopolitan ideals of global justice and individual autonomy. In another interpretation of this argument, liberal nationalists like Kok-Chor Tan (2002) argue that the goals of liberal nationalism and cosmopolitanism are not incompatible. However, these critiques of cosmopolitanism remain limited to defining the ethical limits of the cosmopolitan project mainly through a distinction between a moral obligation to co-nationals and 'outsiders'. The larger engagement with the historical role of anti-colonial nationalism as a liberating discourse is what I attempt below.

Nationalism as Moral Category

To begin with the moral evaluation of nationalism in the cosmopolitan discourse, Martha Nussbaum juxtaposes the 'love of country' against larger obligations we owe to fellow human beings and specifically to strangers. She argues that 'patriotism is a species of love that, by definition, is bounded rather than global particularistic rather than universal' (Nussbaum 2008: 79). I argue that Nussbaum's ignores the simultaneity of the universal ideal and the nationalist project in anti-colonial struggles and maps them as being at polar ends of the discourse of justice. This juxtaposition of nationalism and cosmopolitanism is illustrated in Nussbaum's reading of Rabindranath Tagore's novel *Ghare Baire* ('The Home and the World') (Tagore 2004) where she argues that the novel illustrates Tagore's commitment to broader goals of global solidarity rather than the narrower vision of a nationalist assertion. She understands *Ghare Baire* as a 'tragic story of defeat of reasonable and principled cosmopolitanism by the forces of nationalism and ethnocentrism' thus offering a judgement of nationalism as a negative moral category (Nussbaum 2010: 5). Nussbaum observes that Tagore disavows nationalism in favour of a more globally resonant cosmopolitan ideal. Nussbaum's reading of Tagore has been challenged by Rahul Rao as too simple and he argues that the juxtaposition between nationalism and cosmopolitanism in Tagore's work suggested by Nussbaum may be overstated (Rao 2013: 178). Rao suggests that Tagore's critique of nationalism is related more to the strategies of coercion in the nationalist 'Swadeshi' movement in India rather than the actual goals of the movement (Rao 2013: 180). Even as Tagore offers his critique of the nationalist strategies, he remains committed to the goals of the anti-colonial struggle within which he locates cultural parity for all as the goal of the national movement (ibid.: 182). This does not take away from the broader goals of nationalism but rather provides an alternative channel through which the colonized self may recover its agency. I argue that rather than present a repudiation of nationalism, Tagore epitomizes the predicament of the postcolonial subaltern. This predicament arises both from the universal discourse of imperialism and its enduring legacies of power as well as from the failures of the postcolonial state to deliver on the promise of a just society. Nussbaum's reading of Tagore demonstrates how cosmopolitanism's assumptions of universalism begin to fray in the face of challenge from locality, viz., that of anti-colonial nationalism which successfully accommodates the seemingly opposing concerns of nationalist assertion and the construction of a 'civic nation'. For this we must turn to Gandhi and his understanding of the construction of a 'civic nation' grounded in nationalist assertion. It would appear that Rao's understanding of Tagore and Nussbaum's 'globally sensitive patriotism' both emphasize the need for nationalism as a 'transitional' framework till the conditions for global solidarity and equality are worked out. In contrast, Gandhi's understanding of nationalism provides the context within with both social and national reconstruction must necessarily take place for the creation of a self-aware political community.

Gandhi: Nationalism and the Construction of the Civic Nation

This chapter argues that the Indian National Movement as led by Mahatma Gandhi offered a moral discourse that harmonized the project of nationalism with that of global justice, containing within it an ethical and political critique of liberal values. The moral-political evaluation of anti-colonial nationalism in the chapter is grounded in a discussion of Gandhi's seminal treatise, *Hind Swaraj* (Parel 2011). *Hind Swaraj* or 'Self Rule' was written in 1909, in the context of Gandhi's attempts to revitalize India's National Movement and epitomizes the recovery of the colonial self, cast firmly in the nationalist project. It presents a radical critique not merely of colonialism but of the civilizational underpinning of imperialism that created enduring cultural, political and moral hierarchies. Gandhi sets up the internal weaknesses of the Indian nation by recasting the project of national liberation from that of political equality to that of the recovery of cultural, political and moral agency of the colonized self.

Hind Swaraj has been variously understood as polemic and 'a rather incendiary manifesto' (Erikson 1969: 217), as well as a strident comment on colonial imperialism, industrial capitalism and rationalist materialism that, according to Gandhi, was used to provide the justification for the civilizing mission of the West (Heredia 1999: 1497). The body of the academic critique of Gandhi is too vast to be even mentioned in its entirety in a short chapter. I would just refer to a broad categorization of this critique as those that recognize the centrality of Gandhi not merely as the architect of India's national movement, but as the most unifying force representing the vast diversity of the Indian nation (Nandy 1988; Chatterjee 1992; Chandra 2004). On the other hand, there are long-standing Marxist[1] and subaltern (Guha 1998) critiques of Gandhi. The former critiques Gandhi as representative of the bourgeois nationalist elite that sought to transfer power not to the masses but to themselves, while the latter is a postcolonial critique of nationalism as complicit with imperialism. There is also the counter-response to these critiques from scholars who assert the crucial relevance of Gandhi as a leader and the impact of Gandhian political practice on Indian nationalism. There is critical engagement here with Gandhian social and political thought, as seen in the works of Vinay Lal (2008), Irfan Habib (1995), Aditya Nigam (2009), and Ashis Nandy (1995). The main focus in the work of these scholars is Gandhian political practice and its impact on the nationalist narrative of India. The operative part of Gandhian political practice was non-violence, manifested in the prescription of satyagraha as the preferred strategy for the liberation movement. Responding specifically to the subaltern understanding of Gandhi as not relevant or responsive to the subaltern condition, Irfan Habib argues:

> It seems to me that the lumping everyone in one basket of undifferentiated elites, or very thinly differentiated elites, and treating the subaltern

---

[1] For a representative reading, see Dutt (1930). For a more recent work, see Ghosh (2007).

as autonomous, which means denying the influence of Gandhi on those vast classes of the Indian poor, is a position no serious historian can adopt (Habib 1995: 4).

Underscoring the impact of Gandhian political practice, both as a moral discourse and a mobilization strategy, I locate nationalism as a core value of this moral discourse.

Gandhi's nationalism was centrally premised not on the principle of sovereign equality but as a critique of modernity that created conditions for colonialism. He challenged the relevance of liberal modernity as an aspirational value for all. *Hind Swaraj*, while making a demand for self-rule for India, critiques liberal modernity and its excesses. Gandhi famously declares that 'India is being ground down, not under the English heel, but under that of modern civilization' (Parel 2011: 41). He critiques the essentialist liberal values of progress and growth as against the claims of place, tradition and sustainability. In this, Gandhi's understanding of colonial enslavement goes far beyond the political conception of subjugation to lament the curtailment of moral and political agency in the enslaved through the creation of civilizational hierarchies. Gandhi identified the reason for India's enslavement not in the greater capability of the British nation or western civilization, but India's weakness in yielding to capitalist enterprise as well the internecine political, religious and social conflicts in India. He argued:

> We keep the English in India for our base self-interest. We like their commerce; they please us by their subtle methods and get what they want from us. To blame them for this is to perpetuate their power. We further strengthen their hold by quarrelling amongst ourselves. If you accept the above statements, it is proved that the English entered India for the purposes of trade. They remain in it for the same purpose and we help them to do so. Their arms and ammunition are perfectly useless (ibid.: 40).

Here Gandhi is not looking at replicating the liberal-democratic model under Indian leadership but instead is offering a rejection of the applicability of that model for an independent India. Does this render Gandhi in complete opposition to the moral project of cosmopolitanism based on liberal values? Let us compare the construction of the civic nation in the cosmopolitan discourse and in *Hind Swaraj* to attempt to answer this.

I argue that both Nussbaum and Gandhi advocated the constitution of a civic nation as crucial to the construction of an enabled political community. While Nussbaum located the construction of this civic nation in processes of 'purified patriotism' and 'sacrifice' on the part of the more affluent nations, Gandhi, on the other hand, locates the creation of the civic nation in the nationalist recovery of the self. Anthony Parel encapsulates Gandhi's understanding of the creation of a civic nation as follows: 'A civic nation, a *praja*, as he calls it, is a political community whose basic unit is the individual considered as a bearer of fundamental rights and a subject capable of *swaraj* — i.e., self-determination and self-development' (Parel 2011: xv). The missing piece here is the recognition that these two historical process of construction of the civic nation are mutually constitutive. They differ not in their goal of creating a just world but in their mappings of justice. Further, they differ in the prescriptions of civic institutions as informed by their specific historical trajectories. Nussbaum clearly identifies the aspirational cosmopolitan political community as a 'classically liberal one' that rules out any role for religion in its constitution. This is in contrast to the constitution of a civic nation as envisioned by Gandhi that must specifically make space for religion as a moral discourse. For Gandhi the concept of a civic nation was grounded both in nationalist assertion as well as accommodation of religion in politics. Gandhi is categorical that his civic community can only be achieved through a nationalist resurgence that accommodates its religious and spiritual core. Gandhi chalks out a path for an independent India that accommodates its communitarian basis with *sarva dharma sama bhava* ('equal treatment of all religions') as the framework for accommodating and expressing group identities. Gandhi's path to religious tolerance accepts religion as an integral part of imaginaries of the self. He declares: 'Religion is dear to me, and my first complaint is that India is becoming irreligious' (Parel 2011: 41). He goes on to define his understanding of religion as follows: 'Here I am not thinking of the Hindu, the Mohamedan, or the Zoroastrian religion, but that of religion which underlies all religions. We are turning away from God' (ibid.). To Gandhi, the creation of the civic nation and the accommodation of a religious identity were not antithetical. He declares that 'those who are conscious of the spirit of nationality do not interfere with one another's religions. If they do, they are not fit to be considered a nation' (Parel 2011: 50–51). For him, moving away from India's spiritual core as expressed in its many religions is the cause of moral weakening rather than the strengthening of the nation. Therefore, Gandhi's *Hind Swaraj* saw not a denial of the role of religion in the creation of a civic community, but a transformation of the understanding of religion.

Even as Gandhi chalks out the vision of a secular Indian state, he specifically argues against the secularization of society. These two processes have often been confused in Western comments on Indian secularism as argued by Nalini Rajan (2003). Rajan refutes Jakob de Roover's (2002) contention that Indian secularism lacks systematic theoretical articulation and is instead a series of normative positions on the relationship between religion and politics. She argues instead that de Roover confuses the secular state with secularization of society. Rajan specifically refers to secularism as having varying degrees of separation of religion and politics in different self-avowed secular states, including Western states. The assumption that Western states have been able to make a clear distinction between the secular and the sacred, both conceptually and institutionally, does not then hold up under this argument. What does emerge from this is that the secular and its relationship with the civic have different meaning in different historical contexts. In arguing that the civic is a 'classically liberal' domain separate from religion is to essentialize the understanding of civic within a particular historical context.

Further, nationalism and secularism are not necessarily opposed to each other in the anti-colonial struggle in India. In fact, the concept of a secular Indian state finds its roots in the nationalist discourse. Outlining the intrinsic relationship between secularism and nationalism, Bipan Chandra argues that in India, nationalism and secularism are not antithetical categories.

> In India secularism arose as the ideology of uniting all the Indian people vis-à-vis colonialism and as a part of the process of nation-making. Simultaneously, communalism developed as the most divisive social and political force. Consequently, secularism also came to mean a clear-cut opposition to communalism (Chandra 2004: 6).

In fact, secular nationalism as it evolved in the context of the freedom movement continues to provide the critical response to the rise of right-wing extremism in India. The rise of Hindu

nationalism does not therefore necessarily discredit the project
of nationalism in India. On the other hand, the opposition to
the rise of Hindu nationalism is grounded not in universal categories of humanity but in secular nationalism that privileges the
construction of a secular state in the context of a multi-religious
society. Here nationalism and secularism are not contending but
complementary categories. In the wake of the Gujarat riots, Indian
social scientists debated the form and content of Indian secularism to locate the reasons for the massive failure of the state in
protecting Muslims (Gupta 2002; Kesavan 2003; Rajan 2003;
Sheth 2009). Even as they disagreed with the specific interpretations of secularism, these scholars point to the historical basis of
the Indian concept of secularism that differs from its classically
Western notions. A pertinent example is provided by Mukul
Kesavan as he equates the rise of the Hindu right in India to similar nationalists upsurges in Europe, such as Serbian nationalism,
that are premised in his understanding on an 'exclusionary nationalism that aimed to create a uniform citizenry on tried and tested
European nationalist principles, a shared language, an authorised
history, a dominant religious community, and a common enemy'
(Kesavan 2003: 65). Kesavan refers specifically to the brand of
religious tolerance of the Indian National Congress (INC) led by
Gandhi and Nehru, that 'being secular meant making different
types of Indians equally welcome. In that context, secularism
became a way of being comprehensively nationalist' (ibid.: 62).
This is not a desiccated discourse of the promotion of civic identities denying cultural and religious moorings, but a celebration
of the expression of all identities in equal measure as manifested
in the Indian understanding of secularism. This view of secularism continues to define the relationship between religion, politics
and nation in India. Nationalism then cannot be identified solely
with the rise of the Hindu right but is in fact a critique of the chau-
vinistic and exclusionary discourse of a *Hindu Rashtra* or 'Hindu
nation'. Essentially, there is a clear demarcation between Indian
patriotism that reaffirms the secular state and Hindu nationalism that challenges the secular foundation of the Republic. One
is a discourse of inclusion and the other of exclusion that can be
equated, as Kesavan argues, with the European statist discourse of
nationalism.

Nationalism and Statism

The second strand of cosmopolitan's engagement with nationalism juxtaposes the statism inherent in the latter to the globalism inherent in the former. Here nationality is a morally arbitrary category that cannot be the basis of the construction of a just world order. Gillian Brock argues that nationalism as an historical concept as well as a political identity is incompatible with a cosmopolitan order because nationality places constraints on people's access to resources (Brock 2009: 269) as well as the ability of any global community to take action against the violation of human rights within nation states (Brock 2002). Or, as Brian Barry argues, 'The dirty little secret of nationalism is that the fulfillment of most nationalist aspirations entails stamping on the interests and aspirations of some other nationality' (Barry 1996: 7). Anti-colonial liberation struggles are clearly not a part of Barry's historical mapping of nationalism. Barry understands nationalism

> to be the idea that every nation should have a state and every state should be the institutional embodiment of a nation. Stating it in this way makes it clear that nationalism is in a sense parasitic upon statism, in that it presupposes a world that is a society of states (ibid.).

While Barry does make an exception for struggles for anti-colonial self-determination, he is categorical that this is a one-time exception as nationalism cannot be the basis of the creation of a globally relevant idea of justice (ibid.). In contrast, for postcolonial states, nationalism as a process resonates with ideas of justice and equality, challenging the tyrannies of modernity, that is, imperialism and racism. For anti-colonial movements, the vision is not merely of overthrowing a foreign power and replacing it with the national elite, but of creating a social, national and global order that is based on the ideas of justice and equality. Echoing the underlying universal applicability of the anti-colonial movement, Jawaharlal Nehru, in his historic speech on the eve of Indian independence, exhorted, 'Peace has been said to be indivisible; so is freedom, so is prosperity now, and so also is disaster in this one world that can no longer be split into isolated fragments' (Nehru 1947). This is a powerful statement of a global world in which the responsibility and rights stand on an equal moral footing for all. Similarly, Patrice Lumumba in his vision for an independent Congo linked the independence of his nation not as a mere triumph of the Congolese people, but as a milestone for the liberation of the entire African continent from imperialism (Lumumba 1961). Here the 'universal' imaginaries of the postcolonial future are part of the self-aware and conscious nationalist assertion and they strengthen rather than fragment the notions of a just global world. Similarly, Gandhi's *swaraj* is not restricted to throwing out the British and replacing them with a national elite, but rather about addressing the deep-rooted ills that hamper the creation of a self-aware political community. Or, in other words, it is not merely a call for liberating the colonized subject from imperialism, but to create sovereign cultural, social and political spheres of identity. Gandhi stipulates:

> My patriotism does not teach me that I am to allow people to be crushed under the heel of Indian princes if only the English retire. If I have the power, I should resist the tyranny of Indian princes just as much as that of the English. By patriotism I mean the welfare of the whole people, and if I could secure it at the hands of the English, I should bow down my head to them. If any Englishman dedicated his life to securing the freedom of India, resisting tyranny and serving the land, I should welcome that Englishman as an Indian (Parel 2011: 74).

For Gandhi, in this recovery of the self, along with a societal critique of caste inequalities, the construction of colonial difference was a crucial critique of modernity that underlay political and cultural hierarchies of imperialism. At the same time, there is a strong sense of solidarity on the basis of mutuality of respect. This is contrary to the cosmopolitan assumption of nationalism as a 'bounded' process of statist self-promotion.

The assumption that nationalism is dominantly a statist discourse does not factor its socially transformative role in anti-colonial nationalism. Anti-colonial struggles were not limited to political self-rule, but were the context for profound social transformations within many postcolonial states. For example, the anti-imperialist struggles in both India and China unfolded side by side with programmes for social equality, like the movements against caste-based discrimination and gender equality respectively. Social reform was the context in which nationalism flourished and reached fruition, to the extent that it is not possible to separate the role of social reformers such as Gandhi from his role as a nationalist (Nigam 2009). As Nigam argues, Gandhi's nationalism combined 'dealing with the modern predicament and simultaneously reforming Hinduism and liberating India from colonialism' (ibid.: 42). Nigam insists that Gandhi's programme for social reform did not and in fact could not depend merely on the 'modern' colonial state, or even the postcolonial state to impart its modernity to the colonial subject. Instead this process was essentially grounded away from the state and in the community, challenging the hierarchies of power prevalent both in the colonial and postcolonial states.

Finally, is nationalism an irrelevant discourse once the sovereign equality of nation states is established as argued by Barry? The anti-colonial nationalist project was about the recovery of the self not merely from colonial subjugation but from historical, cultural and social inequalities that plagued colonized nations. As this project became beholden to the postcolonial nation's attempts to 'catch up' with the West, the global hierarchies of power began to be replicated within nation states. Rudolf Heredia argues:

> Thus, our post-colonial world can only be described as a neo-colonial one, internationally divided into developed and developing nations, as also intra-nationally between privileged and underprivileged citizens. Moreover, these divisions are mutually reinforced, not just economically and politically but culturally and socially as well (Heredia 1999: 1498).

Or as Mohanty observes of postcolonial states, that 'while the elite discourse is increasingly fitted into the global perspective on modernization, the social struggle at the grass root level carries on the freedom discourse' (Mohanty 1991: 29). This discourse, he argues, continues to be grounded in nationalist liberation struggles. Dipesh Chakrabarty notes that the postcolonial states slipped into a 'pedagogical style of politics' which re-enacted 'civilizational or cultural hierarchies; between nations, between classes, or between the leaders and the masses' (Chakrabarty 2005: 4812). This is where one may locate the present predicament of the subaltern self for whom the promise of the national liberation movement in terms of equality and justice is yet unachieved.

Conclusion

This chapter argues that anti-colonial nationalism was not framed within a binary or hierarchical understanding of nation versus humanity. The freedom discourse of anti-colonial nationalism was not tied only to the creation of sovereign nation states, creating exclusionary categories of citizenship, but rather it aspired to universal solidarities based on racial, moral and political parity. This does not find place in the current cosmopolitan engagement with nationalism which treats nationalism dominantly as a statist discourse as it unfolded in Europe. Postcolonial societies value the concept of national identity, as it is the embodiment of their struggle against oppression and the context in which they created their aspirational political communities. Nationalism is therefore not a moral-political negative to be transcended, but rather the context within which ideas of global justice maybe most fruitfully negotiated.

The project of anti-colonial nationalism, of aspiring towards a world free of racial, political and economic inequality, is fundamentally relevant today. This project is common between anti-colonial nationalism and cosmopolitanism. While not denying the relevance of the liberal trajectory, I conclude that nationalism understood as a liberating discourse of human equality and not that of statism is the most relevant path towards achieving that goal for postcolonial societies. Denial of nationalism as a concept in the cosmopolitan political and moral space reflects the teleological assumptions inherent in the cosmopolitan project. The universalist foundations of modernity continue to suggest the need to transcend nationalism and also dominate the framework for the transcendence to the post-national moment. To suggest that this transcendence is applicable or should be applicable to other parts of the world is at best exclusionary and at worst coercive.

❧

References

Appadurai, Arjun. 1993. 'Patriotism and Its Futures', *Public Culture* 5(3): 411–29.

Barry, Brian. 1996. 'Nationalism, Intervention and Redistribution', *InIIS-Arbeitspapier Nr. 3/96, Institut für Interkulturelle und Internationale Studien*, Universität Bremen, http://www.iniis.uni-bremen.de/pages/arbeitspapierBeschreibung.php?ID=3&SPRACHE=DE.

———. 2010. 'International Society from a Cosmopolitan Perspective', in Garrett W. Brown and David Held (eds), *The Cosmopolitanism Reader*, Polity Press, Cambridge, 100–114.

Brock, Gillian. 2002. 'Liberal Nationalism versus Cosmopolitanism: Locating the Disputes', *Public Affairs Quarterly* 16(4): 307–27.

———. 2009. *Global Justice: A Cosmopolitan Account*, Oxford University Press, New York.

Chandra, Bipan. 2004. 'Gandhiji, Secularism and Communalism', *Social Scientist* 32(1/2): 3–29.

Chakrabarty, Dipesh. 2005. 'Legacies of Bandung: Decolonisation and the Politics of Culture', *Economic and Political Weekly* 40(46): 4812–18.

Chatterjee, Partha. 1992. *The Nation and Its Fragments*, Oxford University Press, New Delhi.

———. 1998. 'Beyond the Nation? Or within?' *Social Text*, 56: 57–69.

de Roover, Jakob. 2002. 'The Vacuity of Secularism: On the Indian Debate and Its Western Origins', *Economic and Political Weekly* 37(39): 4047–53.

Dutt, Rajani Palme Dutt. 1930. *India Today*, People's Publishing House, New Delhi.

Erikson, Erik H. 1969. *Gandhi's Truth: On the Origins of Militant Non-Violence*, Norton, New York.

Ghosh, Suniti Kumar. 2007. *India and the Raj 1919–1947*, Sahitya Samsad, Kolkata.

Guha, Ranajit. 1998. *Dominance without Hegemony: History and Power in Colonial India*, Harvard University Press, Cambridge, MA.

Gupta, Dipankar. 2002. 'Limits of Tolerance: Prospects of Secularism in India after Gujarat', *Economic and Political Weekly* 37(46): 4615–20.

Habib, Irfan.1995. 'Gandhi and the National Movement', *Social Scientist* 23(4/6): 3–15.

Heredia, Rudolf. 1999. 'Interpreting Gandhi's Hind Swaraj', *Economic and Political Weekly* 34(24): 1497–1502.

Kesavan, Mukul. 2003. 'India's Embattled Secularism', *The Wilson Quarterly* 27(1): 61–67.

Kok-Chor Tan. 2002. 'Liberal Nationalism and Cosmopolitan Justice', *Ethical Theory and Moral Practice* 5(4): 431–61.

Kymlicka, Will. 2010. 'Citizenship in the Era of Globalization', in Garrett W. Brown and David Held (eds), *The Cosmopolitanism Reader*, Polity Press, Cambridge, 435–43.

Lal, Vinay. 2008. 'The Gandhi Everyone Loves to Hate', *Economic and Political Weekly* 43(40): 55–64.

Lumumba, Patrice. 1961. *The Truth about a Monstrous Crime of the Colonialists*, Moscow, Foreign Languages Publishing House.

Mignolo, Walter. 2000. 'The Many Faces of Cosmo-polis: Border Thinking and Critical Cosmopolitanism', *Public Culture* 12(3): 721–48.

———. 2011. *The Darker Side of Western Modernity: Global Futures, Decolonial Options*, Duke University Press, Durham and London.

Miller, David. 2010. 'Cosmopolitanism', in Garrett W. Brown and David Held (eds), *The Cosmopolitanism Reader*, Polity Press, Cambridge, 377–92.

Mohanty, Manoranjan. 1991. 'Swaraj and Jiefang: Freedom Discourse in India and China', *Social Scientist* 19(10/11): 27–34.

Nandy, Ashis. 1988. 'Politics of Secularism and the Recovery of Religious Tolerance', *Alternatives* 13: 177–94.

———. 1995. 'An Anti-secularist Manifesto', *India International Centre Quarterly* 22(1): 35–64.

Nehru, Jawaharlal. 1947. 'Tryst with Destiny', Speech to the Indian Constituent Assembly, 14–15 August, http://www.svc.ac.in/files/TRYST%20WITH%20DESTINY.pdf (accessed 10 May 2013).

Nigam, Aditya. 2009. 'Gandhi — The "Angel of History": Reading Hind Swaraj', *Economic and Political Weekly* 44(11): 41–47.

Nussbaum, Martha. 2008. 'Towards a Globally Sensitive Patriotism', *Daedalus*, 78–93.

———. 2010. 'Patriotism and Cosmopolitanism', in Garrett W. Brown and David Held (eds), *The Cosmopolitanism Reader*, Polity Press, Cambridge, 155–64.

Parel, Anthony J. (ed.). 2011. *Gandhi: Hind Swaraj and Other Writings*, Cambridge University Press, New York.

Rajan, Nalini. 2003. 'Secularism: Revisited', *Economic and Political Weekly* 38(3): 246–48.

Rao, Rahul. 2013. 'Postcolonial Cosmopolitanism: Making Place for the National', in Jyotirmaya Tripathi and Sudarsan Padmanabhan (eds), *The Democratic Predicament: Cultural Diversity in Europe and India*, Routledge, New Delhi, 165–90.

Samaddar, Ranabir. 2012. *The Nation Form: Essays on Indian Nationalism*, Sage Publications, New Delhi.

Sheth, D. L. 2009. 'Political Communalisation of Religions and the Crisis of Secularism', *Economic and Political Weekly* 44(39): 71–79.

Tagore, Rabindranath. 2004 [1916]. *The Home and the World*, Penguin, New Delhi.

Tamir, Yael. 1995. *Liberal Nationalism*, Princeton University Press, Princeton.

Epilogue
Imagining India: The Interplay of the Cosmopolitan and the Vernacular

Sudarsan Padmanabhan

Existing scholarship in cosmopolitanism studies is largely Euro-centric or based on Western social, cultural, political, and economic paradigms.[1] Thinkers such as Walter Mignolo, Eduardo Mendietta, Bryan Turner, Sheldon Pollock, Kwasi Wiredu, Kwame Anthony Appiah, Arjun Appadurai, and Dipesh Chakraborty, to name a few, have problematized the grand narrative of cosmopolitanism in the Western tradition.

The Western grand narrative on cosmopolitanism involves the Stoics, Skeptics, Christians, Medieval religious thinkers, and, most importantly, the Modern thinkers. The cosmopolitanism narrative grows in grandeur only after Kant and modernity. Though Kant was not indulging in speculative metaphysics while proposing his idea of cosmopolitan institutions, subsequent understanding does not engage with the substantive aspect of Kant's cosmopolitanism, while in Kant it is directly linked to the categorical imperative. Kant's cosmopolitanism does lend itself to the idea of the League of Nations and other international institutions and regimes (Kleingeld 1998: 72–90). But the *polis* in cosmopolitanism is only a vacuous append-age unlike the Greek version practised by Hippias or Diogenes. It is also debatable whether the cosmopolitan exhortation of Diogenes or Hippias was merely a rhetorical flourish or a true sentiment encompassing the human race as whole (Plato 1892).

In response to excessive rationalization and formalization of the idea of cosmopolitanism during Modernity, in the later part of the 20th century, several subaltern movements mounted a strong challenge. From this challenge arises the question of whether cosmopolitanism can engage substantively with diversity, oppressed

---

[1] 'Cosmopolitanism', *Stanford Encyclopedia of Philosophy*, http://plato. stanford.edu/entries/cosmopolitanism/ (accessed 27 May 2014).

communities, and marginalized groups. Furthermore, can cosmopolitanism confront existential challenges or is it pure scaffolding that does not form a part of the actual building? Or, in other words, what is the substantive aspect of contemporary cosmopolitanism? Is cosmopolitanism the Holy Grail so much so that its structure or form has attained the status of Plato's Forms or Idea and all other ideas or experiences can only partake in the enterprise of cosmopolitanism? Is the grand narrative of cosmopolitanism complete and the particular experiences are possible only as petit narratives? Let us now consider the postcolonial challenge to cosmopolitanism. Some of the critique is immanent and some other attempts are at returning the gaze. The former exposes the lacuna in the methodological and normative–theoretical framework of cosmopolitanism, while the latter is a more substantive critique that points out what it glosses over. In all contemporary critique, cosmopolitanism has seldom been historicized in non-Western societies. The attendant emphasis on what Etienne Balibar calls the 'eternal kernel of rationalization' seems to create a formal scaffolding of cosmopolitanism (Balibar 2012: 291–301). As a result, the normative aspect of cosmopolitanism is divorced from its political, social and cultural moorings. This is due to the neglect of the study of histories of various non-Western cultures even by postcolonial movements since they are wedded to the 'eternal kernel of rationalization'. There is a need for what Kwasi Wiredu calls conceptual decolonization (Wiredu 1998: 17–46).

Here I attempt two things: first, to utilize the structure of the Western narrative of cosmopolitanism and trace various cosmopolitan tendencies in Indian culture, religions, politics, and society; and, second, I have tried to historicize cosmopolitanism, not in the form of a postcolonial critique or pluralizing cosmopolitanism, but as a project of examining how cosmopolitanism fares when confronted by a subcontinent with mind-boggling diversity of cultures, languages, religions, and an all-pervasive caste system. Has there been a cosmopolitan enterprise in India, independent of the West, with the traditional features of cosmopolitanism, such as universalism and secularism, as a dialogical and hermeneutical engagement with various religions and cultures (Delanty 2012: 4–5)? If yes, what are the contours of such an engagement? The answer is yes and cosmopolitanism in India has not been an imperious — solitary process but a dialectical — dialogical contestation with vernacular

cultures. In due course, the centrality of the contestation and negotiation between the cosmopolitan and the vernacular in Indian
culture and society will emerge. I will eschew the standard char-
acterizations of religious, moral, economic, liberal, and political
cosmopolitanism while I have broadly, for the purpose of comparison, framed my questions around conceptions of equality, justice,
fairness, and tolerance to cultural diversity during various epochs
of Indian history.

In precolonial and postcolonial India, the cosmopolitan–vernacular
contestations in various fields shaped social, political, economic,
and cultural debates. The central argument of this epilogue is that
the cosmopolitan versus vernacular debates have permeated the
Indian sociopolitical and cultural imagination from the beginning.
Furthermore, this conclusion to this volume views Indian society,
culture, economy, religion, and politics against the backdrop of the
politics of language. It also shows how the politics of language has
influenced all other institutions, especially the conception of justice and fairness. Hence, any understanding of the Indian cultural
fabric and the contemporary Indian sociopolitical imaginary requires
an understanding of the cosmopolitan–vernacular debates. In the
first part, this epilogue chronologically describes the cosmopolitan–
vernacular debates, from ancient to contemporary India along the
historical axes, that is, through various epochs. In the second part,
it argues that during the late medieval, modern and contemporary
period the cosmopolitan–vernacular debates assume significance
due to the complete transformation of the peculiarly hierarchical
and startlingly diverse Indian society and polity. Such a transformation of the Indian society and polity was predicated on an understanding of justice (*neeti*) and fairness (*nyaya*), which was also the
fundamental theme that permeated the cosmopolitan–vernacular
contestations.

I will discuss the relationship between the cosmopolitan and the
vernacular in pre- and post-independence India along three trajectories; first, the historical evolution of the cosmopolitan and vernacular cultural traditions in India, a period of broader engagement;
second, the empowerment of vernacular linguistic and cultural traditions and assertion of vernacular identities in post-independence
India, specifically with reference to Tamil Nadu, that was emblem-
atic of vernacular linguistic identity politics (I will substantiate how
the cosmopolitan versus vernacular debate morphs into a battle for

grand narratives during the very process of vernacularization); third, the implications of the cosmopolitan versus vernacular debate for questions of social justice, especially *neeti–nyaya*. This segment will include the challenges faced by Islamic jurisprudence in India, the alternative vision of B. R. Ambedkar *contra* Gandhi along the fault lines engendered by the cosmopolitan versus vernacular debates, and a critique of Amartya Sen's analysis of the *neeti–nyaya* debate in Indian history.

I would argue that without understanding this battle any study of the postcolonial transformation of India could only be ahistorical since all social, political, legal, economic, and cultural institutions have been shaped by the cosmopolitan–vernacular contestation. The entire reorganization of the states of India is based on this contestation, which saved India, the nation-state, from being splintered into different nations and continues to animate current social, political, economic, and cultural debates.

Cosmopolitan and Vernacular Traditions in India: A Historical Perspective

This section begins with the history of the politics of language and literature and the cosmopolitan aspirations of the vernacular traditions. The generative process of dialectical and dialogical interaction between classical Sanskrit and a strong vernacular Indian tradition is discussed in detail. Sheldon Pollock, who has written extensively on the politics of linguistic expansion, argues that the Sanskrit cosmopolis was very distinct from the Latin imperium. Sanskrit, to paraphrase Pollock, was the language of the Gods, while the vernacular languages, which also have a hoary and ancient history like Tamil, Kannada, Telugu, or Marathi, supposedly catered to the world of men. The dialectical process would completely reverse the power equation between the cosmopolitan and the vernacular, which would be reprised over a period of many millennia. As in Rome, the cosmopolitan role reversal between the political and religious spheres could also be observed in the Indian subcontinent.

The cosmopolitan aspect of Sanskrit language and culture during the latter part of the first and second millennium after Christ was known widely all across Asia. Sanskrit was the preferred vehicle of literature, science, law, mathematics, statecraft, religion, and philosophy in the Indian subcontinent during this period. Epics such as the Ramayana and the Mahabharata gained popularity in South and South East Asia. As philosophical and religious schools, Buddhism and Jainism were equally well known (Upadhye 1975: 100–110). Literary productions inspired by Jainism and Buddhism rivalled Sanskrit literature. They played pivotal roles in the expansion of vernacular cultural traditions in the Indian subcontinent and beyond (Pollock 2009: 468–78).

While cosmopolitan Sanskrit created an imaginary of essential Indian culture and literature, at the *vyavaharika satta* (level of everyday reality), it excluded the powerless whose voices were never heard (Pollock 2009: 2–5). But the vernacular languages, which gave a voice to the non-formal or non-textual cultures, increasingly began to envision themselves as classical languages supplementing Sanskrit in the *vyavaharika* realm. This phenomenon was not limited to the process of vernacularization during the late first and early second millennium after Christ when Tamil, Pali, Prakrit, Ardhamagadhi, and several other languages began to replace Sanskrit (ibid.: 44–55). The Tamil country produced both secular and religious literature of very high aesthetic order. Some examples of exquisite poetic-religious literature would be the *Panniru Tirumurai* of the Nayanmars, the Saivites, and the *Nalayira Divya Prabandham* of the Alwars, who were devotees of Vishnu (Champakalakshmi 2005: 47–80). During the 7th century, India was ruled by three very powerful kings — Harshavardhana in the north, Pulakesin-II in the central region and the two greatest Pallava kings, Mahendravarman and his son Narasimhavarman II, in the south. Harshavardhana was a Mahayana Buddhist and a great patron of the arts and literature. The Jains dominated central and eastern India (Basham 1999). Saivism, Vaishnavism, Jainism, and Buddhism were all vying for superiority in south India. But under the Pallavas all four religions flourished. However, with the poetry of the incandescent beauty of the Alwars and Nayanmars appealing to people from all segments of society, the vernacularization had triumphed the cosmopolitan Sanskrit (Lorenzen 2005: 16). However, the influence of Sanskrit *kavya*s on vernacular literary genres is unmistakable. In the Vaishnavite literature, Nammalwar, one of the most important of the Alwars, was hailed as the one who recreated the Vedas in Tamil. But the recreation could be interpreted in two different ways. One, Nammalwar as the translator of the essence of the Vedas into Tamil language, and, the second, the Tamil treatise of *Tiruvaimozhi* which forms a part of the corpus of 4,000 verses called the *Nalayira Divya Prabandham* construed as equivalent to the Vedas (Champakalakshmi 2005: 56, 62). In the Vaishnavite literature, there is a very clear tension between the Northern and Southern sects regarding the status of Tamil and Sanskrit scriptural texts (Stein 2005).

In the 11th century, Ramanuja, who never wrote in Tamil, played a significant part in enshrining the Tamil *Marai* (Veda), which refers to the *Nalayira Divya Prabandham*, on the same pedestal as the Vedas as official scriptural texts in the *Vaishnava parampara* (Stein 2005: 94). Hence, the Vaishnavites were also known as *Ubaya-vedantin*s. Traditional scholars as a rule were required to learn a few other languages along with Sanskrit. Sheldon Pollock argues that Sanskrit was a formal language, initially the mode of religious and ritualistic practices (*vaidika*), then the language of official transactions (*rajabhasha*), and later the language of poets and scholars (*kavya*) (Pollock 2009: 48–52). Hence, Sanskrit as a formal language was also the preferred mode of communication between social, political and economic elites across cultures. Pollock contends that the history of Sanskrit is not only about its glorious literary and cultural past, but also one of domination in the form of Brahmanism. But equally powerful heterodox schools, such as Buddhism and Jainism, while initially refusing to appropriate the scholarly vocabulary of Sanskrit later accepted Sanskrit as a vehicle of scholarly output (ibid.: 55). The Buddhists developed the Pali canon while the Jains wrote most of their important works in Ardhamagadhi. So, the dominance of Sanskrit did not go unchallenged in ancient India as the only language of scholars and philosophers (ibid.: 55–57). Pollock argues that the exclusivity of Sanskrit as a formal language gave ample space for the unhindered development of the vernacular languages in ancient India (ibid.: 104–33). Vernacular language as the repository of cultural discourse also engendered new social, religious and cultural movements in India witnessed during the Bhakti and the Sufi movements in medieval India (Barthwal 2005: 259–64). These movements, interestingly, were humanistic and cosmopolitan in their social and cultural outlook.

*The Bhakti Movement in Medieval India: A Vernacular Response
and its Contemporary Relevance*

The power relationship between Sanskrit and the vernacular languages in terms of access to dominant sources of knowledge or
values was not always equal. For example, women and the lower
classes always had a subordinate role in the Sanskrit cosmopolis,
especially as it venerated the *paramarthika satta* (transcendent
realm). The vernacular dealt with the *vyavaharika satta* of multiple
and dependent realities and became more powerful than the language of the Gods (Pollock 2009: 21–29). The literization and
vernacularization are nowhere more pronounced than in the
Vaishnavite religious and philosophical literature, especially after
Ramanuja. Sanskrit and Tamil became equally important vehicles
for the greatest of *Vaishnava* commentators such as Parasara Bhatta,
Vedanta Desika, Periya Vacchan Pillai, and Pillai Lokacharya.
The Vedantic (philosophical), *sastra* (scientific–formal) and *kavya*
(poetic–aesthetic) genres found expressions in verses of incandescent
beauty. In a manner akin to Ramanuja's philosophy of identity-
in-difference, a concomitant relationship between the formal and
the substantive was established between philosophy and religion,
which permeated the *vyavaharika satta*. Ramanuja was earnestly
concerned about caste discrimination and other forms of social
ills during the 11th and 12th centuries. Ramanuja attempted to
resolve the inequity between the Sanskrit cosmopolis and the Tamil
vernacular, which could be justified on the basis of his philosophy *cit acit visishtam Brahman* (The Ultimate Reality is qualified
by the Conscious and the Unconscious). Ramanuja philosophically questioned the hierarchical complementarity prevalent in the
Indian society and clearly advocated cosmopolitan ideas of social
equality complimented by sensitivity to the aspirations of the vernacular. Ramanuja's attempts to supply a substantive shape to his
cosmopolitan ideas by translating his philosophy into social practice were vehemently opposed and considered politically rebellious
(Tapasyananda 1990).

Several centuries later, Bal Gangadhar Tilak, the great Indian freedom fighter, would write his commentary on the Bhagavad Gita,
known as the *Gitarahasya*, during his incarceration by the British.
Tilak ingeniously utilized the connection established by Ramanuja
between the cosmopolitan and the vernacular. One of the main
conceptual issues that he grappled with was how to reconcile

the concept of *saranagati* or self-surrender so pronounced in the *Vaishnava* tradition in the form of *prapatti* and *niskama karma* (non-attached action) of the Bhagavad Gita to create a moral imperative for the freedom struggle (Goyandhka 2000). Prapatti was total self-surrender and did not have any secular relevance. But *bhakti* was communal, devotional, non-hierarchical, and self-less (Jordens 1975: 266–80). So, Tilak appropriated the concept of *bhakti* from the philosophy of Vaishnavism for its emotive appeal and engagement with the people. The concept of *moksha* or liberation, which was the ultimate ideal of the Hindu way of life, could not be directly utilized to justify a secular struggle (Balasubramanian 2000).[2] But unlike the Advaitic philosophy in which each level of reality is sublatable until the ultimate reality is reached, Ramanuja placed great emphasis on everyday life as well. The concept of *swaraj* or self-rule was at once a spiritual and a political quest for Tilak, but even more so for Gandhi (Brown 1984: 429–41; Gandhi 2009a). The Bhagavad Gita's emphasis on *niskama karma* or renunciation in action conjoined with the religious fervour of *bhakti* towards the achievement of welfare of the world at large (*lokasamgraha*) instead of individual liberation (*moksha*) was Tilak's idea of spiritual nationalism against colonial rule. *Lokasamgraha* was Tilak's moral universal (Tilak 1935: 609). Thus, Ramanuja's cosmopolitan socio-religious outlook inspired Tilak to redefine the moral fibre of the Indian freedom struggle (Harvey 1986: 321–31).

Modern Period: India in the Islamic Imaginary

The *kavya* and *sastra* aspects of the classical Sanskrit culture attracted many scholars such as Alberuni, Amir Khusrau and Abul Fazl during the second millennium after Christ. While Alberuni's mathematical contributions are well known, Amir Khusrau and Abul Fazl were very important in constructing an imaginary of

---

[2] In the Introduction, Professor Balasubramanian refers to the Upanishadic emphasis on the *Brahma-Jiva aikya*. Also refer to Śankara's commentary on the Brihadāraṇyaka Upanishad, Trans. Swami Madhavananda, Calcutta: Advaita Ashrama, 1993. In an interesting passage in Chapter I, Virāj is scared of its attachment to the body and realizes the reality of the Self. In Chapter VI, Sage Yājñavalkya explains to King Janaka that the nature of Brahman is inexpressible in positive terms and describes Brahman as *neti neti*.

India, as Hindawi or Hind. The Hindawi or Hindoo or Hind in
the imaginaries of Khusrau and Fazl are not remotely similar to
the contemporary cultural nationalist conception of Hindu India.
Khusrau mentions various languages, cultures and regions of
India. Khusrau vividly described the cultural diversity of India during the medieval period in his writings. But the Mughal Emperor
Akbar and his friend Abul Fazl conceived the most powerful
imaginary of Hind, as a culturally diverse political entity. From this
was born a new syncretized religion, known as *Din-i-Ilahi*, centred
on the ideal of one supreme reality (Mukhia 2010: 10). Athar Ali
terms this the perception of India as a culturally diverse entity, a
nation and a unified polity (Athar Ali 2008: 215–24).

Pollock's classification of the second millennium after Christ
as the vernacular millennium seems to be justified in the context
of medieval and modern India, especially since literary works in
regional languages increased manifold. Athar Ali argues that
Akbar's secular reflections and his political philosophy created a
perception of India as a nation, a culturally diverse sociopolitical
entity, in the 16th century (ibid.: 215–19). Akbar and Abul Fazl
were intellectually and spiritually engaged with the traditional
forms of Hinduism and Islam. But they were also equally conver-
sant with the philosophical basis of popular devotional movements
in Islam and Hinduism, the Sufi and the Bhakti movements, respectively (Khan 2008: 89). Akbar and Abul Fazl identified religious
bigotry and dogma as the main factors dividing people (Dvivedi
2005; Prasad 2008). So they envisioned a universal religion called
Din-i-Ilahi. Harbans Mukhia clearly demonstrates how Akbar and
Abul Fazl meticulously thought about the import of institutions
and practices, which are manifestations of religions, for example,
the *hijri* calendar in Islam. During Akbar's reign a new calendar
was designed. This was a definite instance of secularization and the
assertion of political authority vis-à-vis religious clergy. All religions
were treated equally in Akbar's court (Mukhia 2010).

Over a period of several centuries, the polity in the Indian subcontinent had to negotiate and contest with a plethora of religions,
ethnicities, cultures, and languages. Thus, the classical refrain of
India's unity in diversity is also the arena of understanding the manifestation of cosmopolitanism in its formal and substantive aspects.
There is a clear shift from the rarefied environs of the Sanskrit cosmopolis to the more horizontal, democratic and dialogical domain

of the vernacular. But the re-emergence and institutionalization of cosmopolitan ideas in the political realm would take a few centuries to evolve, in the form of a parliamentary democracy.

Vernacular Tamil and/or Cosmopolitan Sanskrit: Dravidian vs Aryan Archetypes — A Postcolonial Challenge

After India's independence in 1947, the gargantuan task of forming states within the newly constituted national boundaries was fraught with great risks. So the founders of the Indian nation had the arduous task of creating a political system in which the cosmopolitan and the vernacular would be in a dynamic equilibrium. Gandhi was acutely aware of the need to have a cosmopolitan language, a link language, as a catalyst in the formation of a deliberative democracy. This Indian link language would have been Hindi if not for fierce opposition from many vernacular linguistic communities (Gandhi 1918: 267). The claim of Hindi to be a pan-Indian link language, a cosmopolitan claim, resulted in an aggressive assertion of vernacularism in south India, more particularly in Tamil Nadu. Tamil, a Dravidian language, is the only language in India that can rival Sanskrit in its antiquity, felicity of expression, richness of vocabulary, and quality of literary output. Tamil does not belong to the Indo-European family of languages and has a long history of genres of poetry, prose, drama, and grammar. But Karthigesu Sivathamby poses interesting questions about the history of the term 'Dravidian', which had barely existed for a few decades when the Dravidian movement in various forms began to take shape. Sivathamby even labels the Dravidian consciousness a false consciousness (Sivathamby 2006: 18). Tamil Nadu witnessed a particularly virulent anti-Hindi campaign, not limited to Hindi as a language but against the north Indian/Sanskritic cultural domination of which Hindi was the talismanic symbol (Pandian 2008: 82–83). So, English, the colonial language, continued to serve as the official link language in postcolonial India. But the problem did not end there. English language education was seen as an avenue of modernization and development and many underprivileged and deprived communities in India attempted to transcend the iron-cage of casteism and the perpetuating cultural narrative by disowning native social, political and economic systems and traditions as seen with Pundit Ayothee Thoss, Rettamalai Srinivasan, M. C. Raja

and B. R. Ambedkar (Guha 2008: 201–16). Hence, English education and culture was the new cosmopolitan avenue of transcending the tyranny of the local or vernacular. Sivathamby attributes
the disappearance of Tamil nationalism to the socio-economic
path of India's development. Globalization and market economy
have opened up India as a market for the non-Brahmin Tamils.
The economic interest serves as a glue to bind the non-Brahmin
elites (Sivathamby 2006: 50). Thus, economic cosmopolitanism
annulled vernacular politics.

Bernard Bate analyses how the non-Brahmin, elite-led Justice
Party, established in 1917, captured power in Madras Presidency
during the early part of the 20th century, when India was still under
colonial rule (Bate 2009: 3–5). In order to prevent the north Indian/
Brahmin-dominated Congress Party from gaining power in the
Madras Presidency, the Justice Party even supported British rule in
India. E. V. Ramasamy Naickker, also known as Periyar, suggested
that the Tamil-speaking Dravidian region should join Mohammed
Ali Jinnah's Pakistan during the partition of India in 1947 (More
2008: 55). Jinnah did not entertain Periyar's ideas since the entire
enterprise was impractical and implausible. But Periyar was not
always an anti-Congress politician. He was a strong Congress supporter and participated in several social and political protests. During the Vaikkom satyagraha in Kerala, which finally culminated in
temple entry to the lower-caste people and untouchables in 1936,
Periyar was imprisoned twice and he was hailed as 'Vaikkom Hero'
by the Congress Party in Madras Presidency. Increasingly, Periyar
felt that the Congress Party was not sympathetic to the aspirations and sensitivities of culturally diverse population in the south,
which was different from the Indo-European heritage of the Hindi-
speaking population of north India. Thus, the language of Gods
was being felled by the world of men. Moreover, Periyar felt that
the Congress Party was still dominated by the upper-class interests
and was not interested in complete social transformation (Pandian
2008: 189–93). Ramamurthy, Sivathamby and other Left intellectuals severely criticized the leaders of the Justice Party, Dravida
Kazhagam (DK) and the Dravida Munnetra Kazhagam (DMK) as
opportunists. Periyar was an exception according to Sivathamby
since he consistently advocated social reform and was against exploiting the caste fault-lines to capture political office. Annadurai,
the founder of the DMK, was another leader who understood the

social, political, economic, and cultural dynamics of the times (Sivathamby 2006: 54–55).

The Brahmin community in Tamil Nadu, which dominated the bureaucracy during the colonial period, was disproportionately represented in all governmental positions while it constituted less than 3 per cent of the total population of the Madras Presidency (Pandian 2008: 154–55). The Aryan–Dravidian divide was exacerbated by scholars like Mortimer Wheeler who advocated the theory of Aryan invasion and subsequent destruction of an advanced Dravidian civilization, exemplified by the Indus Valley Civilization (Wheeler 1968: 105). The Justice Party was against caste discrimination, exclusion of lower castes from religious places and the abominable practice of untouchability (Pandian 2008: 146–57). The Justice Party was considered to be a party of landlords and merchants who were only interested in displacing the domination of Brahmins. In Tamil Nadu, the legacy of the Justice Party in the form of DK established in 1944 under Periyar continued in many forms such as attacking Brahmins, garlanding idols with slippers and ridiculing religious practices (ibid.: 193–203). Periyar felt that Tamil literature perpetuated the grand narrative of discrimination and retrograde practices. So he advocated the destruction of ancient works of Tamil literature (ibid.: 210–13). The Communist leaders of Tamil Nadu such as Jeevanandam saved many a *kavya* from being consigned to flames (Sivathamby 2006: viii, 32).

In 1949, a group of ambitious members of the DK, riding on the anti-Hindi and anti-Brahmin sentiment, sensed a great moment to launch a political party. Periyar was averse to exploiting the agenda of social justice, crusading against superstition and eradication of caste discrimination and untouchability to gain political power. A strong dissidence was brewing in the DK. A group led by C. N. Annadurai split the DK and formed the DMK on the quest for a separate *Dravida Nadu* or Dravidian nation (More 2008: 56–57). After India's independence in 1947, the first state to be formed on the basis of language was Andhra Pradesh in 1953. But, quickly, the DMK dropped its demand for a separate nation after the India–China war in 1962 as nationalistic fervour was at its peak. As member of the Rajya Sabha in the Indian Parliament, Annadurai championed the demand for a separate state named Tamil Nadu. Following Annadurai's sudden demise in 1969, just two years into his first term as the chief minister of the state of

Tamil Nadu, the tenor of the state politics changed. M. Karunanidhi took over as the chief minister and conjured up a subliminal connection between Hindi, Sanskrit, Brahmins, north India, Brahminism, and the Congress on one side and Tamil culture on the other (Pandian 2008: 195). This would be the template that Karunanidhi would use with telling effect till the ascent of the charismatic actor-politician M. G. Ramachandran (MGR) as the chief minister of Tamil Nadu in 1977. MGR was unceremoniously expelled from the DMK. During MGR's tenure, the virulent anti-religious and anti-Brahminical feeling cultivated by the DK and the DMK was replaced by a more inclusive but populist approach to politics (Sivathamby 2006: 55).

Whenever in political wilderness, the DMK has consistently gone back to its anti-Brahmin, anti-Sanskrit, anti-Hindi, and anti-north rhetoric whenever it had lost power in the state assembly elections (Guha 2008: 117–20). But what is not to be forgotten is the emphasis on vernacular literature, arts and culture, and the Tamil pride that the DMK stood for during its early days. The socialist–communist movements also influenced the DMK. The DMK was a product of the historical times in the 1950s and 1960s and it passionately defended Tamil culture and pride. Later, the ideal transmogrified into an ideology and from a cadre-based party which prided itself on inner-party democracy powered by fierce Tamil pride, the DMK became a party dominated by a single family in the last two decades. Periyar did anticipate the corrupting influence of political power and forewarned his protégés, who ignored his sagely advice (Sivathamby 2006: 54). The DMK increasingly viewed Tamil as reducible to dramatized film and theatre dialogues through which many of its leaders such as C. N. Annadurai and M. Karunanidhi captured the imagination of the film going public (ibid.: 36–37). Thus the grand narrative of Tamil culture has been reduced to a petty narrative by those who wanted to claim classical status for a language that heralded the process of vernacularization in colonial and postcolonial India (ibid.: 56).

In postcolonial societies, the nation-state relationship continues to be tenuous as the connotations and denotations of what is *natio* is negotiated and contested (Pollock 2002: 36). In some formulations, the cosmopolitan–formal structure of Sanskrit language and literature was given an originary status from which the idea of India is to be derived as a nationalist culture. After independence,

Hindi, a more formal-pragmatic language, with a strong formal foundation based on Sanskrit grammar and literature, was expected to be the lingua franca of India. In terms of reconstruction and reclamation of cultures, the aforementioned attempt is both an involution and an evolution. Sheldon Pollock critiques Niklas Luhmann's systems theory in which 'communication dissemination' is correlated with 'social-system differentiation' (Pollock 2009: 498). This approach reduces cultures and languages to what survives from the past. Pollock attributes cultural naturalist approaches to the disappearance of master narratives, the emancipatory telos that characterized the rationale of nation-state theorists. For example, some cultures are considered naturally civilized and qualified to become nation states, whereas others are not so fortunate. This characterization was very successfully utilized by the vernacular cultures in postcolonial India, but by inverting the grand narrative. The Tamil vernacular tradition laid claims to the grand narrative of which only Sanskrit was the sole claimant hitherto. Thus, the cosmopolitanization of the vernacular cultures in the postcolonial era began.

Pollock criticizes the recent trend in India to demand classical status to various vernacular languages (Pollock 2011: 21). Pollock's assertion about the relationship between the vernacular and the cosmopolitan during the Sanskrit cosmopolis becomes relevant since the vernaculars flourished and new forms evolved without hegemonic interference from the state (Pollock 2002: 34–37). The succinct expression of Nehru about Indian culture and unity in diversity also derives its meaning from the synergistic relationship between Sanskrit and the vernacular languages of India (Sudarsan 2012: 471–73). Thus far, the process of the construction of an Indian imaginary through cosmopolitan–vernacular contestations was analysed. The arena of such contestations was always sociopolitical and led to the emergence of several institutions. But the most important and central theme of cosmopolitan–vernacular contestations in a sociopolitical context has been in jurisprudence and law in general, but, more specifically, *neeti* and *nyaya* in the cultural perception of the people. Both *neeti* and *nyaya* are essential in enunciating the concept of social justice, the central focus of contemporary sociopolitical debates. In fact, *neeti*, *nermai* (honesty) and *nyayam* (fairness) was the slogan coined by C. N. Annadurai, the founder of the DMK.

Neeti–Nyaya: Modern and Contemporary Debates

The cosmopolitan–vernacular relationship in India's long history has to be seen in various institutions and practices. Sheldon Pollock's important distinction between the realm of Sanskrit cosmopolis and the vernacular as the *paramarthika* and *vyavaharika*, respectively, could serve as an archetype to interpret the formal and substantive aspects of social, cultural, economic, religious, and judicial institutions and their evolution over a long period. The *neeti–nyaya* debate (justice versus fairness) should also be analysed on the basis of the cosmopolitan–vernacular relationship, especially on the basis of the *paramarthika-vyavaharika* distinction (Pandian 2008: 82). Most of the problems attributed to the *neeti–nyaya* debate are because of the creation of a binary opposition between the ideational and the experiential realms.

Pollock's analysis of the Indian linguistic, historical and cultural traditions clearly illustrates constant challenges to the Sanskrit cosmopolis from many ancient languages and strong vernacular cultures. The *lakshana-lakshya* categorization in the ancient Indian classical literary theory and musicology, cosmopolitan–vernacular socio-linguistic framework, and the *shariat-tareeqat* distinction in Islamic law and jurisprudence in India demonstrate a highly evolved understanding. Even in the Paninian grammar, rules were framed to explain both the formal and pragmatic aspects of the Sanskrit language and not merely to legislate grammatical rules.

Neeti *and* Nyaya *Debates in Islamic Political Experience*

The Muslim community in India also faced the problem of resolving the conceptual opposition between beliefs, customs and manners, and a secular national ideal. The most well known secular Muslim politicians during the 20th century were Mohammed Iqbal and Mohammed Ali Jinnah. Iqbal's famous poem, still sung today in India as a patriotic song, was an imagining of a nation. The Hindostan of Iqbal was in some ways similar to that of Alberuni, Amir Khusrau and Abul Fazl (Athar Ali 2008: 215–24). Iqbal's Hindostan, at first glance, appears to be a modern conception very amenable to the nation-state discourse. But M. S. Jain argues that Iqbal's love of one's residence or place is different from Islamic nationalism that he advocates in his later years. Jain criticizes Nehru and other non-Muslim political leaders of pre-independence

India who persisted on reading Iqbal as a secular Islamic poet-philosopher rather than a staunch advocate of Islam as a universal religion. For Iqbal, *watan*, or nation, could only be meaningful in the Islamic sense with reference to Madina. Wherever Islam travelled, the *millat* and the *watan* were in consonance. Every other territorial nationalism would lead to war and hence Muslims should oppose such *wataniyat*. For Muslims, Iqbal claimed, China, Arabia and the entire world were *watan* (Jain 2005: 203–15). Iqbal's vision of a *millat* and *watan* were exemplified when Kemal Ataturk ascended to power in Turkey.

From the 17th century onwards, a fierce debate about the role of Islam in the Mughal Empire was raging. Mullah Abdul Qadir Badauni, Shaikh Ahmed Sirhindi, Maulvi Abdul Haq Muhaddis, Shah Wali Ullah, and other religious scholars of the 16th and 17th centuries were appalled by Akbar's syncretistic religious ideas such as *Din-i-Ilahi* (syncretic religion) and *sulh kul*, the concept of universal toleration. Badauni was overshadowed by the brilliance of Abul Fazl and Akbar's strong mystical Sufi influence. Akbar also emphasized the role of reason and encouraged debates among religions (Athar Ali 2008: 215–24).

After Akbar's death, Sirhindi attempted to bring the Sufi order under the Islamic fold. By bringing the Sufi strand under the Islamic legal system (*shariat*), the concept of *sulh kul* could be countered easily. This would also alienate the non-Muslim Sufi influence. By merging liberal and heterodox variants of Islam under the *shariat*, Sirhindi formalized Sufi ideas, which placed emphasis on *tareeqat*, not *shariat*, due to its syncretistic appropriation of non-Islamic thought such as the Bhakti movement (Jain 2005: 36–55). While philosophically Sirhindi seems to have succeeded in creating a direct connection between the authority of the Quran and the authenticity of the *shariat* as the final arbiter of law, jurisprudence and religion, Islam in India remained divided between the immigrant Muslim community and the local Muslims, which culminated in the alienation of Muslims speaking local dialects. This tension created problems in education policy, law, economy, political participation, and social status (ibid.: 55–75). Romila Thapar explains the segmented nature of ancient and medieval Indian society, which had been recognized by Indian rulers and systems of thought. The Chinese Buddhist pilgrims, Fa Hsien and Hsüan Tsang, also recognized the distinctions among various philosophical and religious systems. Thapar also refers to the geographical connotation of the term Hindu in Iranian and Arabic sources (2005: 335–48).

During the medieval centuries, especially during Akbar's rule, the association between the state and Islam, the dominant religion, especially Sunni, was severed (Eaton 2005: 105–27). A secular imagined political territory ruled by an equanimous emperor gave a model of a nation that was not merely formal but also substantive (Jain 2005: 28–39). The emperor did appeal to the divine origins of his moral legitimacy but the political authority was the ultimate authority and not the ulema (ibid.: 30). This historic reversal of the power equation between religious and political authorities was a deliberate decision by Akbar, which is clearly noted by Abul Fazl. Abul Fazl refers to Akbar as *Insan-i-Kamil* (the perfect man), which for Sufis did not necessarily refer to Prophet Mohammed as an individual perforce but the divine spirit associated with the Prophet, a spiritually awakened human being capable of understanding the purest nature of the ultimate reality (Khan 2008: 89). Ibn-Arabi, one of the greatest Sufi philosophers, explained the concept of perfect human being in great detail. Akbar was influenced by the similarities between the pantheism of the Sufis and many other saints of the Bhakti movement. Abul Fazl claimed that Akbar remarked frequently that one should follow the path of justice guided by reason (Beveridge 1926: 271). Akbar changed the *hijri* calendar, emphasized *sulh kul* (universal toleration) and *Din-i-Ilahi* (universal religion), encouraged spirituality inspired by the Sufis instead of dogmatic adherence to rituals and religious tenets, emphasized the role of reason, and facilitated intellectual debates in his court. Akbar was also anointed by the *ulema* as the religious authority even higher than the *mujtahid* (a scholar of Islamic jurisprudence) (ibid.: 269–74).

After Akbar, Jehangir abandoned the project of universal religion, which has been described as a vague ideal by many scholars. It was only meant for the intellectuals and enlightened scholars. While politically the *ulema* were still under the mercy of the emperor, Jehangir was more favourably inclined towards the *ulema* than Akbar. Aurangazeb, who was the last powerful Mughal emperor, was a staunch follower of orthodox Islam. After his rule, the Mughal Empire started to crumble. Many of the non-Islamic rulers began to reclaim their territories. The *ulema* did not have

the support of a strong political power to Islamize the newly con-
verted population. They sought the support of rulers from outside
India, like Nadir Shah and Ahmad Shah Abdali, to prevent the
dismemberment of the Mughal Empire (Jain 2005: 57). Many
Islamic scholars considered the sphere of politics as a distraction
and advocated an inward turn, especially the Deoband School. The
Deoband School produced Islamic scholars of repute but did not
participate either in the creation of the political *millat*, which would
form the basis of the post-independence Pakistan or engage in the
watan or nation-state discourse (ibid.: viii–xi). Thus, the Islamic
jurisprudence in India could not reach its logical conclusion.

Cosmopolitan and Vernacular: The Alternative Vision

This section deals with the tension between different cosmopolitan visions. The alternative vision proposed by Pundit Ayothee
Thoss, Rettamalai Srinivasan and B. R. Ambedkar also questions
the validity and the primacy of the nation-state vis-à-vis social
equality. In this context, it widens the debate about democracy
and equality beyond the confines of the nation-state boundaries,
thus founding the concept of *neeti* or justice on human dignity and
individual rights. In the late 19th and early 20th centuries, the
deprived classes began asserting their rights. Especially in southern India, Ayothidas Pandithar (Pundit C. Ayothee Thoss) in the
1870s and later Rettamalai Srinivasan were pioneers who led
the struggle for equality and social democracy within the fold of
the Hindu society. Ayothidas Pundit initiated the Buddhist conversion movement among the Dalits of Tamil Nadu. Ayothidas argued
that the original religion of the Adi-Dravidas was Buddhism and the
invading Aryans imposed Hinduism on the native population. The
movement for equality and abolition of untouchability practiced
by the caste Hindus against the deprived classes has not been given
importance that it deserves in comparison to the more elitist non-
Brahmin Justice Party (Pandian 2008: 103–20). Both Pundit and
Srinivasan cooperated with Dr B. R. Ambedkar in questioning the
fairness of the nationalistic agenda of the Indian National Congress
(INC) without resolving the social conflict arising out of the injustice perpetrated upon the deprived classes. Ambedkar participated
in all the three Round Table Conferences convened by the British
government. Rettamalai Srinivasan and Ambedkar put forth a very

strong case for the rights of the deprived classes (Jaffrelot 2005: 56–59). Another powerful Dalit leader from Tamil Nadu, M. C. Raja, was also very active in promoting the cause of the deprived communities (ibid.: 70).

B. R. Ambedkar advocated a procedural approach to eradicate social discrimination and injustice. Ambedkar was able to incorporate many legal provisions against untouchability, caste and gender discrimination and other inhumane practices while simultaneously introducing legislations empowering the deprived classes, as the leader of the Indian Constitution Drafting Committee. Ambedkar's recommendations were based on an analysis of constitutions of liberal democracies and their justice system (Ambedkar 1933).[3] He was also influenced by the *sramana* opposition to caste hierarchy and religious rituals, especially that of Buddhism. Buddha belonged to the Sakya clan. Both Licchavi and Sakya clans were part of ancient confederacies, *gana sangha*s, groups of various sanghas or social groups. The *gana sangha*s were ancient Indian republics with horizontal social structure, participatory and dialogical political organization (Thapar 2002: 149). Ambedkar's emphasis on social democracy, first and foremost as the substantive aspect of any liberal democracy, was based on the model of *gana sangha*s. Ambedkar's conversion to Buddhism was an assiduously calculated move. Philosophically, Buddhism was the most logically sound, non-metaphysical and ethics-centred system. Buddhism was an immanent and not a transcendental critique of Hinduism (Jaffrelot 2005: 41). Socially, Buddhism was all-inclusive and welcomed followers from any caste, creed, gender, and social status. Politically, the Buddha belonged to the Sakya clan, which was part of the *gana sangha*s. All his life, Buddha strove to facilitate consensus among warring republics. The Buddha preached detachment from any claims about absolute entities or eternal truths. Most of the ills, according to the Buddha, were due to ignorance. Desire stems from the ignorance of the ephemeral nature of what one desires. Once *avidya* or ignorance as the reason for one's suffering

---

[3] 'Evidence before Joint Committee on Indian Constitutional Reform', http://www.ambedkar.org/ambcd/16A.%20Evidence%20Taken%20 Before%20The%20Joint%20Committee%20PART%20I.htm (accessed 27 May 2014).

is realized, as explained by Buddha's four noble truths, the eight-fold path leads to liberation or nirvana, which is the cessation of suffering (Sangharakshita 1975: 87). The absence of an absolute centre, such as the concept of a soul (*anatta*), and the concept of emptiness or *sunyata*, the absence of an ultimate essence, paves the way for the middle path that eschews extremes of nihilism and essentialism. Buddhism also emphasizes the direct relationship between knowledge and ethics. The dharmic life begins with the knowledge of the basis of human suffering.

Ambedkar's knowledge of Buddhism as a republican social, political and religious movement provided him with a strong phil-osophical framework to launch an incisive critique of various dis-criminatory practices prevalent in Hindu society (Jaffrelot 2005: 131–33). While Ambedkar was not against the political democracy of India which was achieved after a long struggle for independence against British rule, he argued that social justice, which means ensuring equality for all citizens of a nation state, would not be realized unless all sections of the population feel a sense of equal-ity. Political democracy is a formal requirement whereas social democracy is the substantive aspect that ensures fairness.

Neeti *and* Nyaya: *Contemporary Moral and Political Challenges*

While imagining cosmopolitan social, political and legal institu-tions on the bases of liberal democratic and republican ideals was not a serious problem for a nation that had attained independence recently from foreign rule, imagining and institutionalizing the organization of constituent states was going to be very difficult. Initially, the moral legitimacy of the INC and the charisma of its leaders like Jawaharlal Nehru were able to hold the vernacular interests of the individual states under the moral thrall of progress of the nation (Chandra et al. 2002; Iyengar 2007). But the power of formal institutions that evolved from the Constitution of India did not reverberate with the vernacular constituents. Amartya Sen points out the difference between the formal conception of justice (*neeti*) and the substantive idea of fairness (*nyaya*). But Sen seems to consider *neeti* as a purely formal and ideational construct and *nyaya* as the justice in practice (Sen 2009: 20). Sen's critique of Rawlsian theory of justice, conceived in an advanced liberal democracy that emphasizes formal access to justice rather than ensuring capabil-ities, is relevant to a postcolonial society like India (ibid.: 253–59).

In an asymmetrical sociopolitical system like India, there is a lack of consensus about how justice could be ensured in a postcolonial democracy where ideas of government, public sphere, public good, law, justice, society, rights, secularism, subsidiarity, and solidarity are constantly being negotiated and contested.

The concept of formal justice (*neeti*) and fairness (*nyaya*) have been discussed by Amartya Sen in *Idea of Justice* which evaluates various theories of justice in which justice is conceptualized only as an ideal (ibid.: 5–8). Sen argues that in the process of construct-ing purely formal institutions of justice, the objective of a justice system more often than not remains appreciated. A justice system should necessarily redress injustice and facilitate the emergence of a more just and fair society in which public institutions and practices are based on fairness of laws, rules and regulations. Here, fairness means equal opportunities and access to various goods where social, political and legal institutions function as enablers. Amartya Sen's analysis of *neeti* and *nyaya* needs to be understood in two parts. The first part involves an understanding of classical Indian *neeti* works called *Dharmasastra*s, which prescribe various codes of conduct in a fractured polity, with innumerable castes and cultural practices; the second involves the actual impact of the *Dharmasastra*s on statecraft (Thapar 2002: 111). The rajas treated the *Dharmasastra*s as formal frameworks of justice, as guiding principles of jurispru-dence or ethics.[4] There has been a long argumentative tradition of Indian jurisprudence, which has been modified and revised based on

---

[4] Nagaswami, a great archaeologist and epigraphist, who was the doyen of research and documentation of ancient Tamil inscriptions, in a recent article, emphasized the need to rely on documentary evidence citing several *Dharmasastra*s. According to Nagaswami, the *Dharmasastra*s mention four types of evidences in property disputes, namely the written documentary evidence (*lekhya pramana*), property enjoyed over a period of time (*bhukti*), eyewitness accounts (*sakshi*), and divine evidence (*daivikam*). At present, one of the most interesting legal disputes confronting the Supreme Count of India concerns the discovery of huge treasure in the Anantha Padmanabha Swamy Temple at Thiruvananthapuram in Kerala. While astrologers in Kerala have decided to appeal to the *daivikam*, which has been rejected in many legal battles in ancient India. Nagaswami cites many inscriptions and religious chronicles like Sekkizhar's *Periyapuranam* and 8th century Pandya court inscriptions (Nagaswami 2011).

kala (time), *desa* (place) and *varthamana* (contemporary context). This principle has been enunciated in the Tamil Sangam classic *Tirukkural*, beyond any doubt, in which there are several references to formal justice (*neeti*) and fairness (*nyaya*) in which the role of prudence is strongly emphasized (Diaz 2005).

Romila Thapar describes the Indian imaginary as multi-hued, even in the realm of the religious, which defied any unitary or unified understanding (Thapar 2005: 335). This was well understood by rulers in various parts of the Indian subcontinent throughout its history, with a few exceptions. So, the question one faces is whether a conception of *neeti* in the classical sense is an attempt to create a formal framework amidst mind-boggling diversity. While various *Neetisastras* were in vogue, *Itihasas* and the *Puranas* were also used to illustrate ethical dilemma in various existential situations, most importantly, in the Ramayana and the Mahabharata (Basham 1999: 85–87). For example, Yudhisthira, who is also known as the Dharmaputra, makes decisions, which could be termed unjust according to *neeti*. The epics, in India or in the West, constantly illustrate the tension between *neeti* and *nyaya*. Vidura and Bhishma, in the Mahabharata, part ways based on their sense of duty and righteousness, respectively. So, do Kumbhakarna and Vibhishana in the Ramayana. Citing Sen's own position of broad consequentialism, there needs to be a balance between *neeti* and *nyaya*, as in Rawlsian reflective equilibrium (Sen 2009: 22–24).

Sen has a philosophical reason to choose *nyaya* over *neeti* (Sen 2005). The *nyaya* school of Indian thought is also known as the science of reasoning or logic. The argumentative tradition of ancient India was not only religious and soteriological but also this worldly and oriented towards solving problems of people and promoting happiness. To illustrate this point, Sen's collection of essays were published in the form of a book, *The Argumentative Indian*, in which he discusses the contribution of heterodox systems like Buddhism, Jainism and Charvaka philosophies all through India's historical past. India's argumentative tradition promoted critical reasoning as the defining feature of acquisition of knowledge and learning. But Sen's ascription of *Neetisastras* as static and *Nyayasutras* as critical, argumentative and logical does not do justice to the dialogical-argumentative tradition common to most strands of Indian thought. Both the *astika* and the *nastika* traditions utilized the *nyaya* method. All philosophical schools of India mandated training in the *nyaya* tradition (Matilal 1986).[5]

Sen also creates a binary opposition between the contractarian and consequentialist political models. While criticizing the Rawlsian theory of justice, Sen does a balancing act with his broad deontological and broad consequentialism formulation (Sen 1983: 132). Sen accepts most of the fundamental assumptions of John Rawls' theory of justice in an advanced liberal democracy (Sen 2009: 52–69). Sen's emphasis on *nyaya* also stems from important philosophical assumptions, especially in relation to ethics. As less of a broad deontological and more of a broad consequential theorist, Sen has to espouse an ethical framework that does not merely emphasize formal justice but also the consequences of actual behaviour (ibid.: 62–70). But utilitarianism was pejoratively defined as an ethical theory that is only concerned with consequences and not with the means of an action. J. S. Mill (1985) questions Kant's deontological ethics on the ground that ethics is all about consequences, not for action for action sake or duty for duty sake.

During mid-20th century, Rawls' theory of justice gave liberalism and deontology a strong political and moral foundation. While questioning utilitarian ethics and political philosophy, Rawls explicitly argued that a theory of justice should also focus on outcomes and hence cannot be merely deontological in the formal sense of the term. Rawls questioned the fundamental moral assumptions of social, political, legal, and economic institutions in the post-world war America that did not seem to address the rampant socio-economic inequalities (Freeman 2007: 337–38). Most Americans

---

[5] The philosophical differences were due to the variations in metaphysical and epistemological positions of various schools. But at the *vyavaharika* level, explanation of suffering was attributed to ignorance (*avidhya*). The emphasis on dharma was also common to all schools of Indian philosophy. In the realm of metaphysics, the path to liberation from suffering either by appealing to scriptural authority, divine beings and Gods, or one's own conduct separates the orthodox and the heterodox schools. The Bhagavad Gita beautifully expounds the tension between *neeti* and *nyaya*. The social status of various actors, their moral character, tragic events that defy rational justification, moral dilemma and the classic Socratic question about the status of justice illustrate some of the difficult moral issues pertaining to the *neeti–nyaya* debate.

construed morality in relation to religion and community. Therefore, a popular conception of morality was a hindrance in redress-
ing historical injustices such as racism, oppression of women and
ethnic strife. As a result, Rawls separated the moral assumptions
that emanated from the religious-communal realm from those that
arise from public reason and public sphere (ibid.: 31). Rawls was
influenced by Abraham Lincoln's position that moral outrage cannot be the basis of justice. Clearly, Lincoln's opposition to slavery
was solely situated on the American constitution, that is, based
on *neeti* or justice.[6] Thus, it could be strongly demonstrated that
neeti cannot be divorced from *nyaya* and vice versa. Sen's approach
seems to create a false dichotomy between the *neeti* and *nyaya* distinction unless the categorizations are purely formal-ideal and not
pragmatic-dialogical. Sen also contrasts Tagore and Gandhi whose
views differed on several aspects such as nationalism, tradition, culture, politics, secularism, diversity, and morality (Raghavan Iyer
1990). Gandhi exemplifies deontology, while Tagore represents
the quintessential cosmopolitan liberal, not tethered to doctrinaire
deontology, probably whom Sen would consider a Millian liberal
(Erikson 1969; Aravamudan 2007). Tagore's fascination was with
reasoned freedom and the fearless pursuit of knowledge (Sen 2005:
89–109).

The present day Indian judicial system uses *neeti* and *nyaya*, not
entirely in the classical sense, but in a much more modern sense
to include secularism, tolerance, equality, equity, and also social,
political, economic, and cultural rights enshrined in the Indian
constitution. In some states, courts, interestingly, are known as
Neeti-manram and in some others, *Nyayalaya*. Sen's emphasis on
evaluator relativity and consequential evaluation is also included

---

[6] The Lincoln–Douglas debates are centred on the issue of slavery.
Lincoln attacks Stephen Douglas in Kansas for not taking a stand on the constitutional issue of slavery and defends himself in Freeboro on the question
of the powers of the federal government vis-à-vis the state legislature.
I have used the works of Abraham Lincoln from the digitization project
of the Northern Illinois University, Dekalb, Illinois. Lincoln's earliest
speech to the young men at Lyceum, Illinois, is replete with pleas for
strengthening institutions that would bolster the Constitution of America.
See 'The Lincoln/Douglas Debates of 1858', http://lincoln.lib.niu.edu/
lincolndouglas/commentary.html (accessed 27 May 2014).

within both these formulations. In another context, Sen's capability approach is an extension of the liberalism of Rawls rather than a trenchant critique. Sen's fundamental philosophical position would also not permit him to entirely endorse Marx or other thinkers who approached justice in the particular context of enlightenment and universal class conflict caused by imperialism and massive industrialization. Sen does argue that Marxian philosophy is more concerned with fairness than formal justice vis-à-vis Kant. In his book, *Modern Social Imaginaries* (2004), Charles Taylor traces the evolution of modern social imaginaries not only in terms of ideas but also in terms of the evolution of various institutions that defined modernity. Taylor delineates how public sphere, economy and the state developed into separate spheres but were regulated by one another. But what transformed modernity most importantly was the moral order that led to various strands of cosmopolitan outlook in the social, political, legal, religious, and economic spheres (Taylor 2004).

Howard Wiarda's work on civil society classifies the Western political thought post-Enlightenment into the liberal and the republican strands (2003: 18–24). The former is procedural, emphasizes the inviolability of individual and property rights, based on rule of law and established institutions that are public, which are clearly the bulwark of a procedural democracy. The latter derives its political legitimacy from majoritarian/popular support of the citizenry. In the liberal thought, popular opinion plays an important role but cannot supersede the political process, judiciary, executive or legislature. The best example of liberalism during modernity would be John Locke's political writings and, more recently, John Rawls' liberalism (Sen 2009: 52–65). Justice is the thread that links the social, political, judicial, and economical. The republican model emphasizes direct democracy, a direct reflection of people's aspirations, beliefs and opinions. Ancient Rome, and contemporary France, Spain, Ireland, and Portugal would be the examples of a republican polity that encourages revolutions and envisages revolutionary potential universally. In a successful democracy, justice (*neeti*) and fairness (*nyaya*) need to be in a reflective equilibrium. This has always been the refrain of great thinkers, ancient or modern or contemporary, depending upon their sociopolitical understanding that characterized their epoch. Liberal or social democracies operate on universal principles of human, economic, social, and political rights and justice and hence they are fervent proponents of cosmopolitanism. Similarly, throughout Indian history, there have been attempts to understand various processes in a cosmopolitan–universalistic framework, notwithstanding the caste system.

Conclusion

An understanding of the Indian social imaginary requires a foundational historical understanding of various institutions past and present. In this conclusion, I have explained the paradigm shift from the cosmopolitan to the vernacular, its importance for a syncretistic understanding of a multicultural India during the medieval period, the ascendancy of vernacular politics in post-independence India, the appeal to the cosmopolitan ideals by the elites and downtrodden alike from different vantage points that influenced the framers of the Indian constitution, the importance of the cosmopolitan and the vernacular contestations in establishing social, political, economic, and judicial institutions and creating a constitutional morality. In the *neeti–nyaya* debate, India has seen titanic battles. Tilak and Gandhi, Tagore and Gandhi, Gandhi and Subash Chandra Bose, Gandhi and Ambedkar are a few historical ones. The Gandhi–Ambedkar debate is probably the finest and rivals the debate between Abraham Lincoln and Stephen Douglas in the 1860 American Presidential Election. The Gandhi–Ambedkar debate in many ways transformed India by shaping the Indian constitution. The Gandhi–Ambedkar debate revealed the tension between Gandhi's moral cosmopolitanism based on universal humanism and Ambedkar's liberal cosmopolitanism (Raghavan Iyer 1990). Gandhi wanted to nurse the soul of India, back from the throes of moral abyss, mauled by colonialism, casteism, feudalism, internal colonization, structural violence, and religious schism that led to unimaginable violence during the partition of India (Dalton 1996). Gandhi refused to believe that violence could ever be cathartic. Ambedkar sought constitutional equality for the deprived classes by guaranteeing fundamental political rights, social equality and economic empowerment of a population repressed for millenia, a political nirvana of sorts. Gandhi envisaged an Indian Supreme Court, justice for Indians, whereas Ambedkar championed the Constitution of India (Gandhi 2009b: 82–117). Gandhi illustrated the difference between justice (*neeti*) and fairness (*nyaya*) to the Indians and the British alike, while Ambedkar institutionalized a *neeti* always cognizant of the *nyaya*, a *nyaya* that does not only serve the cause of the majority or bend to the will of a morally outraged populace.[7]

❧

References

Aravamudan, S. 2007. *Guru English*, Penguin Books, London.

Athar Ali, M. 2008. 'The Perception of India in Akbar and Abu'l Fazl', in Irfan Habib (ed.), *Akbar and His India*, Oxford University Press, New Delhi, 215–24.

Balasubramanian, R. (ed.) 2000. *Advaita Vedānta*, Vol. II, Part 2, *History of Science, Philosophy and Culture in Indian Civilization*, Centre for Studies in Civilization, New Delhi.

Balibar, Etienne. 2012. 'Citizenship of the World Revisited', in Gerard Delanty (ed.), *Routledge Handbook of Cosmopolitanism Studies*, Routledge, London, 291–301.

Barthwal, P. D. 2005. 'The Times and their Need', in D. N. Lorenzen (ed.), *Religious Movements in South Asia*, Oxford University Press, New Delhi, 253–68.

Basham, A. L. 1975. *A Cultural History of India*, Oxford University Press, New Delhi.

———. 1999. *The Wonder that was India*, Rupa & Co, New Delhi.

Bate, Bernard. 2009. *Tamil Oratory and the Dravidian Aesthetic*, Oxford University Press, New Delhi.

Beveridge, H. 1926. 'Akbar', in James Hastings and John A. (eds), *Encyclopaedia of Religion and Ethics, Part 1*, Charles Schreibner's Sons, New York.

Brown, M. C. 1984. 'Svarāj, the Indian Ideal of Freedom: A Political or Religious Concept?', *Religious Studies* 20(3): 429–41.

Champakalakshmi, R. 2005. 'From Devotion and Dissent to Dominance: The Bhakti of the Tamil Alvars and Nayanars', in D. N. Lorenzen (ed.), *Religious Movements in South Asia*, Oxford University Press, New Delhi, 47–80.

Chandra, B., M. Mukherjee and A. Mukherjee. 2002. *India after Independence, 1947–2000*, Penguin Books, New Delhi.

Dalton, D. (ed.) 1996. *Mahatma Gandhi: Selected Political Writings*, Hackett Publishing Co., Indianapolis.

---

[7] Refer to two important cases involving Gandhi: (*a*) 'Was it contempt of the Court?' and (*b*) 'The Great Trial' (Gandhi 2009b).

Delanty, G. 2012. 'Introduction: The Emerging Field of Cosmopolitan Studies', in Gerard Delanty (ed.), *Routledge Handbook of Cosmopolitanism*, Routledge, London, 1–8.

Diaz, R. M. 2005. *Tirukkural*, Vardhaman Publishers, Chennai.

Dvivedi, H. 2005. 'Kabir's Place in Indian Religious Practice', in D. N. Lorenzen (ed.), *Religious Movements in South Asia*, Oxford University Press, New Delhi, 269–88.

Erikson, E. H. 1969. *Gandhi's Truth*, Norton & Company, New York.

Freeman, S. 2007. *Rawls*, Routledge, New York.

Gandhi, M. K. 1918. 'Education through the Vernacular', *The Indian Review*, April.

———. 2009a. *The Bhagavad Gita According to Gandhi*, edited by J. Stohmeier, North Atlantic Books, Berkeley.

———. 2009b. *The Law and the Lawyers*, edited by S. B. Kher, Navajivan Publishing House, Ahmedabad.

Goyandka, J. 2000. *The Bhagawad Gita*, Gita Press, Gorakhpur.

Guha, R. 2008. *India After Gandhi*, Picador, New Delhi.

Harvey, M. J. 1986. 'The Secular as Sacred? — The Religio-Political Rationalization of B. G. Tilak', *Modern Asian Studies* 20(2): 321–31.

Iyengar, U. (ed.). 2007. *The Oxford India Nehru*, Oxford University Press, New Delhi.

Iyer, R. (ed.). 1990. *The Essential Writings of Mahatma Gandhi*, Oxford University Press, New Delhi.

Jain, M. S. 2005. *Muslim Political Identity*, Rawat Publications, Jaipur.

Jaffrelot, C. 2005. *Dr Ambedkar and Untouchability: Analysing and Fighting Caste*, C. Hurst & Co, London.

Jordens, J. T. F. 1975. 'Medieval Hindu Devotionalism' in A. L. Basham (ed.) *A Cultural History of India*, Oxford University Press, New Delhi, 266–80.

Khan, I. A. 2008. 'Akbar's Personality Traits and World Outlook — A Critical Reappraisal', in Irfan Habib (ed.), *Akbar and His India*, Oxford University Press, New Delhi, 79–96.

Kleingeld, P. 1998. 'Kant's Cosmopolitan Law: World Citizenship for a Global Order', *Kantian Review* (2): 72–90.

Lorenzen, D. N. (ed.). 2005. *Religious Movements in South Asia*, Oxford University Press, New Delhi, 1–44.

Matilal, B. K. 1986. *Perception: An Essay on Classical Indian Theories of Knowledge*, Clarendon Press, Oxford.

Mill, J. S. 1985. *The Collected Works of John Stuart Mill, Volume X — Essays on Ethics, Religion, and Society*, edited by John M. Robson, University of Toronto Press, Toronto.

More, J. B. P. 2008. *Partition of India: Players and Partners*, Irish, Kannur.

Mukhia, Harbans. 2010. *Exploring India's Medieval Centuries: Essays in History, Society, Culture and Technology*, Aakar Books, Delhi.

Nagaswami, R. 2011. 'Rely on Documentary Evidence', *The Hindu*, 10 September.

Pandian, M. S. S. 2008. *Brahmin & Non-Brahmin*, Permanent Black, Ranikhet.

Plato. 1892. *The Dialogues of Plato, Vol 1*, trans. B. Jowett, Oxford University Press, London, http://oll.libertyfund.org/title/111 (accessed 2 August 2013).

Pollock, S. 2002. 'Cosmopolitanism and Vernacular in History', in C. A. Breckenridge, S. Pollock, H. K. Bhabha, and D. Chakrabarty (eds), *Cosmopolitanism*, Duke University Press, Durham, NC, 15–53.

———. 2009. *The Language of Gods in the World of Men*, Permanent Black, New Delhi.

———. 2011. 'Crisis in the Classics', *Social Research: An International Quarterly* 78(1): 21–48.

Prasad, P. 2008. 'Akbar and Jains', in Irfan Habib (ed.), *Akbar and His India*, Oxford University Press, New Delhi.

Sangharakshita, B. 1975. 'Buddhism', in A. L. Basham (ed.), *A Cultural History of India*, Oxford University Press, New Delhi, 83–99.

Sen, A. K. 1983. 'Evaluator Relativity and Consequential Evaluation', *Philosophy & Public Affairs* 12(2): 113–32.

———. 2005. *The Argumentative Indian*, Penguin Books, New Delhi.

———. 2009. *The Idea of Justice*, Belknap Press, Cambridge, MA.

Sivathamby, K. 2006. *Understanding Dravidian Movement Problems and Perspectives*, New Century Book House, Chennai.

Stein, B. 2005. 'Social Mobility and Medieval South Indian Hindu Sects', in D. N. Lorenzen (ed.), *Religious Movement in South Asia*, Oxford University Press, New Delhi, 81–102.

Sudarsan, P. 2012. 'Unity in Diversity — Indian Cosmopolitan Idea', in Gerard Delanty (ed.), *Routledge Handbook of Cosmopolitanism Studies*, Routledge, London, 463–76.

Tapasyānanda, Sw. 1990. *Bhakti Schools of Vedānta*, Sri Ramakrishna Math, Madras.

Taylor, C. 2004. *Modern Social Imaginaries*, Duke University Press, Durham.

Thapar, R. 2002. *Early India*, Penguin Books, New Delhi.

———. 2005. 'Imagined Religious Communities', in D. N. Lorenzen (ed.), *Religious Movements in South Asia*, Oxford University Press, New Delhi, 333–59.

Tilak, B. G. 1935. *Sri Bhagavadgita-Rahasya, Vol 1*, trans. B. S. Sukthankar, Bombay Vaibhav Press, Bombay.

Upadhye, A. N. 1975. 'Jainism', in A. L. Basham (ed.), *A Cultural History of India*, Oxford University Press, Oxford, 100–110.

Wheeler, M. 1968. *The Indus Civilization*, Cambridge University Press, London.

Wiarda, H. J. 2003. *Civil Society*, Westview Press, Colorado.

Wiredu, K. 1998. 'Toward Decolonizing African Philosophy and Religion', *African Studies Quarterly*, University of Florida, 1(4): 17–46.

About the Editors

Sonika Gupta is Associate Professor of International Relations and Chinese Politics in the Department of Humanities and Social Sciences, Indian Institute of Technology Madras (IITM), India. She is the founder of and currently heads the China Studies Centre at IITM. She has co-edited *Nuclear Stability in Southern Asia* (with P. R. Chari and Arpit Rajain, 2003) and *Human Security in South Asia: Gender, Energy, Migration and Globalisation* (with P. R. Chari, 2002), as well as contributed articles in edited volumes. Her research interests lie at the intersection of international political theory and area studies with specialization in Chinese domestic politics.

Sudarsan Padmanabhan is Associate Professor in the Department of Humanities and Social Sciences, Indian Institute of Technology Madras, India. His recent publications include the co-edited volumes, *Becoming Minority* (with Jyotirmaya Tripathy, forthcoming) and *The Democratic Predicament: Cultural Diversity in Europe and India* (with Jyotirmaya Tripathy, 2013) and research articles in journals and edited volumes. Sudarsan specializes in social and political philosophy, Indian philosophy and culture. His research focus is on the confluence of law, politics and ethics in the public sphere. Currently, he is working on an understanding of an Indian social imaginary and its effect on the Constitution of India.

Notes on Contributors

Daniele Archibugi is Research Director at the Italian National Research Council (CNR-IRPPS) in Rome, Italy and Professor of Innovation, Governance and Public Policy at Birkbeck College, University of London, UK. His most recent publications include *Global Democracy: Normative and Empirical Perspectives* (co-edited with Mathias Koenig-Archibugi and Raffaele Marchetti, 2011), *The Global Commonwealth of Citizens: Toward Cosmopolitan Democracy* (2008), which has been translated in several languages, and *Debating Cosmopolitics* (as editor, 2003).

Garrett Wallace Brown is Reader in Political Theory and Global Ethics in the Department of Politics, University of Sheffield, UK. He has authored *Grounding Cosmopolitanism: From Kant to the Idea of a Cosmopolitan Constitution* (2009), and co-edited *The Handbook of Global Health Policy* (with Gavin Yamey and Sarah Wamala, 2012) and *The Cosmopolitanism Reader* (with David Held, 2010).

Eva Erman is Associate Professor of Political Theory at Uppsala University, Sweden. She is also founder and Chief Editor of *Ethics & Global Politics*. Erman has authored *Human Rights and Democracy: Discourse Theory and Global Rights Institutions* (2005), co-edited *Territories of Citizenship* (with Ludvig Beckman, 2012) and *Legitimacy Beyond the State? Re-examining the Democratic Credentials of Transnational Actors* (with Anders Uhlin, 2010), and published numerous articles on democracy, communicative action and discourse ethics in international journals.

David Held is Master of University College, Durham and Professor of Politics and International Relations at the University of Durham, UK. He is co-founder and Director of Polity Press, and General Editor of *Global Policy*. His recent publications include *Climate Governance in the Developing World* (with Charles Roger and

Eva-Maria Nag, 2013), *Gridlock: Why Global Cooperation is Failing When We Need It Most* (with Thomas Hale and Kevin Young, 2013) and *Cosmopolitanism: Ideals and Realities* (2010).

Véronique Pin-Fat is Senior Lecturer in International Politics at the University of Manchester, UK. She has authored *Universality, Ethics and International Relations: A Grammatical Reading* (2010), and co-edited *Sovereign Lives: Power in Global Politics* (with Jenny Edkins and Michael J. Shapiro, 2004) and *Sovereignty and Subjectivity* (with Jenny Edkins and Nalini Persram, 1999).

Francesco Ragazzi is Assistant Professor in International Relations at the University of Leiden, Netherlands, and Associate Researcher at the Centre for International Studies and Research, Sciences Po Paris, France. His current research, supported by the Marie-Curie program and the Netherlands Organization for Scientific Research (NWO) focuses on the relation between counter-terrorism and ethnic relations in France, Netherlands and the United Kingdom.

Sudhir Chella Rajan is Professor in the Department of Humanities and Social Sciences, Indian Institute of Technology Madras, Chennai. He was formerly Senior Fellow at Tellus Institute, USA. Rajan has co-edited *The Suicidal Planet: How to Prevent Global Climate Catastrophe* (with Mayer Hillman and Tina Fawcett, 2007) and contributed articles in journals and edited volumes.

Rahul Rao is Lecturer in Politics at SOAS, University of London, UK. He has authored *Third World Protest: Between Home and the World* (2010), and numerous articles in the fields of IR, political theory, and gender studies. He blogs occasionally at *The Disorder of Things*.

Arvind Sivaramakrishnan is Senior Deputy Editor of *The Hindu* and Adjunct Professor at the Asian College of Journalism, Chennai, India. His publications include *Public Policy and Citizenship* (2012), *Short on Democracy: Issues Facing Indian Political Parties* (2007) and *Through a Glass Wall* (2007).

Latha Varadarajan is Associate Professor of Political Science at San Diego State University, USA. Her research focuses on the political economic dimensions of the various manifestations of transnationalism. She has authored *The Domestic Abroad: Diasporas in International Relations* (2010) and published articles in journals including *Review of International Studies, Millennium: Journal of International Studies, New Political Science,* and *International Political Sociology.*

Index

Abdali, Ahmad Shah, 251
Abel, M., 125
Actions: consequences of, 133; intentional, 131, 133; just/unjust, 131–32
Advaita Ashrama, 241n2
Advaitic philosophy, 241
Advani, L. K., 176, 180
Agreement on Trade-Related Aspects of Intellectual Property Rights (TRIPS Agreement), 45
Akbar, Emperor, 242, 249–50
al-Bashir, Omar, 22
Alberuni, 241
Ali, Athar, 242
Alighieri, Dante, 150
Alwars, 238
Ambedkar, B. R., 12, 237, 244, 251–53
Anderson, Benedict, 198
Annadurai, C. N., 245, 247
anti-colonial nationalism, 216–17
anti-discrimination law, 126–27
Appadurai, Arjun, 198
Archibugi, Daniele, 6–7, 121
Ardhamagadhi, 238–39
Aryan–Dravidian divide, 245
Association of Indian Engineering Industry (AIEI), 181
Aurangazeb, emperor, 250

Badauni, Mullah Abdul Qadir, 249
Balibar, Etienne, 235
Bancroft Treaties, 147
Bate, Bernard, 244
Beck, Ulrich, 18, 86
Beitz, Charles, 93
Benhabib, Seyla, 108–9, 140
Bhagavad Gita, 240–49, 256

bhakti, 241
Bhakti movement, 12, 239–42, 249–58
biomes, 115
Biome Stewardship Council (BSC), 115–19
Bohman, James, 66
Boojum ethics, 97–100
Bose, Amar, 183
Bose, Subhas Chandra, 207
bourgeois nationalism, 179
Brahman, 241
Brahmanism, 239
Brahmin community in Tamil Nadu, 245
Bretton Woods agreement, 113, 181
Brubaker, Rogers, 148
Buddha, Lord, 252–53
Buddhism, 238–39, 251–52

Çali, Başak, 86
Carroll, Lewis, 8, 97, 100
Casey and *Webster*, 126
Cass, Deborah, 46
Caste system, 12, 235, 259
Chakrabarty, Dipesh, 202
Chatterjee, Partha, 218
cit acit visishtam Brahman, 240
citizenship, 3. *See also* territorialization of citizenship; acquisition of, 150; ambiguities of, 146; de-securitization of migrant citizens, 154; diasporic, 138–42, 157; dual, 137, 146–47, 154, 167, 176; evolution of, 138; flexibility of, 180–85; freedom to choose one's, 147; global, 176–85; laws of emigration,

146; national heterogeneity of, 143; notions of perpetual allegiance and, 143–48; post-national, 142; post-territorial, 138, 142–44, 153–58; security and, 143; sovereign-subject relationship, 144; territorial, 147–48; transnational migrations and, 140–42

Citizenship Act (1955), 185

civil code 1803, 145

civil society, 64, 76, 112, 118, 258; normative role of, 65

comparative political thought (CPT), 193, 201–6

conceptual decolonization, 235

Conflict of Nationality Laws, 147

consequential evaluation, 257–58

constitutionalization, 7; codification and specification of rights and duties into international law, 41; conceptualization issues of, 48–49; constitutional arrangements for legal adjudication, 44–45; and constraints on human conduct, 46; and cosmopolitan theory, 50; definition, 39; and economic crisis, 44–45; establishment of formal legal processes, role in, 39–44; EU integration and, 41, 47; of global norms, 48; of international law and international institutions, 37; at international level, 40; language of, 37; normative principles of, 47–49, 51–54; progressive, 48; Schachterian notion of, 42; scholarship and research on, 47–49; socializing processes of, 46; use of, 39; vertical, 43

constitutional patriotism, 53

cosmopolis, 84, 99; Latin cosmopolis, 199; Sanskrit cosmopolis, 12, 237, 240, 242, 247–48

cosmopolitan democracy, 1, 53, 105; as academic discourse, 18; citizens' participation, influence of, 24; impact of globalization on, 18; international courts, role of, 22; international law and, 23; international relations and, 18; lawful conflict resolutions, 23; national foreign policy priorities for, 20–21; path towards, 19–20; political communities and, 25–26; role and functions of IOs and, 21; rule of law and its enforcement, effect of, 21–24; states as champions of, 20; in textbooks, 17; top-down and bottom-up agents of, 26–35

cosmopolitan enquiry, 5

cosmopolitan global justice, 53

cosmopolitan international condition, 127

cosmopolitanism, 1, 121, 197, 259. *See also* India, cosmopolitanism in; Beitz's, 93–94; commitments to universality and humanity, 90–91; cosmopolitan practices, 198; cosmopolitan–vernacular contestations, 236–48; critiques of, 1; definitions, 83–87; deformed, 86; ethical basis of, 2; foundational ontology of, 86; global history comparison, 205–11; global social changes and, 3; hard *vs* soft ontologies of, 8, 87–91, 93; and identification of foundations, 86; indigenous concepts of, 5; institutional, 51; institutionalization of cosmopolitan norms, 4; legal, 84–85; liberal, 2; liberalism and, 134; localism, 5; during modernity, 234–35; moral, 4, 51, 84–85; non-deformed, 86; normative considerations, 47–49; *polis* in,

177–80, 186, 197, 234; political, 4, 84–85; as a political theory, 50; with practice turn, 198–201; principles of, 124; transformative changes, 3; universal focus of, 51; and vernacularism, 199–200; Western narrative of, 234–35; West/non-West distinction, 11, 199–205; Wittgenstein's language game metaphor, 8, 87–90
cosmopolitanization, 43–47
cosmopolitan project, 1, 3, 5–6, 8, 32, 54, 220–21, 231
cosmopolitans, 28–29, 195
cosmopolitan state, 20; challenges from migration, 20
cosmopolitan thought zones, 206, 209
Council of Europe, 20
Croatian Law on Citizenship of 1991, 158
cultural cosmopolitanism, 123

Dabashi, Hamid, 200
Dahl, Robert, 18
Dahrendorf, Ralf, 18
de-constitutionalization, 40
Delanty, Gerard, 121–122, 124
democracy, 7; arrangement to qualify as democratic, 63; civil society and, 64, 76; equal influence principle, 75; Forst's path to, 69–73; global, 61, 66; Habermas' discourse theory of, 73–74; normative elements in, 61; political equality and political bindingness, 61; role of non-state actors, 64, 76; stakeholder interest in decision-making, 65; at transnational level, 62–67
democratic accountability, 65
democratic agents, 61–62, 76
democratic citizenship, 66

democratic decision-making, 63, 65–67; between individual rights and collective decision-making, 66
democratic legitimacy, 77
democratic minimum, 66
democratic rights, 72
Deoband School, 251
Dharmasastras, 254
diasporas, 200; cosmopolitan diasporas and diasporic cosmopolitianism, 168–75; Indian citizenship and diaspora policy initiatives, 176–85; limits of global citizenship, 176–85; state actors and, 167
diasporic citizenship, 138–42, 157
Din-i-Ilahi (universal religion), 242, 249–50
Diogenes, 234
disaggregated sovereignty, 112
dispossessed (the bottom billion), 26–27
Donzelot, Jacques, 148
Douglas, Stephen, 259
Dravida Kazhagam (DK), 244–45
Dravida Munnetra Kazhagam (DMK), 244–46
Dravidian movement, 243
dual citizenship, 137, 146–47, 154, 167, 176
DuBois, W. E. B., 208

economic cosmopolitanism, 244
English language education, 243–44
equal influence principle, 61, 74
equal respect principle, 69–70
EU Maastricht Treaty, 41
Eurocentrism, 196
European Court of Human Rights, 40–41, 127
European territorial 'nationalizing state', 153

European Union (EU), 3, 20, 113, 122, 124, 154; form of constitutionalization in, 40

Falk, Richard, 18, 112
Fazl, Abul, 241–42, 250
Federation of Indian Chambers of Commerce and Industry (FICCI), 176
Forst, Rainer, 61
Fossum, John Erik, 84
Foucault, Michel, 144
Fraser, Nancy, 111
freedom of speech, 72
free market, 123–24, 131, 133
French Revolution of 1709, 148

G20, 114
*gana sangha*s, 252
Gandhi, M. K., 12, 207–8, 237, 257
Genocide Convention, 84
German citizenship law, 1913, 146
Gill, Stephen, 46
Gitarahasya, 240
global citizenship, 10, 112, 172, 176–85
global civil society, 29–30
global constitutionalism, 38–43, 52–53; form of legal processes, 41
global democracy, 61, 66; human rights approach to, 66, 71–72
global economic constitution, 45
global governance, 19
globalization, 7, 40, 48, 85, 138, 167, 244; cosmopolitan democracy, impact on, 18; negative effects of, 37
globalized civil society, 65
global judicial authorities, 21–24
global justice, 193–197
Global Legislators for a Balanced Environment (GLOBE), 114

global normative order, 8, 61–62; contexts of justification, 61; layers of, 67–76; multiple citizenship and, 76–77
global parliament, 9, 112–13
global stakeholders, 29
global taxation mechanisms, 127
Godrej, Farah, 202–5
Goodhart, Michael, 66
Goto-Jones, Chris, 202
group rights, 130

Habermas, Jurgen, 18, 41–42, 61, 122
Hammer, Dean, 104
Harshavardhana, 238
Harvey, David, 196
Hayek, Friedrich von, 123, 131–34
Held, David, 6–7, 121–25, 127–28, 131
Herman, Edward, 125
Hind, Hindawi, Hindoo, 242
Hind Swaraj, 11, 222–26, 229
Hinduism, 242, 251–52
Hippias, 234
Holton, Robert J., 83
Holy Grail, 235
Hsien, Fa, 249
humanity, 97–101
human rights, 70, 75–77, 105, 124–25, 127–28, 228; approach to global democracy, 66, 71–72; democratic legitimacy of transnational and global governance via, 65–66; global, 85; global economic order and, 128; IOs and, 28; language games of universal, 91; norms, 140–41; protection of, 51; status of citizenship, 77

Ibn-Arabi, 250
identity, 3
identity-in-difference, 240

imagined communities, 198
India, cosmopolitanism in, 11–12, 235. *See also* cosmopolitanism; Bhakti movement, 240–41; cosmopolitan *vs* vernacular debates, 236–48; Islamic imaginary, 241–43; *neeti–nyaya* debate, 237, 248–59; Sanskrit language and culture, 237–38
Indian jurisprudence, argumentative tradition of, 254–55
Indian National Congress (INC), 178, 251
international constitutionalization, 41
International Court of Justice (ICJ), 23
International Criminal Court (ICC), 22, 84, 122, 127
International Labour Organization (ILO), 31
International Organizations (IOs), 21
Iqbal, Mohammed, 248–49
Isin, Engin, 152
Islam in India, 248–51
Islamic jurisprudence, 237, 251
Itihasas, 255

Jabri, Vivienne, 5
Jacobs, Jane, 111
Jainism, 238–39
Japan, 124
Jehangir, emperor, 250
Jinnah, Mohammed Ali, 244, 248

Kaldor, Mary, 18, 32
Kant, Immanuel, 5, 84, 106–8, 110, 234–35
Kapany, Narendra Singh, 183
Karunanidhi, M., 246
kavya, 238–41, 245
Khilafat movement, 207
Khusrau, Amir, 241

Klabbers, Jan, 37
Korkman, Petter, 197
Koskenniemi, Marrti, 51
Koslowski, Rey, 146
Kymlicka, Will, 199, 221

labour movements, 30–31
lakshana-lakshya categorization, 248
Latin cosmopolis, 199
Law of Return, 152
Law on Citizenship, 152
Lecomte, Maxime, 149
Lefebvre, Henri, 111
Lefort, Claude, 105
legal cosmopolitanism, 84–85
lex mercatoria, 6, 23
liberal cosmopolitanism, 2, 4, 6, 11
liberalism, 135; advanced liberal, 153; critique of, 6; economic liberalization, 182; Hayek's market liberalism, 131–34; during modernity, 258; problems with, 129–30
Lincoln, Abraham, 257, 259
Lincoln-Douglas debates, 257n6
literization, 240
Locke, John, 258
lokasamgraha, 241
Luhmann, Niklas, 247

Macdonald, Terry, 65
MacIntyre, Alasdair, 130
Mahabharata, 238, 255
Manjapra, Kris, 209–11
Marai, 247
March, Andrew, 201
Marshall, T. H., 123
material rights, 128–29
McChesney, Robert, 125
McGrew, Tony, 18
methodical imaginary, 204
Mignolo, Walter, 220

migration/immigration, 140, 209–20

Mill, J. S., 256

millat, 249, 251

Miller, David, 18, 220

moral cosmopolitanism, 51, 84–85, 106

moral equality, 73

moral justification, 67–68, 75; criterion of generality and reciprocity, 69*n*7

Muhaddis, Maulvi Abdul Haq, 249

mujtahid, 250

Mukhia, Harbans, 242

multiculturalism, 155

multinational corporations (MNCs), 7, 30–32

multiple citizenship, 61

Muslim community in India, 248–51

mysticism, 97–101

Naickker, E. V. Ramasamy (Periyar), 244–45

Nairn, Tom, 199

Nalayira Divya Prabandham, 238–39

Nammalwar, 238–39

Nandy, Ashis, 219–20

Narasimhavarman II, 238

natio, 246

national homogenization, 148

nationalism, 141; in contemporary India, 219; in Europe, 217–18; Gandhi and Indian National Movement, 222–27; liberal, 221; moral evaluation of, 220–22; negation/disregard of, 220; in postcolonial states, 218–19; spiritual, 241; Statism and, 228–30

Nayanmars, 238

neeti, 236, 247, 253–67, 268

neeti–nyaya debate, 237, 248–59; contemporary moral and political challenges, 253–59; in Islamic political experience, 248–51

Neetisastras, 255

negative rights, 128

Nehru, Jawaharlal, 12, 177, 247, 253

neo-liberalism, 182; form of governmentality, 153; Hayek's argument, 131; practical knowledge, role of, 131

nermai, 247

niskama karma, 241

non-governmental organizations (NGOs), 19, 21, 27, 29, 64–65, 114, 117, 122

North American Free Trade Association (NAFTA), 124

Nuclear Non-Proliferation Treaty (NPT), 113

Nuremberg Charter, 84

Nuremberg trials, 126

Nussbaum, Martha, 121, 220

nyaya, 236, 247, 253–67, 260

'one person, one vote,' 72

Ong, Aihwa, 140

Opinion Tribunals, 22

Pagden, Anthony, 197

Pali, 238–39

Pandithar, Ayothidas, 251

Paninian grammar, 248

Panniru Tirumurai, 238

paramarthika satta, 240

paramarthika-vyavaharika distinction, 248

parampara, 239

people, political significance of, 104; cosmopolitans, 105, 119; global people, 111–13; law of world citizenship, 106–7;

legitimacy and cultural identity, 110–11; liberal and non-liberal, 108–9; liberals *vs* Marxists, 104; Machiavelli's, 104; pluralistic conception of the people, 119; Rawls' ideal structure of people, 107–9; single-identity requirement of the people, 113–19; sovereign, 104; tensions between 'I' and 'we,' 103
Peters, Anne, 52
Plant, Raymond, 128
Plato's Noble Lie, 133
political bindingness, 61, 63
political cosmopolitanism, 84–85, 122
political equality, 72–73
political justification, 67, 69, 71
political parties: international, 30
Pollock, Sheldon, 199, 237, 247
positive rights, 128
post-territorial citizenship, 10, 138, 153–58; emigration context, 156–58; immigration context, 154–56
Prakrit, 238
prapatti, 241
Pravasi Bharatiya Diwas celebrations, 175, 179–80
procedural rights, 129
proto-constitution of international law and international legitimacy, 42
Pulakesin-II, 238
Puranas, 255
Purie, Aroon, 184

Raja, M. C., 243, 252
rajabhasha, 239
Ramachandran, M. G. (MGR), 246
Ramamurthy, 244
Ramanuja, 239
Ramayana, 238, 255

Rawls, John, 107–108, 110, 194–96, 256–58
recursive principle, 71
republican, 52, 66, 109, 253, 258
republican federalism, 66
republicanism, 110
Responsibility to Protect, 84
rights and rights discourses, 126–30; civil rights, 128–29; clashes of rights, 134; global taxation mechanisms and, 128; human. *See* human rights; idea of a cosmopolitan international condition, 127; impact of rights and rights instruments, 126–27; material rights, 128–29; political rights, 129; procedural rights, 129; rights-based constraints, 128–30; social and economic rights, 128; universal validity of rights, 125–26
rights-based liberalism, 9
right to health care, 72
right to justification, 70–71, 75; in democratic contexts, 72
right to vote, 72
Robbins, Brue, 198
Roe v Wade, 126
Rome Treaty of 1963, 41
Rose, Nikolas, 153, 155
Roy, M. N., 209–11
rule of law, 42, 53

Sachs, Albie, 125
Saivism, 238
Saivites, 238
Sakya clan, 252
Samaddar, Ranabir, 218
Sanskrit cosmopolis, 12, 237, 240, 242, 247–48
Sanskrit language and culture, 237–38, 240, 243–47; as a formal language, 239; influence on vernacular literary genres,

238; poetic-religious literature, 238; Sanskrit cosmopolis, 247; *vyavaharika satta*, 238
saranagati, 241
Sassen, Saskia, 18
sastra, 240–41
Schmitter, Philippe, 18
Scholte, Jan Aart, 18, 64
secularism, 219–20, 257
Sen, Amartya, 237; capability approach, 258; critique of Rawlsian theory of justice, 253, 256; evaluator relativity and consequential evaluation, 257–58; formal justice (*neeti*) and fairness (*nyaya*), 254; India's argumentative tradition, 255–56; on Marxian philosophy, 258
Seth, Sanjay, 201–2
Shah, Nadir, 251
shariat-tareeqat distinction, 248
Sharon, Ariel, 157
Shue, Henry, 194
Singer, Peter, 194
Sirhindi, Shaikh Ahmed, 249
Sivathamby, Karthigesu, 243–44
Slate, Nico, 208
Slaughter, Anne-Marie, 112–13
smart borders, 155
social imaginary, 9, 104, 106, 111–12, 117, 258–67
Soysal, Yasemin, 140
Spiro, Peter, 146
sramana, 252
Srinivasan, Rettamalai, 243, 251
state sovereignty, 127, 140, 144
Strauss, Andrew, 112
Sufi movement, 12, 239, 242
Sufism, 248–49
sulh kul, 249–50
swaraj, 229, 241. *See also* Hind Swaraj

Tagore, Rabindranath, 196, 207, 221–22, 257; critique of nationalism, 221–22; *Ghare Baire*, 221; *vs* Gandhi, 257
Tamil: culture, 246–47; language, 238–40, 243–47; literature, 245; nationalism, 244
Tamir, Yael, 221
Taylor, Charles, 258
territorialization of citizenship, 142–43. *See also* citizenship; assimilation policies, 150–51; defending territorialized citizens, 148–53; immigrant rights, 152; migration issues, 149–50; notion of solidarity, 148; principle of territorial homogeneity, 152; territorializing project of state of Israel, 152–53
Thapar, Romila, 249, 255
Thoreau, Henry David, 208
Thoss, Pundit Ayothee, 243, 251
Tilak, Bal Gangadhar, 240–41
Tirukkural, 255
Tiruvaimozhi, 239
trade unions, 30–31
transnational democracy, 66
transnationalism, 167
Treaty of Westphalia, 122
Tsang, Hsuan, 249

Ubaya-vedantins, 239
ulema, 250–51
Ullah, Shah Wali, 249
UN General Assembly, 24
UN Human Rights Council, 20
UN human rights declarations, 127
United Nations Security Council (UNSC), 127
United Nations (UN), 3, 122
Universal Declaration of Human Rights, 84
universalism/universality, ethico-political practice of, 91–97
utilitarianism, 256

vaidika, 239
Vaikkom satyagraha, 244
Vaishnava: commentators, 240; *parampara*, 239; tradition, 241
Vaishnavism, 238, 241
Vaishnavite literature, 246–48
Vaishnavites, 239
Vedantic genre, 240
Vedas, 238–39
vernacularization, 237–38, 240, 246
vernacular languages: influence of Sanskrit, 238; as repository of cultural discourse, 239
vertical constitutionalization, 43
Vitoria, Francisco de, 5
vyavaharika, 238, 248, 256n5
vyavaharika satta, 238, 240

Washington, Booker T., 208
watan, 249, 251
Weale, Albert, 125
Weiss, Yfaat, 152

Western cosmopolitanism, 196, 204
Westphalian system of nation-states, 84
Westphalia treaty, 144
Wiarda, Howard, 258
Wiredu, Kwasi, 234–35
Wittgenstein, Ludwig, 8, 87–88, 97–98
Wolin, Richard, 127
World Economic Forum, 19
World Health Organization (WHO), 3
World Parliamentary Assembly, 6, 24, 26
World Social Forum, 19
World Trade Organization (WTO), 31, 45, 113, 122

Yudhisthira (*Dharmaputra*), 255

Zeno of Citium, 197

www.ingramcontent.com/pod-product-compliance
Ingram Content Group UK Ltd.
Pitfield, Milton Keynes, MK11 3LW, UK
UKHW020411010325
455677UK00029B/849